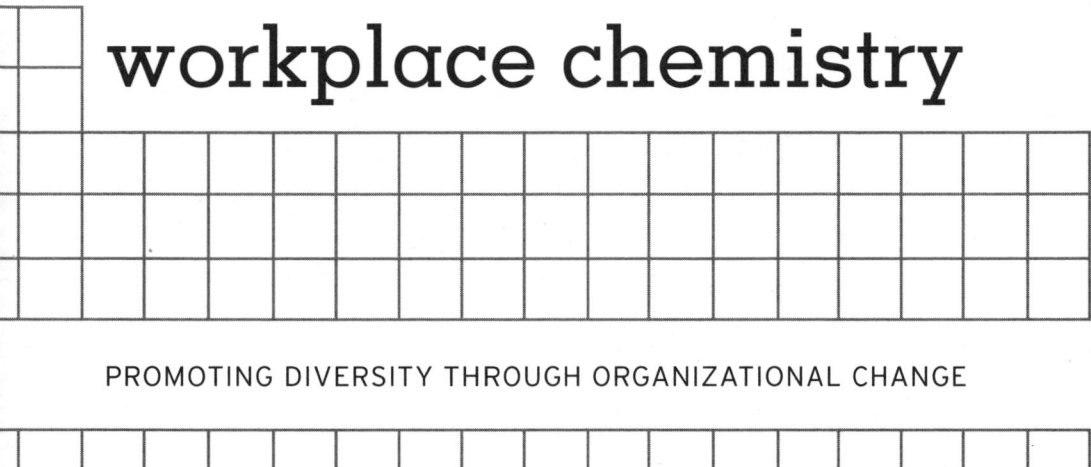

workplace chemistry

PROMOTING DIVERSITY THROUGH ORGANIZATIONAL CHANGE

meg a. bond

university press of new england

HANOVER AND LONDON

Published by University Press of New England,
One Court Street, Lebanon, NH 03766
www.upne.com
© 2007 by University Press of New England
Printed in the United States of America
5 4 3 2 1

Library of Congress Cataloging-in-Publication Data
Bond, Meg A.
Workplace chemistry : promoting diversity through organizational change /
Meg A. Bond
      p.   cm.
Includes bibliographical references and index.
ISBN-13: 978-1-58465-652-4 (cloth : alk. paper)
ISBN-10: 1-58465-652-2 (cloth : alk. paper)
   1. Diversity in the workplace.   2. Organizational change.   3. Organizational culture.
   I. Title.
HF5549.5.M5B66   2007
658.3008—dc22   2007025945

 University Press of New England is a member of the Green
Press Initiative. The paper used in this book meets their
minimum requirement for recycled paper.

contents

figures

tables

acknowledgments

While the cover of this book may bear my name, this story could not have been written without the help of many colleagues and friends. *Workplace Chemistry* came into being backed up by a diverse community of support—both in the doing of the work and in the writing of the book.

First and foremost, I want to acknowledge all the people at ChemPro who invited me into their world. At the outset, I had a hunch that they would teach me a lot, and indeed they did. Keitha is an inspiring woman whose commitment and clarity about diversity is both calming and challenging. Rich has been an indefatigable ally—open minded and deeply committed to doing the right thing. Our cotrainers and the many managers who partnered with us along the way were courageous and willing to take risks that gave this initiative wings. Without Warren's support, it simply would never have happened. I admire them all and thank them for the opportunity to do this work.

My foray into "workplace diversity" as a topic started with a partner, economist Jean Pyle. In 1993, with seed funding from the Committee on Industrial Theory and Assessment at University of Massachusetts Lowell, Jean and I gathered whatever materials we could find, spread articles and books over every surface of our offices and homes, and spent hours together talking and carving out our interdisciplinary take on the topic. Although Jean has since moved to Florida, her voice can be heard in the pages of this book. Robin Toof became an invaluable partner in designing the training and consultation. She contributed her expertise in experiential learning, which enriched our joint enterprise.

The Center for Women and Work (CWW) and the Department of Psychology at UMass Lowell have been my professional homes for over eighteen years and have provided me with critical supports for this project—pragmatic, emotional, and intellectual. CWW, with all of its interdisciplinary energy and collegiality, will be the platform for taking the ideas presented here forward in the future. The UMass Lowell students who were involved over the years included an incredible group of bright, curious, and engaged people: Beth Adler, Dianne Cazeca, Jennifer Gooch, Raji Kanniyapan, Yael Keren, Steve Lockney, Erin Lynch, Eileen Maloney, Gabriela Pashturro, Manjula Sastry, Ana Valdez, and Melissa Wall. I am hopeful others will sign on as we continue this type of work.

When it comes to the writing, I have had many colleagues encourage me, but the most consistent and generous support has been from the Social Issues Research Working Group at the Women's Studies Research Center at Brandeis University. It was during a 2003–4 sabbatical from UMass Lowell that I met these wonderful women, and they still urge me onward: Rhoda Unger, Evelyn Murphy, Linda Pololi, Phyllis Silverman, Hilda Kahne, Louise Lopman, Helen Regan, Linda Brimm, June Ellen Mendelson, Margaret Gullette, and Rajashree Ghosh. These are the kind souls who first suggested I turn this story into a book, and they have willingly offered their feedback on drafts chapter by chapter. They have been challenging *and* supportive—a perfect combination particularly given the focus of my writing. It is because of their amazing minds and hearts that I so value the feminist community at WSRC, where I have continued as a Resident Scholar even after resuming my academic position in Lowell.

I am a glutton for feedback and want to thank several other people who indulged me by reading portions of my numerous drafts. The feedback from my community psychology colleagues who share my value for thinking ecologically about diversity—Shelly Harrell, Chris Keys, and Cary Cherniss— has been particularly constructive and has pushed my analysis deeper. I am also grateful to Paula Rayman, who shared her interest in dignity at work though her review and her coaching to think about an impact beyond the book. The thoughtful feedback from Paula Alexander and Tom Tardiff has made me more confident about the usefulness of the lessons I have tried to convey.

For the last lap, I was blessed with technical, statistical, and clerical help from Dianne Cazeca, BongKyoo Choi, Heather Norcross, Ekaterina Konolova, Lyndsey Tarsia, and Jamie Weller. Margaret Farrar was a great resource as she tolerated my silly questions about chemistry and guided me in the development of this imagery. Margaret Scarsdale provided invaluable reviews particularly when I could no longer see the forest for the trees. My editor, Phyllis Deutsch, has been wonderfully supportive throughout the process of writing this book, providing steady and patient encouragement.

The most important supports are often not the professional ones. My gratitude to my family is hard to put into words. Bill Madsen has been my cherished partner in all ways—as a coparent, as an intellectual sounding board, as an adviser, and as an escape from work. Arlyn and Erik have been busy growing up during the ten years since I started working with ChemPro. I am inspired by their abilities to both delight in life and critique their social worlds. I am confident they are becoming well-equipped to live and work in a diverse society. I hope we have given them some important tools as parents, but I am sure they will soon be guiding us.

This book is dedicated to my mother (1921–2005). After receiving her B.A. at Swarthmore College, Winifred Cammack Bond was awarded the Lucretia Mott Fellowship, which she used to attend a program in personnel management at Radcliffe College. This was in 1944, during an era when women were not allowed to attend Harvard Business School. The "males only" sign was still on the door, and the yearbooks pictured row after row of white men. While a "certificate" from Radcliffe was the only alternative for women, many of her classmates were the people who first challenged the glass ceiling for women in management. Winnie was not among them, however. She devoted her life to the jobs of mother and wife. After her field placements in various factories standing next to Rosie the Riveter, she never again worked for a wage. Yet I truly believe that had she been raised in a different time or under a different set of circumstances, she would have worked as an organizational change agent. Raised with a strong commitment to Quaker values in a family of modest means, I believe she would have championed women's equality and fought against injustice to workers at the bottom of the ladder. I think about my mother as one of those women who was personally stifled by the gendered expectations of her time, yet she did not impose those barriers on others. I thank her and my father in more ways than I can express for instilling in me the belief in the possibility for change.

workplace chemistry

introduction

THE WORD "CHEMISTRY" is often used to describe relationships between people. When there is "good chemistry," we understand it to mean that things are going well because of naturally occurring forces of nature. The basic elements—or individuals—involved seem to mix and complement one another well. They not only coexist with relative ease but may also synergistically bring out something new and positive in one another. "Bad chemistry" implies an interpersonal mess—or even explosion—as personal elements collide and refuse to transform peacefully on contact. The players in this second chemical drama may simply not mix, like oil and water, or worse, may bring out something quite negative in one another. In our personal lives, we can choose friends based on a "natural" chemistry and decide to foster those relationships that offer a relatively effortless or spontaneous connection. In the workplace, however, people often need to work closely with people in situations where there is little natural or organic connection. As the workplaces of the future become more and more diverse in terms of race, gender, ethnicity, and sexual orientation, this challenge will only intensify, making it imperative to identify and nurture catalysts for positive change.

Achieving "good chemistry" among diverse workers is not a simple seven-step program. Nor is it primarily a matter of increasing diversity through hiring more women or more workers from racial and ethnic minority groups. It is a long-term commitment to changing an organization's culture such that it fully supports people who vary on key identity and demographic characteristics. It is also a multilayered challenge that requires change in individuals and also in work groups and in organizational dynamics. In today's workplaces, we need to learn how to maximize the good chemistry of diversity—to create it, not just happen upon it—through understanding the relationships between the basic elements (i.e., workers) and the medium within which they work (i.e., the team and organizational contexts).

Books providing advice on the tremendously popular topic of workplace diversity abound. Some offer advice to the would-be manager; some summarize issues for subsets of workers from various racial and ethnic groups; some focus on the unique issues for women; and some are highly theoretical and define a psychological or sociological research agenda. While many of these books provide valuable general guidance, the current book addresses an important void in the literature by sharing the specifics of a long-term, site-specific collaborative case study. *Workplace Chemistry* is unique in that it is both practical and analytical. It describes the theoretical foundation for the work and illustrates how the details of the intervention emerged from the guiding principles. The book has four primary goals: first, to provide a way of thinking about effective diversity as an ongoing organizational process; second, to articulate issues for a participatory change process aimed at developing a healthy organizational culture for diverse employees; third, to illustrate the complex and subtle systems dynamics behind many workplace diversity initiatives; and fourth, to draw out lessons for others invested in fostering organizations that truly support diversity. The book seeks to provide insights useful to both organizational change agents and students of organizational dynamics.

Workplace Chemistry is based on a multiyear collaboration within a manufacturing firm in northeastern Massachusetts, which I will refer to as Chemical Products or ChemPro.[1] Through the story of one organization's thoughtful and long-term effort to address diversity, the challenges of change are brought to life. When the collaboration began in 1995, the plant had a predominantly Caucasian male workforce. However, the company's desire to promote a workforce that was able to work effectively across a wide range of differences led it to make a serious commitment to a change process. Even though the focus was primarily on racial and gender diversity, ChemPro set as its goal "to establish a workplace where every individual is respected, valued, and allowed to contribute to their full potential without advantaging or disadvantaging anyone." While working with this midsize plant, my role was one of researcher, consultant, and trainer combined. From this unique vantage point, my team and I were able to both help guide and document the organizational efforts. In the process, we became familiar with the inner dynamics of the company's initiatives and were trusted with the personal reflections of those involved. My hope is that telling the story of this one organization will provide a nuanced view of the dynamics and the process of organizational change as ChemPro worked to create a more inclusive and welcoming setting. Kurt Lewin, a pioneer in systems theories, observed that the best way to understand the intricacies of a system is to try to change it.[2] That is certainly what happened here.

why bother?

Before exploring the details of the organizational change process itself, it is essential to step back and address the broader question, why bother? Even though the topic of workplace diversity has been tremendously popular over the last decade, it is nonetheless important to consider why achieving effective diversity might be worth the investment of time and resources for today's organizations. There are at least four aspects to the guiding rationale: Organizations *cannot* avoid it. Organizations *should not* ignore it. Organizational *approach* matters. And besides, attending to diversity is, quite simply, the *right thing* to do.

ORGANIZATIONS *CANNOT* AVOID DIVERSITY

Diversity is a fact of organizational life—diversity among workers is growing in scope and relevance to work practices. Population estimates and projections made by the U.S. Census Bureau in 2004, coupled with the findings of the 2000 census, provide ample evidence that the U.S. population is becoming more diverse. In the decade between 1990 and 2000, the percentages of individuals in the U.S. population who identified themselves as Hispanic and Asian rose 58 percent for Hispanics or Latino/as (of any race) and 72 percent for Asians. The percentage rose a bit more slowly for African Americans but was still up nearly 22 percent.[3]

In 2004, the U.S. Census Bureau estimated that Hispanics or Latino/as of all races numbered about 41 million, non-Hispanic blacks nearly 36 million, and Asians around 12 million. Non-Hispanic whites remained the largest group at nearly 198 million, but their growth has been slower (only up 5 percent between 1990 and 2000). Further, the U.S. Census Bureau's 2004 projections indicate that by the year 2020 Non-Hispanic whites will make up 61.3 percent of the population, compared with 69.4 percent in 2000. By the year 2050, it is projected that this number will decrease to about 50.1 percent of the population. The combined percentage of Native Americans, Alaska Natives, and Pacific Islanders is predicted to grow from 2.5 percent in 2000 to 3.5 percent in 2020 and 5.3 percent in 2050. As of the 2000 census, an increasing number of individuals identified themselves as mixed race (2.4 percent of the U.S. population or 6.8 million). In 2000, 30 million (11 percent of the U.S. population) indicated that they were foreign-born. According to a Bureau of Labor Statistics (BLS) annual report, *Labor Force Characteristics of Foreign-Born Workers,* in 2004 the foreign-born population over sixteen years of age reached nearly 31.8 million. An estimated 12 million new immigrants arrived legally between 1990 and 2000.[4]

As our population grows more diverse, so does the potential workforce. In 1997, Judy and D'Amico, in their celebrated Hudson Institute *Workforce 2020* report, predicted that the workforce would steadily grow more ethnically diverse and that women would constitute about half of the workforce by 2020.[5] We are already almost there. According to the BLS, in 2003 women already constituted 46.6 percent of the workforce, and, looked at from a slightly different angle, about 60 percent of adult women were in the workforce during that year.[6] This compares with a 75 percent participation rate for men. According to the BLS, 2005 participation rates for women and men parallel those of 2003. The patterns of participation include a dramatic increase for women during the 1970s and 1980s, then a more gradual upward trend since. The more striking change has been the very steady increase in the proportion of women who are working full-time, year-round (at about 40 percent in the 1980s but up to about 60 percent in 2003) such that workforce participation rates for women over their life cycles have become more like men's. The trends no longer reflect a dip around child-rearing ages, as was the case for women in the 1970s.[7]

The Hudson Institute Report predicted that by 2020 only two-thirds of workers would be non-Hispanic whites. During 2003, the workforce was roughly 84 percent white (including Hispanic and Latino/a), 5 percent Asian, and 11 percent black. In terms of ethnicity, 12 percent of the workforce was Hispanic or Latino/a (black and white). According to the BLS annual report cited above, *Labor Force Characteristics,* foreign-born workers comprised 14.5 percent of the U.S. labor force during 2004. Native Americans and other ethnic/racial minority groups made up such a small proportion of the workforce that they are not described in the Hudson Institute Report or in the BLS statistics.

At the same time that we see increasing gender, racial, and ethnic diversity among those participating in the workforce, the *relevance* of this diversity is also intensifying with changes in the context, structure, and global nature of work. Organizations are placing greater and greater explicit emphasis on teams to get work done. Reliance on teams involves not only departmental collaboration among immediate coworkers but also cross-functional teams, which are increasingly common structures and demand attention to a wider range of differences. This increased interdependence both within work groups and across work functions has obvious implications for the types of interpersonal skills that are needed to bridge differences in culture, expectations, styles, attitudes, and values among coworkers. The increased ease of electronic communication has reduced the importance of physical proximity in the definition of a team and, with the increased geographic distance, has also intensified the potential for diversity among those who need to work closely together. People need to be able to negotiate these differences.

Other trends in our economy have also rendered diversity dynamics more salient over the last decade. The instability of the U.S. economy has contributed to downsizing and leaner staffing patterns, which not only push some people out of the organization but also put many of those who remain into closer, more highly interdependent working relationships. Mergers present workers with unique challenges around bridging cultures—both among the individuals involved and between the organizations being merged. Additionally, globalization signals not just an increase in the number of international ties and partnerships but also the need for all organizations to learn how to attract, support, and retain a diverse group of workers in order to develop rapport with international clients or constituents, to be responsive to varied markets, to understand differing standards for services, and to reach across borders to solve organizational challenges. All these changes in the structure of work increase the importance of knowing how to work with diversity.

Organizations need to face the fact that their potential pool of employees is increasingly diverse. Simultaneously, today's organizations are confronted with workplace trends that make this diversity essential to their survival. These forces—changing demographics *and* the changing context of work— combine to send a clear message to today's organizations that the challenges associated with a diverse workforce are *not* going to simply pass them by. Diversity *cannot* be avoided.

DIVERSITY *SHOULD NOT* BE IGNORED

Diversity may be inevitable, but some may still wonder, What's the big deal? We're all just people, so why should increased diversity really change anything? The fact is that changes in the demographic makeup of an organization have an impact on individuals, on team dynamics, and on organizational effectiveness. These impacts—both the positive and the problematic—should not be ignored.

On the positive front, increased diversity among workers can open doors to new ways of thinking and approaching work. Diversity within a work team has been associated with greater creativity and innovation.[8] Individuals often thrive. Incorporating a more diverse group of workers signals that broader pools of people are valued by and thus will be attracted to the workplace. People who work in organizations that are free of discrimination tend to be healthier and more satisfied with their jobs.[9] Attendance can even be affected. In a study of bank employees, Ng and Tung found lower absenteeism and higher productivity in heterogeneous branches when compared with more homogeneous branches of the same bank.[10] In some studies focused on the bottom line, companies with positive diversity management records and diverse boards of directors outperformed those with less diversity.[11] Companies with greater diversity also tend to be better business partners and to merge more smoothly with other companies—presumably because they have already learned to accept some cultural differences.[12]

Yet we also know that diverse work groups and organizations face considerable challenges. Clearly, diversity in and of itself is not *automatically* good for business or, for that matter, good for the health and well-being of workers. The simple introduction of individuals of different races, ethnicities, and genders is not necessarily going to precipitate improvement in the effectiveness or financial success of an organization. Working with people from backgrounds that differ from one's own is often not easy. Although diverse teams *can* be more creative than more homogeneous work groups, they can also experience less cohesion, greater turnover, and lower morale.[13] Diverse groups also bump up against increased communication difficulties, misunderstandings, and interpersonal and team conflicts.[14] It is more challenging to work with people who do not share the same assumptions, expectations, values, and worldview. Subtle style differences as well as more blatant biases and discrimination can get in the way. For members of the majority group and those most comfortable in an organization, diversification disrupts predictable patterns and signals changing expectations without a clear promise of improved conditions. For example, in one study, as gender diversity increased, the organizational attachment of white men decreased.[15]

Downplaying the significance of the increased diversity does not help. "We are all just people" is likely to be an ineffective management strategy. In fact, the price of ignoring diversity can be quite high. Title VII of the 1964 Civil Rights Act made it illegal to engage in employment practices that discriminate on the basis of race, color, religion, sex, and national origin. Age and disability were added in subsequent legislation. Discrimination charges, wrongful termination suits, and other violations of fair employment practices can be costly—in terms of time and the direct legal and settlement costs, and also in terms of the indirect impact on worker morale and productivity. In 2005, the Equal Employment Opportunity Commission (EEOC) received 23,094 charges of sex-based discrimination, 12,679 charges of sexual harassment, and 26,740 charges of race discrimination.[16] In a 2003 survey of three hundred privately held firms across the United States, 22 percent of the executives indicated that an employee had filed a discrimination or harassment complaint with the EEOC or a state agency in the previous few years— and the percentage was higher among the larger firms. Half of the company representatives felt that it was likely that such a complaint would be filed in the upcoming year.[17]

The challenge here is to get the most out of the opportunity presented by diversity within work groups while avoiding the potential difficulties. Organizations that pay attention can capitalize on the potential synergy and energy; inaction will not make the challenges go away. Diversity *should not* be ignored.

APPROACH MATTERS

The impact that increased diversity has on organizational effectiveness has everything to do with how organizations go about addressing it. In order to be effective in promoting active collaboration across diverse groups, organizations must recognize the diversity within groups, value the varied resources different groups can bring, and actively support teamwork.[18] Research points to particular elements of organizational settings important for promoting diversity, including an explicit value for diversity among members, openness to alternative approaches, tolerance of ambiguity, and opportunities for cooperative exchanges.[19]

Kochan and colleagues engaged a national group in a five-year research project to assess what conditions might lead to a positive impact of diversity in organizations.[20] Through four case studies conducted by pairs of researchers, they collectively concluded that the effect that diversity has on an organization depends on the organization's business strategy, values, and practices. Conditions that exacerbate the negative effects of racial diversity include an organizational culture that fosters competition within the organization. Diversity seems to have the most positive impact when organizations foster an organizational culture that "promotes learning from diversity"[21] through firmwide approaches that embrace managerial strategies, human resource policies, and employee attitudes that actively value and attend to varied demographics and life demands among workers.

Two of the researchers involved in this collective effort, Thomas and Ely, argue more pointedly that the outcomes for organizations that address diversity are largely dependent on the perspective that guides the initiative.[22] They distinguish among three guiding perspectives: (1) discrimination-and-fairness (i.e., fair treatment agenda), (2) access-and-legitimacy (reaching niche markets), and (3) integration-and-learning (integrated approach). They found that all three perspectives could motivate managers to diversify their staff, but only the most integrated approach yielded sustained benefits for the organization.

Attention to recruitment and fair treatment of women and people of color can successfully broaden demographic diversity among coworkers, but it does not necessarily incorporate a value for the different experiences, ideas, and perspectives that would make diversity a real asset for the organizational work. Seeking diversity will likely increase hiring and initial access to jobs, but it does not necessarily translate into creating a positive climate for all groups once hired or promoted. Access-and-legitimacy efforts to tap new markets with diverse staff can create positive niches within the organization where diversity expertise is valued, but they do not necessarily promote the institutionalization of these values or generalize the same level of acceptance to other parts of the organization. Thus, with this approach, women and people of color may feel valued but tend to be clustered only at the organization's margins. Integration-and-learning is the only approach that considers issues of fairness through all organizational systems and functions, and thus is the approach that is associated with the most positive effects of diversity at work.

Similarly, Harrison, Price, and Bell argue that the *depth* to which diversity is addressed will influence how that diversity affects group and organizational functioning.[23] They distinguish between surface-level (demographic) and deeper-level (attitudinal) diversity. They argue that if an organization goes beyond surface-level demographic markers of race and gender and attends to deeper levels involving appreciation of varied perspectives, then diversity is much more likely to become a resource for the organization instead of a contributor to conflict. They conclude that organizational efforts to attend to the surface level by hiring diverse workers are necessary but not sufficient for effective diversity, and that it is essential to attend to varied attitudes, beliefs, and values through extended contact over time.

Clearly, an organization is not guaranteed benefits from diversity by simply hiring a wider range of demographic groups. Rather, the benefits of diversity are directly shaped by the organizational context and approach, and only realized when the value for diversity is integrated throughout organizational structures and practices. Diversity is not just unavoidable and to be tolerated. Rather, it takes thoughtful and proactive attention *and* a serious investment on the part of the full organization in order to realize the potential benefits. *Approach matters.*

DIVERSITY IS THE *RIGHT THING* TO DO

The incentives of improved group and organizational effectiveness have at times been contrasted with concerns for fairness or equity. However, concern for profitability and values for social justice can be compatible and even synergistic. In fact, workplace diversity advocates are increasingly recognizing that to be successful, diversity initiatives cannot be motivated by the bottom line alone. Paying attention to diversity is often the right—moral, respectful, equitable, just—thing to do.

The rationale behind organizational diversity initiatives has evolved over time. The civil rights movements of the 1960s were accompanied by legal changes that prohibited discrimination in the workforce and established affirmative action guidelines. These new laws provided a wake-up call for many organizations. Yet, by the late 1970s and 1980s, there was increasing recognition that legal mandates were helpful but not sufficient. Diversity training was introduced in many workplaces out of a desire to foster understanding across differences, reduce the more subtle forms of discrimination, and aid the cause of fair employment.

However, in the 1980s, there was a concerted shift away from promoting attention to workplace diversity on the basis of fairness, and increasing attention was put into arguing the "business case." The emphasis was on developing the rationale that diversity is a business necessity, that is, essential for organizations to retain their competitive edge.[24] The social values of fairness, equity, and/or justice per se were not considered compelling enough for organizations to invest in the hard (and potentially costly) work of integrating diverse workers across all job categories and all levels of the organizational hierarchy. In fact, there was some worry that attending to diversity would actually threaten employee satisfaction based on the notion that responding to unique needs of various demographic groups would constitute differential treatment and would compromise the principles of merit and "equal treatment."[25] After a couple of decades of research on the impact of organizational diversity, we now know that there is not a *simplistic* business case to be made.[26] There is no *guarantee* that simply increasing diversity among workers will produce increased profits—particularly in organizations that are not fully committed to institutionalizing the values for working across differences.

We have circled back to value-based rationales. Wise organizational leaders realize that support for people who differ on a wide range of identity and demographic factors can be good business *as well as* the "right" thing to do. They also realize that the complications in relations across differences at work are a reflection of our society—not something unique to the peculiarities of their hired workforce. Societal attitudes and values are the medium within which workforce dynamics are shaped. Stereotypes about women and people of color abound in our society. They shape interpersonal biases, expectations, and assumptions—and thus influence how people treat one another at work. Additionally, a very interesting line of research has shown that when people are reminded of negative societal stereotypes about some group to which they belong (e.g., women, African American, Asian American, etc.), they can stumble even on tasks where they are usually extremely competent.[27]

Simultaneously, the workplace presents us with a unique opportunity to address societal biases and inequities. It is one of the few settings where people learn about issues outside their often-insular personal worlds. In many realms of our lives, people tend to seek out others who are like themselves.[28] Friendship networks, neighborhoods, and even whole cities and towns tend to be composed of people who are similar socioeconomically, racially, and ethnically. Men, whites, and those with greater economic resources are particularly able to shield themselves from the influence of people from less powerful economic, racial, or cultural groups. Thus, members of the majority group are even less often in situations where they find they need to understand people who are "different" and/or who do not share their assumptions and experiences of the world. The reverse is often true for members of minority groups, who typically *must* pay attention to majority group members who have control over important aspects of their lives (e.g., their bosses, their landlords). Jean Baker Miller argued that this is also true for women, who tend to be the less powerful partner in most of their relationships with men. As a result, women tend to be better informed about the ways of men than men are about the ways of women.[29]

As values for diverse ways of being in the world are integrated into our work lives, lessons of tolerance can be taken back to families and communities. There is, in essence, a recursive relationship between diversity dynamics at work and values in the community—with each shaping the other. The potential for positive radiating effects from workplace diversity efforts is tremendous. It is conceivable that if we reduce inequities and insensitivities on the job, our workplaces will be more productive, supportive, and satisfying, *and* individuals who are freed from the constraints of discrimination will be better equipped physically, mentally, and financially to care for their families; to support local institutions like schools, service agencies, and places of worship; and to contribute to their broader communities. Justice and profits can indeed coexist. The social justice rationale is not less pragmatic than the bottom line version—both demand results. The social dividends are just less tangible (and more long-term) than immediate financial returns. The social justice rationale also emphasizes a bigger picture, incorporates the impact on society, and recognizes that inequalities at work take an intense toll on the mental and physical health of a large portion of our population.[30] Fostering settings that are free from discrimination and harassment can, alternatively, provide participants with a sense of dignity and purpose.[31] This is particularly important for groups that have a history of marginalization within U.S. organizations—including women; people of color; lesbian, gay, and bisexual individuals; people of non-U.S. national origin; and people with disabilities.

basic elements: a social ecological perspective

This book is about the process of helping an organization develop the capacity to welcome and make the most out of the differences among employees. Any such organizational change effort is guided by a set of assumptions. The framework that guided the case study presented here is rooted in a social ecological perspective about how systems work.[32]

Consistent with the chemical imagery, an ecological perspective focuses on understanding the natural resources, working with the "medium" or context within which relations across differences have developed, identifying catalysts for change, and clarifying formulas for action that enhance synergy and prevent combustion. The complex nature of the phenomena of workplace diversity makes clear the need for analyses that avoid looking for a single, one-dimensional "cause" but, rather, consider the interaction among multiple levels of analysis from the individual level to the broader societal level.[33]

More specifically, organizational change agents need to consider how individual skill requirements are situated in team contexts, how team dynamics are situated in organizational processes, how organizational issues are situated in national cultural contexts, and how all the issues are situated in broader social, economic, and policy trends. Ultimately, we must consider how factors at all these levels of analysis interact to shape one another and the final outcomes for organizations. Moreover, we also need to push beyond a simplistic "everything is related to everything else" and attend to the power differences and dynamics that mean that some elements of the social ecosystem have more influence than others.[34]

The social ecological perspective is useful here since it is rooted in the notion that the arrangement of the environment (and particularly the distribution of resources) exerts powerful effects on human behavior and that people's behavior can be understood only when viewed in context.[35] You can no more extract a person from his or her family, neighborhood, or workplace to understand her or his behavior than you can take a fish out of water to learn how it swims. The perspective originally drew on concepts from environmental biology and applied them to social systems, thereby challenging traditional psychological theories that locate explanations for human behavior primarily *within* individuals.[36] Levine and Perkins summarize the application as follows: "Social ecology accepts that organismic [i.e., individual] characteristics set certain limits for development. Within those limits, however, the variance among organisms is strongly related to available resources and to necessary adaptations."[37] In other words, people indeed have their own unique characteristics, capabilities, and preferences. But what gets highlighted and developed at any particular time depends, in large part, on what the setting or environment offers in terms of supports and constraints, including structural inequalities.

Some elements of this paradigm that are particularly important for work with organizations revolve around the following principles:

1. *Multileveled analyses.* The relevant ecosystem includes individuals, groups, *and* their environment, where "environment" refers not only to the physical setting but also to the social rules, roles, customs, and laws or policies that affect people's access to opportunities and resources. In terms of supporting a diverse workforce that enables all employees to work to their full potential, this ecological perspective means attending to individual, group, interpersonal, and organizational levels of analysis. At the individual level, there

are beliefs, group identities, attitudes, biases, assumptions, skills, and perspectives of workers. At the group level, there are the interpersonal dynamics that emerge within and among project groups, work teams, and departments. At an organizational level, there are policies, practices, and structures that determine social arrangements. There are also informal ways that values about diversity are expressed and permeate the organizational culture. Additionally, an ecological perspective requires us to consider relationships among various levels of analysis and the way in which power differentials shape those relationships. A critical component of this is the "fit" between, on the one hand, individuals' and/or groups' *needs and competencies* and, on the other, the *demands and resources* provided by a setting.[38] For example, when a woman is not contributing to the team, it is worth considering *both* whether she has the requisite skills *and* whether the team is functioning in a way that facilitates her involvement. A solo woman electrician who is rarely called on by her male manager to address emergencies or who endures sexist comments from coworkers will not perform as well in that context as she will when working with men who trust her skills.

2. *Person-environment adaptation.* The ecological perspective also puts this notion of "multiple levels" into motion by looking at how the individual and the environment continually shape one another. The "fit" between persons and their environments is not a static state, but rather people and their environments are constantly mutually influencing each other and adapting to one another over time. Organizations evolve their own unique ways in which resources— such as money, power, and influence—are created, defined, and distributed among members. Organization members then vary their styles and approaches to cope with available or changing norms and resources. Through the process of mutual adaptation, organizational traditions, structures, and values exert a strong influence on how workers treat one another. At the same time, employees' attitudes, values, and styles help to shape the organizational culture— with majority and minority group members usually having different levels of influence. For example, as the manufacturing sector has encountered tougher international competition, many U.S. firms have been forced to downsize and readjust production procedures to work with leaner staffing. This environmental press can shape a

context where many are worried about the security of their own jobs. In some organizations, workers may feel compelled to constantly advocate for themselves as individuals, the result being that an organizational emphasis on teamwork is hard to maintain. In another organization with a strong tradition of collective accountability for meeting production goals, workers may respond with *increased* attention to team functioning and thus further strengthen the organizational values for teamwork. The reactions of women and people of color in both types of organization are likely to be shaped by a heightened sense of vulnerability during reductions in workforce size.

3. *Phenomenological attitude.* When thinking ecologically, the focus is on people's *experiences* of events—not just on external assessments or descriptions.[39] Understanding some essential or objective "reality" as defined by an "unbiased" observer does not capture how an individual is influenced by her/his environment. This is in sync with feminist standpoint theories, which emphasize constructing knowledge based on participants' experiences of their particular contexts.[40] A phenomenological approach is essential for diversity work in that it allows for an understanding of how *experiences* of the same events might differ for members of different groups depending on their standpoint—both in the moment and historically. Individuals' lived experiences are largely shaped by (and interact with) both group identity issues and differential access to organizational power and resources. The cumulative effect of gender-based and/or race-based person-environment adaptations over time is that the ways women, people of color, and white men experience the same workplace may be quite divergent. Further, it is their lived *experience* of the situation that shapes their response. A solo woman may feel marginalized by a discussion around the watercooler about last Saturday night's parties, while the men find it a bonding experience. Even though they all experience the same conversation, she may withdraw, while the men may find it easier to ask for help on the job as a result of the sharing. Even promotions and rewards can be experienced differently by virtue of membership in various demographically defined identity groups. For example, when a promotion means leaving a mixed-gender or mixed-race group behind to join a group where you will be in a noticeable minority, it is an entirely different experience than when a promo-

tion means you will be interacting with people who look like you, have backgrounds and life experiences similar to yours, and return home to a similar set of family demands at the end of the day. Sensitivity to these varied experiences is an essential element of understanding organizational dynamics around diversity. The search for a single "truth" is fruitless and irrelevant.

4. *Attention to interdependencies.* From an ecological perspective, an organizational system is much like a mobile: touching one part affects the balance of all other parts.

> Visualize a mobile with four or five pieces suspended from the ceiling, gently moving in the air. The whole is in balance, steady yet moving. A breeze catching only one segment of the mobile immediately influences movement of every piece, some more than others, and the pace picks up with some pieces unbalancing themselves and moving chaotically about for a time. Gradually the whole exerts its influence on the errant parts and balance is re-established but not before a decided change in direction of the whole may have taken place. Coalitions of movement may be observed between two pieces. Or one piece may persistently appear isolated from the others; yet its position of isolation is essential to the balancing of the entire system.[41]

All elements making up a system interact and exert influence on one another such that a touch affecting one component will have reverberating effects on other components. Workers are more highly interdependent with one another than they often recognize, and the actions of one person can shape (either open up or limit) the options for the next. For example, when Joe and Tom try to help Ruth out by repairing her tools, she may be tremendously relieved but she does not learn how to do it on her own. Over time, the "guys" may come to resent the extra work without understanding that their behavior has contributed to what they now label as Ruth's "incompetence" and their conclusion that "women can't do this job." Ruth may not understand that her comfort with the initial arrangement contributed to Joe's and Tom's growing resentment. The story leaks out, and the impact radiates to produce a broader attitude that "women don't belong in production." In a parallel manner, formal organizational policies, procedures, and structures shape, but then are also shaped by, informal practices and expectations. For example, even when an organization's formal policies support

TABLE I.1 · QUALITIES OF SETTINGS THAT SUPPORT DIVERSITY

SETTING CHARACTERISTICS	RELEVANT ECOLOGICAL PRINCIPLES
Contextualized understanding	Multiple levels of analysis Person-environment adaptation
Culture of connection	Person-environment adaptation Attention to interdependencies
Recognition of multiple "realities"	Phenomenological attitude
Accountability for impact	Attention to interdependencies

diversity (e.g., nondiscriminatory hiring and promotion policies, family-friendly benefits), subtle disapproval by one's supervisors or peers may keep a woman from lodging a complaint and/or making use of family leave. Alternatively, creating new opportunities for people to come together informally (e.g., at breaks/lunch or during training) may foster new connections across gender and racial differences and thus contribute to creating a more welcoming, inclusive organizational culture. It is essential to remember that a formal organizational intervention cannot determine—or even predict— all the effects that will radiate throughout the organizational system.

QUALITIES OF SETTINGS THAT SUPPORT DIVERSITY

Based on these social ecological principles, the goal of diversity work with ChemPro was to create *organizational settings* that would support diversity.[42] The characteristics of settings that emerged as important through this work are: (1) contextualized understanding, (2) culture of connection, (3) recognition of multiple realities, and (4) accountability for impact. These dimensions will be introduced below and explored further throughout the book (see table I.1).

Contextualized Understanding: Putting Differences into Context. Understanding issues at multiple ecological levels is essential for appreciating the diversity dynamics in any setting or organization. A basic characteristic of settings that support diversity is an emphasis on understanding people in relationship to their contexts. Contextualized thinking is rooted in the ecological value for multileveled analyses and also takes into account the process of adaptation whereby people and contexts shape and mutually influence each other. In some ways, recognition that the environment has an impact on people is common sense. However, in practice it often requires a collective paradigm shift away from locating problems *within* people and toward an emphasis on how multiple contextual factors influence individuals and shape patterns within systems over time. For example, interpersonal dynamics such as stereotyping, self-fulfilling prophecies, and microinequities establish distinctly adverse environmental conditions at work for women and for people of color, with each group facing a unique combination of challenges, constraints, and lack of power and resources. Structural issues such as being few in numbers or lack of policies that prohibit harassment are barriers to empowerment and greater legitimacy. Team dynamics can be subtle yet powerful forces in the creation and maintenance of an organizational culture that keeps women and minorities at the margin.

Contextualized thinking helps to support a less pathologizing stance such that no single individual or group is "blamed" for inequities among diverse groups. The profound ways that informal organizational processes can exclude certain groups help to illustrate why there needs to be attention to issues that range from policies at the organizational level to everyday interpersonal interactions.[43] Constricting change efforts to one level is more likely to produce temporary shifts. It is valuable to consider multiple nested contexts in order to understand any important aspect of organizational life, and diversity is no exception.

Culture of Connection: Bridging Differences. A second key characteristic of settings that value diversity is a sense of connection among members.[44] Sharing overarching goals has long been considered a strategy for bridging differences.[45] A culture of connection adds to those shared goals a sense of "being in it together" and valuing each team member's unique contributions to meeting the goals. This emphasis on the interconnections among coworkers is rooted in the ecological notions of adaptation and interdependence— that is, recognition that coworkers have profound impacts on one another in both formal and informal ways.

The emphasis here is on relationships that are empathetic and reciprocal, that reach beyond differences, and that are sustained over time. Not all types of connection would be expected to be constructive and to support members of marginalized groups. Although "connection" can conjure up images of coming together through what people have in common, it does not necessarily mean we have to be alike. In fact, Trickett, Watts, and Birman put it well when they counseled that "a call for connections should not be a mandate for convergence."[46] Basing connections primarily on similarities can serve a hegemonic function, such that critical differences tied to individuals' identities are not allowed to be expressed (or, if they are, they are defined as dysfunctional). Thus, a critical accompanying theme for settings that support diversity is that they are contexts that actively acknowledge and legitimize differences.

Multiple Realities: Acknowledging Differences. A third characteristic of settings that value diversity is recognition of multiple "realities." The notion of multiple realities is based in a phenomenological attitude and involves awareness that the way coworkers experience the world is shaped by their race, ethnicity, gender, class, and/or other core identities. It involves challenging the stance that "if I've never seen it, felt it, or heard it, it's not there." Phenomenologically, women and people of color often inhabit different workplaces than their white male counterparts. Indeed, sometimes their experiential sense of work varies quite a bit from one to another. Experiences of family policies, overtime demands, inflexible hours, meeting procedures, as well as of the themes of informal exchanges (jokes, teasing, and hallway banter), for example, are often affected by identity-based societal expectations and forces. For example, when company events include "spouses," lesbian or gay male workers are faced with a worry about acceptance of their partners that their heterosexual coworkers do not even begin to ponder. The only African American man on a team with all white coworkers may experience heightened awareness of his race and, unlike his white peers, may be concerned that his comments or requests will be heard not just as his opinion but as a "black" perspective. So when white workers describe their team as open and cohesive, this man is not likely to share the perception.

Creating contexts that value multiple "realities" involves not just recognizing the differences but also understanding the forces that have rendered some "realities" less visible and less legitimate than others. It includes making room for marginalized groups to define their own "reality" rather than having their experiences named and defined for them. It involves challenging many taken-for-granted assumptions. Thus, the challenge vis-à-vis workplace diversity is to create organizational settings that recognize how participants' *experiences* of settings and events vary within and among race and gender groups. Also critical is that communication about those differences is managed such that multiple views are allowed to coexist and the dynamics that privilege one reality over others can be actively addressed.

Accountability for Impact: Going beyond Intent. A fourth characteristic of settings that value diversity is that individuals are held accountable for the impact (versus intent) of their actions. Building on the ecological notions of interdependence and radiating effects, there is an emphasis on promoting awareness and responsibility of workers for their impact on others (e.g., on other individuals, on the team, and even on the organizational culture). Although one's intent in making a comment or taking a particular action is important for understanding motivation and/or the intended goals, it is the *impact* that triggers and shapes the organizational consequences—that is, the ripple effects on coworkers, on team dynamics, and on broader organizational processes. The male facilities supervisor who consistently talks about "the guys" and uses "he" when describing members of his team may do so without any intention to exclude his female carpenter. Yet his language can leave her feeling marginalized and also make her less visible to her coworkers.

Raising awareness of and responsibility for how one's actions affect others may be uncomfortable (it is harder to control than intention), but it is also essential for promoting sensitivity to a wide range of differences among coworkers. A stance of holding people accountable to one another can require some radical revising of organizational cultures in that it contrasts with values for independence and self-advocacy common in many organizations.

PUTTING IT ALL TOGETHER

These ecologically driven aspirations for organizational settings are both commonsense and radical. *Of course* people are affected by their environments, yet building an organizational approach that fully recognizes these influences is rarely done. *Of course* a worker will be able to do a more effective job when s/he is given the resources necessary to do the work. Yet it requires broader thinking to recognize that a secretary's negativity and "gossip" with other secretaries is not necessarily a personal proclivity but, rather, may be shaped by the general lack of respect from others in the organization.[47] *Of course* the way workers feel about their teammates influences the work environment. Yet what about the person who says, "I just want to come in, do my work, and leave—as long as I do a good job, why should anyone care?" or "Nobody said I have to be friends with people around here." While friendships are not required, it represents a major shift to emphasize that what happens *between* coworkers is just as critical to the job as what happens *within* people. *Of course* it's not hard to see how coworkers might experience increased night hours differently from one another based on their sense of safety when traveling home at late hours and based on the family demands that face them once they get there. Yet incorporating such factors into job redesign efforts can be unsettling and raise concerns about special treatment or "pandering" to one group over another. Thinking and acting ecologically can truly be a challenge!

PROCESS CONSIDERATIONS: CONNECTED DISRUPTION

Along with particular ways of understanding system dynamics and the requirements for settings that support diversity, the ecological perspective frames particular ways of approaching the process of inquiry and change. A change effort will be most successful if it is attentive to the unique culture, opportunities, and resources of the setting (context-specific) and is developed collaboratively with respect for the voice of participants in the organization. Yet it nonetheless must be ready to disrupt problematic patterns and challenge complacency.

Connected disruption is how I describe the stance I am suggesting.[48] It is an approach that is nonblaming and attends to the specifics of the context. It involves recognizing the current resources within an organization and seeking to engage in a collaborative process toward change. This stance involves developing settings that promote support for diversity. Being sensitive to the way the environment influences individuals (e.g., attending to multiple levels) and promoting connections with and among participants (e.g., promoting a culture of connection) helps to establish a culture that does not isolate or blame individuals for "getting it wrong," but rather works to promote understanding and make differences acceptable. Missteps can be rendered nonfatal—even, perhaps, understandable. At the same time, *connected disruption* is a stance that involves disrupting the status quo, challenging the current arrangements, and holding people accountable in new ways. Paying attention to multiple levels of context and fostering a culture of connection are perhaps the preconditions for promoting honest recognition of multiple realities and emphasizing accountability for impact. If you ask people to incorporate different ways of viewing the world without also validating their views, the dissonance is often too great to allow them to open up to change. If holding people accountable for their impact is paired with a stance that blames or shames individuals for their actions, resistance will become too great for more constructive processes to emerge. However, if reevaluating one group's lock on defining "reality" and increasing accountability for impact are fostered through a process that is context-specific, collaborative, and respectful, then you can open up possibilities to disrupt "business as usual" and work toward change.

structure of *workplace chemistry*

The ecological perspective and ecologically derived goals form the backdrop for the case example explored in this book. I will tell a story about one company's diversity initiative undertaken through an organizational change process. I will interpret it through an ecological lens, and I will share the principles for action that emerged from the experience. The book is based on a long-term, multilevel partnership with a New England manufacturing firm that recognized both the value for and the inevitability of increased diversity in their ranks. The purpose of the book is to trace the dynamics involved as this organization made a serious and sustained commitment to help *all* employees work to their fullest potential. To provide a nuanced picture of the change process, the story told here includes not only the successes but also the complex subtleties, messy dilemmas, and delicate balancing acts that emerged during the work with this one organization. Through the telling of this story, the book illustrates a way of thinking about the development of a healthy organizational culture for diversity and the process of working toward change through a participative and sustained effort.

The team that worked with me on this project included an often-changing cast of faculty, staff, and students from the University of Massachusetts Lowell with interests in workplace diversity.[49] Although I was the team leader and the only constant across all the activities and all the years, I have worked with numerous teammates along the way. An early partner was Jean Pyle, an economist and collaborator on other theoretical work on workplace diversity. As the work with ChemPro evolved and focused more on intervention activities, several "waves" of students and colleagues were involved through course work, master's theses and projects, internships, research assistantships, and as paid consultants.[50] Robin Toof, from the UMass Lowell Center for Family, Work, and Community, was an important collaborator in designing and facilitating the training sessions. In addition, we all partnered with a core group of ChemPro employees whom I will introduce as this story unfolds.

In the fall of 1993, Jean Pyle and I approached the director of human resources (HR) about doing a case study of ChemPro. We were interested in working with an organization to develop a portrait of the multiple factors and dynamics involved in developing and supporting organizational diversity.[51] The HR director had done a master's project under my supervision on workplace diversity, and we knew she was invested in the topic. When we met, we found she was indeed very interested in establishing a partnership and convinced that the organization would benefit from looking more closely at its diversity dynamics. At that time, however, she was doubtful that the president would make this a priority. Almost exactly a year later, she called and announced that the conditions were now right—circumstances had opened the door. Little did I know at the time that this work would evolve into a longer-term collaboration.

What had led me to ChemPro was the combination of circumstances just described: my relationship with an ex-student alongside some fortuitous timing. My long-term involvement, however, grew out of a deep appreciation (dare I say affection?) that I developed for the people with whom I was working and a mutual respect that emerged out of our shared commitments to equity, justice, and fairness. My distinctly professional-class background certainly did not prepare me for this blue-collar setting; my feminist values did not make a white male setting a "logical" fit; and my many years of research and organizational consulting in the nonprofit human service sector did not make a for-profit, manufacturing company a natural choice. Yet I found I was drawn to this organization and the people in it. I somehow knew that they could teach me at least as much as I could teach them. This book is my way of sharing those lessons.

It is important to note before going much further that the work with ChemPro focused primarily on issues of race and gender. Although the dynamics that emerged and challenges that ensued might have parallels for projects dealing with other types of diversity, our primary focus was fairly specific. The choice to focus on two primary dimensions of the broader topic of "diversity" was guided by two factors—one pragmatic and the other more philosophical and paradigmatic. First, the concerns felt most deeply by the organization revolved around race and gender. There were also ethnic differences among workers (e.g., many of Portuguese descent), and issues related to disabilities and sexual orientation did enter the dialogue during the course of training. However, the most palpable and visible interpersonal tensions had to do with race, and the most intractable structural barriers were tied to sex segregation and gender stereotyping.

Second, the initiative was based on a belief that not all differences are created equal—some are more loaded than others. The focus in this case study has been on dimensions of diversity that reflect power imbalances. Many of the observations offered in this book may be relevant to other groups affected by differential privilege and limited access to resources (e.g., based on sexual orientation or disabilities), even though I will not address them as directly as I will race and gender. The initiative described here was *not* geared toward differences along such dimensions as personal style or personality, where group-based power differences and group identity issues do not emerge. This emphasis on power differences contrasts with the approaches of some consultants who either feel that diversity dynamics easily generalize across all types of difference[52] or worry that dealing directly with race and/or gender produces too much backlash to be useful.[53]

Clearly, power-related differences carry more intensity. An intervention to address these loaded dimensions requires tremendous attention to the development of a safe and respectful approach. It is more delicate; it is more difficult. However, if differences based on race and gender are treated as though they are parallel to differences on such dimensions as personality, the discussion loses the focus on inequality and stigmatization.[54] Folding the high-intensity dimensions into a discussion of more mundane differences that do not carry with them any comparable historical and structural "baggage" ignores the distinctive dynamics of privilege and oppression. The work described here keeps a focus on differential access to resources and addresses the challenges of crafting a change process that allows such work to be done constructively.

In this analysis, "effective support for diversity" includes not only the actual representation of diverse workers at all levels of the organization (i.e., a representational component) but also an interactional component (e.g., members of different groups working well together) and an organizational culture component (e.g., well-established organizational values for supporting diverse peoples).[55] Support for diversity is not a stable "state of being" for an organization; neither is it akin to a production goal. Rather, it involves incorporating organizational processes and values that permeate every aspect of organizational life. It is also not the achievement of some level of perfection or a state where organizational members never make mistakes or missteps. The goal is more akin to the chemical notion of "dynamic equilibrium," where what looks like a steady state is achieved only through constant recalibration as new elements are added and as environmental conditions change. It is the adoption of values and strategies for grappling effectively and honestly with diversity issues whenever such problems emerge. In line with this definition, *Workplace Chemistry* not only documents this organization's efforts to achieve greater diversity in its workforce but also describes lessons learned from the dilemmas faced along the way.

The book begins by introducing the reader to the organization. In chapter 1, I describe ChemPro and place the current initiative into historical context. Chapters 2 through 5 describe the change initiative in depth, starting with the initial assessment and work to provide a foundation for change (chapter 2),

TABLE I.2 · OVERVIEW OF ECOLOGICAL REFLECTIONS ABOUT
ORGANIZATIONAL CHANGE

Chapter 1	
Understanding the organization	Anchoring organizational change in context · Recognizing the indigenous resources · Attending to organizational momentum · Working in sync with the organizational culture

Chapter 2	
Setting the stage for collaborative action	Recognizing assessment as an opportunity to create energy for change · Incorporating multiple voices · Putting "resistance" into context · Broadening the support base

Chapter 3	
Developing and delivering the training	Connecting training to everyday life · Integrating new realities through storytelling · Addressing privilege in a group that does not feel privileged · Managing the tension between individual awareness and team cultures

Chapter 4	
Working with team dynamics	Understanding team culture as the essential medium for change · Challenging team cultures that press for sameness · Confronting contradictions between organizational values for participation and diversity · Understanding leaders in relation to their teams

Chapter 5	
Assessing and institutionalizing change	Appreciating the motion of organizational life · Recognizing that systems are in perpetual motion · Allowing for change in the meaning of measures · Attending to social locations

then moving to descriptions of the training workshops (chapter 3), consultation with work teams (chapter 4), and finally evaluation and institutionalization efforts (chapter 5). The chapters describe the substance of the initiative
and trace the dynamics that unfolded at each phase. The insights gained
through the organizational change experience are interpreted through an
ecological lens to yield a set of lessons about systems change. Lessons relevant to each phase are summarized at the end of each chapter. These lessons
are framed more in terms of dilemmas or balancing acts than as prescriptive
"how tos" because of my belief that approaches to diversity must be contex-
tually grounded and derived from the particularities of the system involved. I
will refer to them as "Ecological Reflections." They are lessons about system

dynamics to consider, forces working against diversity to contend with, opportunities to capitalize on, and stances to take as a change agent. Taken together, the reflections describe the essence of what I have referred to as *connected disruption*. The final chapter pulls together the various threads from all aspects of this work and presents a framework to guide future change initiatives. (See table I.2 for an overview).

> Chemical change occurs everywhere: in the processes of respiration that permit us to live, in the slow geological transformations that shape the earth's surface, in the formation of molecules deep in interstellar space. Some of these changes are slow, some fast, some are barely detectable, some strikingly dramatic. Chemistry is the study of these changes.[56]

This book is a study of organizational changes ... some slow, some fast, some barely detectable, and some strikingly dramatic.

1

chempro

CHEMICAL PRODUCTS (ChemPro) is located in an industrial city of about fifty thousand in the northeastern United States and is a subsidiary of a major national corporation. The company employs about two hundred full-time workers and produces a specialized chemical needed for one of the major products of the parent corporation. The physical plant has been producing related products for almost two hundred years, long before ChemPro took over the facility in 1930. The facility has 700,000 square feet of production space in over forty buildings on a 500-acre site.

the workforce

ChemPro is divided into five manufacturing units, two research labs, facilities (including maintenance, security, and power plants), and administration (including an environmental health and safety unit as well as financial and clerical staff) (see figures 1.1 and 1.2).

The production process involves turning animal materials into substances usable for other purposes. The workers on the production units do the nitty-gritty work of combining and washing raw materials, processing and "cooking" them under highly controlled conditions, then filtering and drying so that the crystals are highly uniform and ready for use.

The Research Labs are responsible for both quality control and research and development activities. The Facilities Department primarily employs people in the skilled trades and is responsible for the upkeep of the equipment, security, and the maintenance of the grounds. Workers in the power plant, water system, and waste treatment plant are somewhat physically separated from the rest of production. Turnover at ChemPro was almost nonexistent owing to a combination of good wages and benefits, a sense that com-

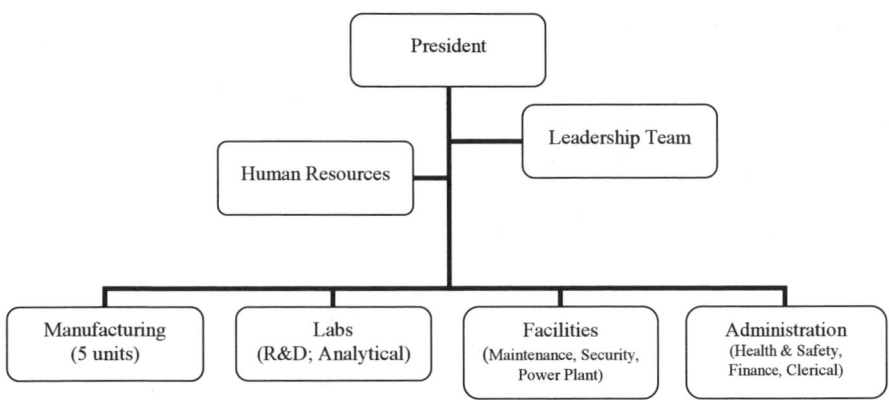

FIGURE 1.1 ChemPro Organizational Chart

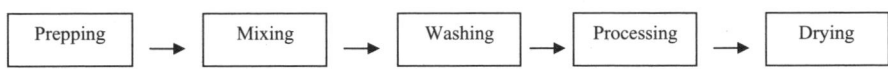

FIGURE 1.2 Manufacturing Units

parable jobs were not available elsewhere, and a general commitment to the organization fostered by the fact that many people were the second or third generation in their families to work there.

When we began our collaboration in 1995, the workforce of 211 was largely white and male (71.1 percent white men). The next-largest group was white women (14.7 percent). The remaining 14.2 percent were people of color—mostly black men (9.5 percent) but also a few Asian men (2.4 percent), three black women (1.4 percent), one Asian woman (0.5 percent), and one Latina (0.5 percent) (see figure 1.3). In our interviews, one white woman described ChemPro as "Mr. 40-year-old-white-male plant."

There was clear sex and racial segregation in jobs. In 1995, about two-thirds of all women were in office or lab positions. The majority of people of color were men (85 percent) and worked in production as operators and technicians. The distribution of people of color and women was uneven across the five production units. The percentage of white men within different production units ranged from 56.5 percent to 92.6 percent, and the percentage of men of color ranged from 4.3 percent to 22.7 percent. The percentage of women ranged from 0 to 39.1 percent. The majority of women—and *all* the women of color—in production were clustered in one unit (Drying), whereas an entirely different production unit had the highest percentage of people

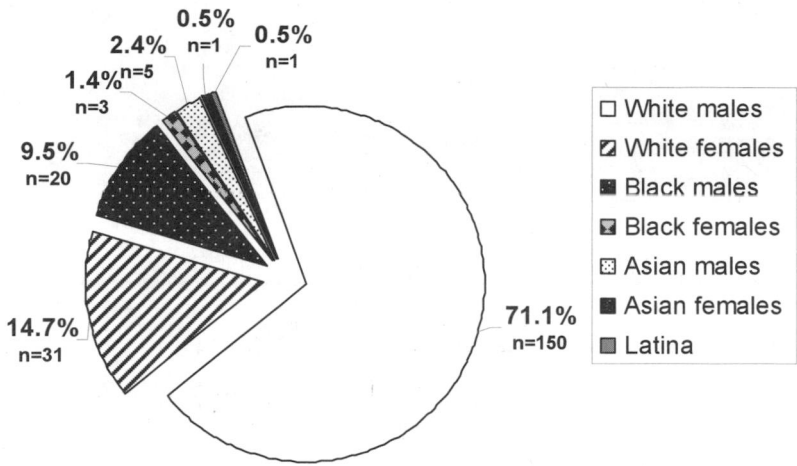

FIGURE 1.3 Race and Sex of ChemPro Workforce (n = 211)

of color, all of whom were men (Prepping) (see figure 1.4). When we began our partnership at ChemPro, the top leadership team consisted of five white men, one Asian man, and one white woman.

changing business context

The company has a history not unlike that of many manufacturing firms established in the first half of the twentieth century—although its status as a subsidiary of a larger international company has added some important twists. The history that led up to our work with ChemPro can be described in three phases.

BEFORE 1980

Up until the early 1980s, the plant had only one customer for its product—its corporate parent. Thus, there was absolutely no need for a marketing strategy and little press for detailed business plans or strategic planning. Production levels were not driven by "customer need" but rather set by organizational planners. There were limited customer specifications and no enforced quality standards for the product. There was no tracking of worldwide inventories and no regular measurement of financial performance.

The company was run in what could be described as a fairly "paternalistic" fashion—kindly but without much employee involvement. The company was generally generous with pay and benefits particularly when compared with other local employers. The skills needed by plant managers were primarily

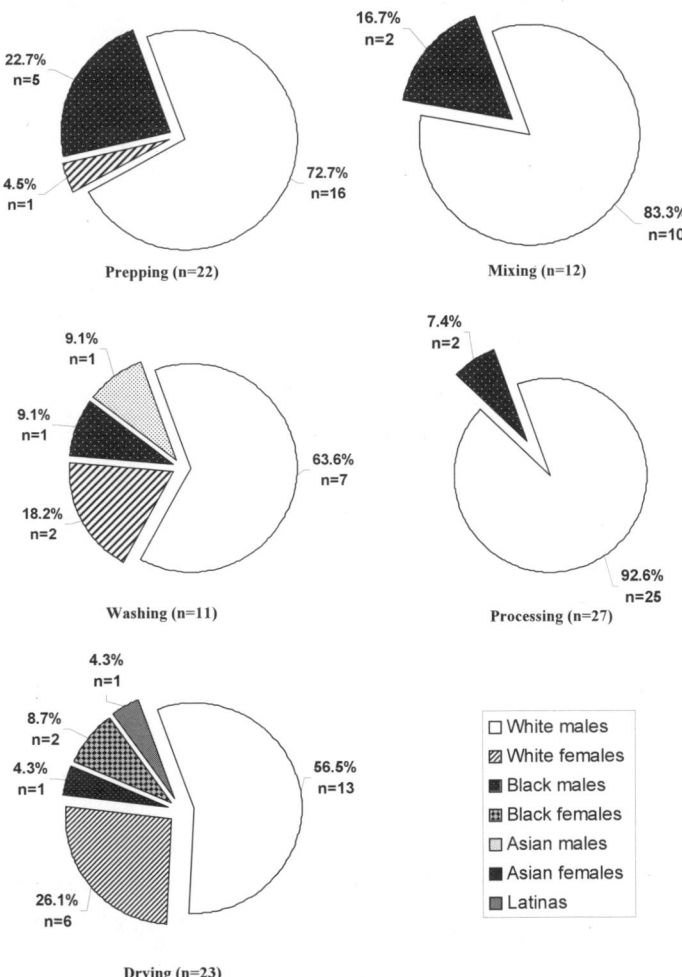

FIGURE 1.4   Race and Sex of Workers in Manufacturing Units

technical proficiency and operational knowledge. The managers gave direc-tives to workers; delegation was minimal. Employee involvement in problem solving and innovation were not even considered. Managers did have to be responsive to requests from the single customer (and owner), but there was no real need for innovation or change. In fact, the standards of operating were, explicitly, to continue with the way things had always been done—stability and standardized approaches were valued. Given this context, the technical skills needed from operators were minimal; physical strength and endurance were important requirements.

The surrounding community demanded only limited accountability. There were few environmental restraints or rules imposed by the city, county, or state. The company was the largest taxpayer in the city, the largest employer, and had the highest pay scales. Most employees were local, and many were related by blood or marriage to one another. The community generally accepted whatever negative impacts the company may have had on the neighborhood. People were not inclined to complain, because it was assumed that with jobs came some annoying but unavoidable negatives. The community had grown up on the tanning industry, one not known for its largess or sensitivity to local concerns. By contrast, ChemPro was considered responsive and had a long history of community involvement through contributing land, money, and expertise to the community. Environmental concerns were not on the community agenda until a national movement increased awareness in the 1980s.

During this period, there were also no state or federal regulatory agencies such as the Occupational Safety and Health Administration (OSHA) or Environmental Protection Agency (EPA). There were no affirmative action or equal opportunity requirements. Close relationships with the local government were based largely on the economic clout of the company and facilitated by some employees who served in important community positions, both appointed and elective.

SHIFT IN THE GLOBAL CONTEXT: THE 1980S

In the 1980s the world of ChemPro changed dramatically. Four other companies—all in other countries—were producing similar products. The quality of the competitors' products had improved, and the costs had remained steady or actually decreased. Some competitors not only offered higher quality but also focused on consistent quality. All this whetted the parent company's appetite for improvements in quality and reductions in costs. The parent corporation (which I will refer to as "Corporate") began to more actively monitor and evaluate the ChemPro subsidiary—basing evaluations largely on its financial performance and its ability to compete with the other manufacturers. In essence, ChemPro was moving from being a simple production arm of a larger corporation to a company with worldwide business competitors.

These dramatic shifts created a need for changes on many fronts, but particularly in the role of managers and in their relationships with workers. Managers increasingly needed to develop financial measures (return on assets, return on investments, productivity rates, etc.) and to understand competition, especially as it was being played out in international markets. Strategic planning and benchmarking against competitors were essential. Managers were being asked to *drive* change rather than *prevent* it; innovation became highly valued. Thus, they needed to develop very different leadership skills such as coaching, delegating, and motivating their workers. This was no simple matter in that all the existing mangers—both senior and midlevel—were engineers or scientists and, at least initially, had some difficulty with the concept that supervisors should serve as inspirational coaches and not just as experts who told workers what to do. They had an average seniority of twenty years but an average age of fifty. So, while they were well indoctrinated in the ways of the past, retirement was not close at hand.

With the shift in global context, plant workers were required to have expanded skill sets. Previously, workers had not even needed to be literate, but now they needed not only to be able to read but also to have strong math, problem-solving, and communication skills. Workers now needed a greater understanding of the production process, and technical skills became a must. They could no longer rely solely on their physical abilities.

At the same time, a host of new legislation affected the day-to-day operation of a manufacturing business. The Environmental Protection Agency (EPA) and state environmental agencies established environmental standards. New federal employment and discrimination laws, retirement and pension laws, and specific legislation affecting foreign companies all influenced how Chem-Pro had to operate.

This was also a time of increased community awareness and activism around environmental issues. There was greater public demand for information and greater concern about any chemicals that the plant might be releasing into the water, soil, and/or air. The neighbors were becoming less likely to tolerate noise, dust, odors, and traffic congestion emanating from the plant. City services were being cut because of budget constraints, and there was growing public expectation that companies would take on additional civic duties and contribute constructively to the community in such areas as education and cultural affairs.

CHANGES IN VISION: THE 1990S

The 1990s brought further challenges as ChemPro continued to have to deal with international competition and changing technologies. Its competitors—particularly those in Asia and Europe—had highly skilled and technically educated workforces and continued to improve product quality and services. The pressure for short-term results complicated the challenge of shifting to more strategic thinking and long-term planning.

In the early 1990s, there was a marked change in the company philoso-phy as the leadership increasingly emphasized team-based management. The demands on managers for broader skill sets intensified. Managers needed to understand both long-term and short-term strategic planning, both the inter-national arena and local customer needs, both the fiscal and the production issues. Alongside the ability to see the "big picture," managers also needed to better understand how to create and coach employee teams. They needed to delegate day-to-day operational decisions as well as to initiate, drive, and manage change within their teams. Soft skills (interpersonal, teamwork, etc.) were now added to the technical and physical skills required of operators. Several reorganizations were done to facilitate team-based decision making and employee empowerment. Even though early retirements were creating some openings, turnover continued to be low. Thus, the changes primarily meant retooling and retraining a current workforce that had become comfort-able with old ways of operating.

With government agencies and the local community demanding in-creased accountability for environmental and employment issues, ChemPro had to find constructive ways to respond. It moved to make the plant entirely self-sustaining. Water was pumped from numerous wells on the ChemPro property; the company developed waste treatment operations to clean all the water used in the production process; and it maintained its own power plant. It developed the ability to recycle all the solid waste from the manufacturing process for use in other products. To support these efforts, ChemPro shifted resources into these operations such that about 9 percent of the total yearly budget began going into projects dealing with environmental issues.

It was in this context of changing technological, environmental, and fiscal demands that we entered the scene in the mid-1990s. It quickly became clear that the playing field would never stand still again. Over the years in which we worked with the company, we witnessed further technological changes, reorgani-zations, and even downsizing as the pressure continued for a leaner production process. Like most manufacturing firms in the twenty-first century, ChemPro continues to adapt to rapid changes in technology and in the global economy.

key players

Our primary partner from the beginning was Keitha, the director of Human Resources (HR). Keitha was an African American woman who began her career at ChemPro in her midtwenties. A single mother with a high school degree, she started as a clerical assistant in the HR Department. From there she moved to the plant floor and became the first woman to ever hold a supervisory position in manufacturing. While working full-time, she earned her bachelor's degree and then, several years later, went back to school to earn a master's degree. She returned to the personnel aspects of the company and served as assistant director of HR for several years. I met her while she was a student in our master's program in community social psychology, where I advised her thesis on workplace diversity. Keitha was extremely well respected throughout the plant and was particularly sought out by other people of color when they felt marginalized or treated unfairly. She was an important sounding board for those in the minority. In 1992, after about seventeen years in the plant, she was promoted to director of the department. She became one of only two women in management roles and the highest-ranking black manager, but was not initially given the same access to the leadership group that her predecessor, an African American man, had enjoyed. She was not invited to become a full member of the leadership team until a couple years *after* we began our work with the company—a move bolstered by our feedback to the president that her lack of status was sending a message to the plant that the contributions of women and minorities were not valued.

The white male president was another central player in the organizational change process. Even though we worked primarily through HR, Warren supported our work and initiated several parallel activities related to diversity. He was committed to a "zero tolerance" policy prohibiting discrimination and harassment of any kind in the plant. He had been sent from Corporate headquarters in the early 1990s to be the ninth president of ChemPro. In his initial years, he was generally well regarded but mocked for being formal and meticulously groomed—for "never having a hair out of place." Many saw his demeanor as a sign of "hard-nosed" rigidity. He was not a "local," and many worried that he was out of step with the blue-collar world of production. He was to earn tremendous respect from all corners of the plant, however, as he began to listen to feedback, increase communication, and prove himself to be an advocate for the workers on several fronts. Many were surprised by how open and responsive he was when faced with a crisis of confidence and subsequent business and structural changes. As one worker reflected, "When he knew there were issues inside the plant, he responded. I didn't think it was possible for somebody to change. I thought you could change for three months and you could change for so many days but eventually you would revert back to your old behavior. But he never did—still to this day has not reverted back." By the time he retired, he was widely respected by workers at all levels.

The third key player was Rich. Like Keitha, Rich began his career at ChemPro in an entry-level job. His Irish-American father was working in the plant when Rich got a job as an operator at the age of twenty-one. He started out in what he described as "the worst job in the plant," working in the "hot rooms" and cleaning huge kettles. He was miserable. "I remember almost crying coming in here 'cause it was *so* brutal . . . what we had to do back then was so much different. Today is so much more modernized." However, he stuck it out—with just a GED in hand he did not see a lot of other options that paid as well. When there was an opening in the R&D Lab five years later, he applied and was taken under the wing of the lab manager. He spent thirteen years there working his way up from a technician to a team leader. Although a self-described "troublemaker" when in production, he grew to be very well liked and respected by others during his years at the plant. "I got myself a reputation, and a bad one, and I deserved it. And it took me a long time to change that. And what happened was the R&D manager took me in . . . basically he just kinda, ya know, put the screws down, and said 'This is the way. You're screwing yourself up, and you gotta straighten out' and this and that. And I did, and I just started working hard."

I initially met Rich during a consultation with the R&D Lab, but closer collaboration began when he accepted a promotion to training coordinator in the HR Department. In this role, he became our partner in the design and facilitation of the Workplace Chemistry training workshops. Keitha continued to be deeply involved, but Rich was a cotrainer and, given his history in the plant, a key to designing training that was relevant to the lives of the "guys" on the floor. After a couple of years, Rich's job as training coordinator evolved into a position as a general HR assistant, and he was helping Keitha in most HR functions. In 2001, when Keitha was promoted to work in HR at Corporate headquarters, Rich became director of HR at ChemPro. This was an unusual move and vote of confidence since Rich did not have a college degree. He had proven himself on the job and was promoted to take Keitha's place through the strong advocacy of Warren and Keitha. From that point forward, our primary connection to ChemPro was through Rich. The succession of leadership in HR was fortuitous for our diversity initiative, as the commitment to diversity transferred relatively smoothly into Rich's hands.

eye-opening moments

Even with many organizational supports in place, it often takes a specific catalyst to move an organization to action. This was indeed the case here. A
couple of specific situations heightened leadership awareness and resolve to
address employee concerns about isolation, differentials in disciplinary action,
and greater dissatisfaction among women and people of color than among
white men.

As mentioned above, the organization had gone through multiple reorganizations prior to our arrival in 1995. Employees felt pressed to work harder
and faster. There were also cuts in the hiring of supplemental workers, resulting in increased workloads and considerable mandated overtime. Dissatisfaction had also been fueled by proposed changes in benefits (particularly
higher health premiums). About a year and a half before we began working
at ChemPro, this unhappiness had led to rumblings about a union. A black
employee described the situation as follows: "A lot of that stuff [union organ-
izing] had to do with . . . Corporate forgot about the worker. They just wanted
more and more and more and they forgot about the person, and I think they
got a wake-up call when this [the union bid] happened."

The prospect of a union was so counter to the organization's self-image
(i.e., as generous, responsive, and worker-friendly) that the pro-union organizing signaled a crisis of identity. Many workers were also ambivalent about
a union. As the key organizer put it, "We didn't really want a union—we just
wanted Corporate to listen." Indeed, the organizing got the attention of both
ChemPro and Corporate. As the lead worker put it:

> We started off focused on benefits but [the organizing] triggered a
> whole lot more about how they treated workers. It created a lot of extra
> work for Warren, for everyone . . . I didn't mean to do all that but, we
> came out in a much better place. I took this thing about as far as I
> could. We got a good response so the activity pretty much ceased . . . I
> tried to tell others, I said, "You could still go forward," but I really
> didn't want them to.

The spreading dissatisfaction had quickly motivated the president to
become much more proactive in reaching out to workers. He shed his tie,
rolled up his sleeves, and began spending more time on the plant floor. As
his awareness of workers' concerns grew, Warren publicly apologized to the
plant and worked to explain better the fiscal pressures that had led to the pro-

posed changes. He began holding weekly open meetings with the entire workforce. In these meetings, workers identified a wide range of issues, including concerns about fairness, consistency, and respect for differences.

As a result, many came to believe they could work *with* Warren toward the desired changes. The workers, while not totally united, generally understood that many of the upsetting changes had not been proposed locally but rather had come down as policy dictates from above. Warren's active outreach not only shifted the discontented workers' focus to Corporate headquarters; it allowed for greater coordination within the plant to build a case to get Corporate to better understand the distinctive situation at ChemPro (e.g., the higher cost of living in the Northeast in comparison to the midwestern site of the Corporate offices). Warren was able to shift his role from "messenger of bad news" to one of responsive advocate, particularly as he grew to better understand the stresses ChemPro workers were experiencing. As Keitha put it, "It was a humbling experience for him—for us. It humbled management enough to get us to really listen."

As a result of increased contact with employees, Warren also became sensitized to the subtle ways in which race and gender had been affecting the ability of workers to perform their jobs. Racial and gender issues were part of the problem. As one white woman said about this period: "We already had a bunch of racial issues here—and gender issues too—but it became much more obvious in the last year. I think a lot of people issues were let go for a long time, but they all came out."

Keitha had fielded—and experienced—concerns about the racial and gender dynamics at ChemPro for many years. She took the opportunity presented by the crisis to again raise concerns about the differential impact of the changes on subgroups within the plant. It had become apparent that, with the increased demands for teamwork, more workers of color and immigrant workers with English as a second language were having problems than were the majority white, English-speaking workers. Most of the people targeted as "poor performers" were black. With the increased stress and focus on worker accountability, the diversity among workers became more visible, motivating Warren, with encouragement from Keitha, to consider what factors beyond individual skill levels were contributing to problems.

One situation was described by Warren as particularly eye-opening. A black employee had complained about lack of support from his white coworkers. He felt like an outcast, left out of decisions and unfairly criticized, and yet his concerns were generally ignored by others on his shift. He became increasingly unreliable and late. The company eventually had to let him go because he stopped showing up for work, but Warren, with Keitha's support, came to see how the issues that led to this man's dismissal had been shaped by his exclusion by white coworkers. Warren became convinced that had all the players involved been more sensitive to the racial undertones, the situation would not have unraveled.

These events opened the door to some new ways of understanding and proceeding. Recognizing that external resources could help, the president and HR manager (Warren and Keitha) invited our team to conduct the case study we had proposed a full year prior. There was now a *readiness* to commit to a process of organizational change. Keitha actually described it as a sense of urgency: "We were realizing that if we didn't make the changes, we weren't going to survive."

the company in broader context

The broader environment exerts a powerful influence—whether we are talking about how temperature affects the rate of a chemical reaction or how community and societal forces affect organizational change. Thus, it was not only important to understand the evolution of events and forces *within* ChemPro; it was equally important to understand how the local organization was embedded in larger systems. The two most critical ones for ChemPro involved the parent corporation and the local community.

THE PARENT CORPORATION

The parent corporation (which I have been referring to as "Corporate") was a major international company established in the late 1800s—successful and diversifying ever since. Corporate wholly owned ChemPro and was its sole customer. The president of ChemPro was responsible for all the production activities at the plant and reported to a supervisor at Corporate headquarters. ChemPro was located in the northeastern United States; Corporate was located in the Midwest. By the mid-1990s, Corporate employed almost ninety thousand people.

Not only was the business environment changing for ChemPro during the 1980s and 1990s, but parallel forces were also influencing Corporate. Just prior to our partnership with ChemPro in the early 1990s, Corporate had expanded into new markets and been hit with hard times. It had been forced to lay off thousands of workers. By the time we began our consultation, a new

Corporate president had taken over and refocused the basic mission of the company. There was a generally optimistic sense of the future, even though there was continued tightening of the belt and streamlining of operations. The new CEO introduced five core values to guide the company, which in essence codified how Corporate expected employees to behave toward one another. These values included respect for employee dignity, integrity, trust, credibility, and continuous improvement. This new leadership signaled a significant shift in management style and values—as well as in opportunity and accountability structures. There was increased emphasis on fostering a more informed and more involved workforce and on promoting a "coaching" approach for managers.

The emphasis on the core value of "respect for the dignity of individuals" became a foundation for many new diversity-related initiatives, and the new Corporate CEO articulated the affirmation of diversity as a priority. In some ways this focus was not new. There had already been some effort to recruit a more gender- and racially diverse workforce, and Corporate had been early to adopt a family leave policy in the 1980s before the Family and Medical Leave Act (FMLA) was enacted into law. However, in the 1990s the company made its commitment to diversity even more explicit. It recognized that simply employing a diverse group of employees would not be enough. The Corporate vision was revised to include developing an "inclusive organizational environment" based on the belief that when provided with a work environment that fosters dignity and trust, employees will be better able to put their creative energy toward their work. Corporate was supportive of Chem-Pro's efforts to proactively address diversity. It was actively engaged in several parallel activities and, in fact, on several occasions looked at the work we were doing at ChemPro as a model.

THE COMMUNITY

ChemPro was, in some ways, an extension of Corporate, yet it was also tightly embedded in its own unique local community. There was a long history of involvement of individual ChemPro employees in community activities through contributions of time, expertise, and money. The company had also donated over 30 acres of land to various city and county groups—some for land conservation and some for the construction of community facilities such as museums, gymnasiums, municipal offices, and parks. The company was particularly proud of its partnerships with local school science programs.

More than 50 percent of ChemPro employees lived in the city where the plant was located. This city of about 50,000 was largely white working class. Census data indicated that, in 1990, 96.8 percent of the population was white; in 2000 it was still almost 94 percent white. However, the company was located in an increasingly Hispanic neighborhood, and Hispanics were the largest and fastest-growing ethnic group in the city. The surrounding communities from which ChemPro drew most other workers were similarly majority white, but changing even more rapidly. In one neighboring community of about 40,000 where whites decreased from 93 percent to 85.4 percent of the population during the 1990s, groups of color grew from 6.1 percent to 14.6 percent over the same period. The Latino/a proportion of the population (some whites and some people of color) almost doubled (6.7 percent in 1990, 11.2 percent in 2000). In another nearby town (of about 89,000), the white population dropped from 83 percent in 1990 to about 68 percent in 2000. Latino/a representation grew from around 9 percent to over 18 percent, and all people of color from 17 percent to over 32 percent.[1] Additionally, Asians and Asian-Americans were moving to this area and were a rapidly growing segment of the population. In one community, it was estimated that the Asian population grew more than 90 percent, from just under 3,000 people to over 5,000, with the largest Asian group being Cambodians.

The overall growth in the immigrant population in this region has been dramatic. In one local school system, it was estimated that there were over twenty-five first languages spoken among families. During the 1990s, the state recorded the largest growth in immigrants in nearly a century. By 2000, foreign immigrants represented just under 13 percent of the total U.S. labor force. In the northeast region of the state near ChemPro, they made up over 16 percent of labor force participants—and the numbers continue to grow. The newest arrivals have come largely from the Caribbean, Central and South America, as well as from Southeast Asia, Portugal, Russia, and India. These immigration trends have significantly changed the face of the entire northeastern United States and have accounted for similarly high portions of the population growth in surrounding states.

While the overall size of the civilian labor force is not changing rapidly, its complexion is. ChemPro could not ignore the fact that it is located in a region with a pool of employees that, while still predominately white, is increasingly ethnically and racially diverse. At the same time, it is an area of modest means. The per capita income, according to the 2000 U.S. Census, was below $25,000 in all three communities closest to ChemPro, yet the cost of living was well above the national average. It is also an area where the propor-

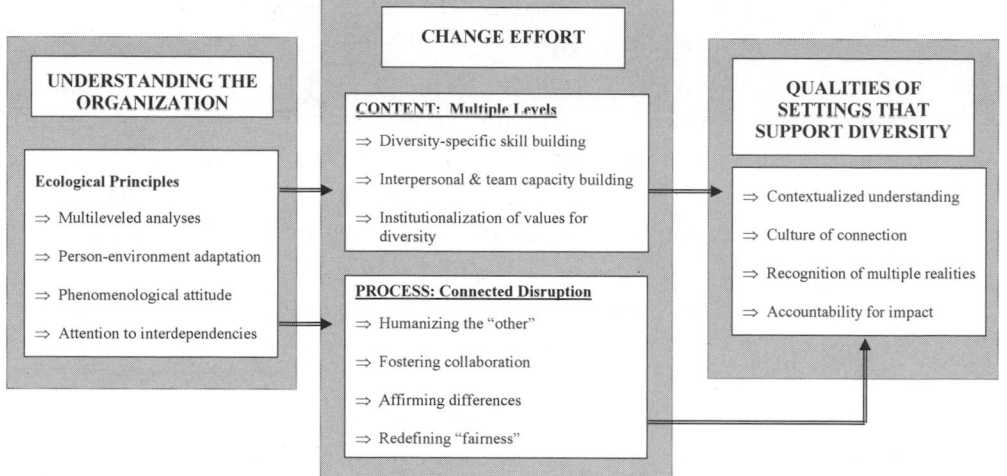

FIGURE 1.5 Workplace Chemistry Initiative Overview

tion of families living below the poverty level rivals national rates (with one community at 5.3 percent and the other two at 9.7 and 16.5 percent, while national rates are around 12.4 percent). ChemPro has been an important employer within the city for over sixty years, and one of two major employers for much of that time. During the late 1980s and 1990s, an industrial park with several comparably sized companies opened, but ChemPro remains one of the top ten employers in the area today. The demographics, the economics, and the company's historical relationships with the community all helped shape the challenges that it faced.

the initiative for diversity

We titled the project the "Workplace Chemistry Initiative" and organized activities along three interwoven dimensions: (1) diversity-specific activities, (2) team capacity building, and (3) institutionalization of a value for diversity (see figures 1.5 and 1.6). The adoption of this three-layered approach was rooted in principles of the social ecological paradigm. In line with the emphasis on addressing multiple levels of analysis, we sought to address individual awareness and skills around diversity, provide consultation to improve general interpersonal dynamics and teamwork, as well as support the adoption of

	Prelim Work	Year 1	Year 2	Year 3	Year 4	Year 5	Year 6	Year 7
DIVERSITY-SPECIFIC SKILL BUILDING	Interviews Feedback	Survey Feedback	Diversity curriculum developed with team	Diversity classes began	Interim evaluation interviews	Continued training	Training evaluation / File reviews	Survey Feedback
		Ongoing: Organizational leaders communicating a value for diversity, 'zero tolerance policy,' diversity awareness activities						
TEAM CAPACITY BUILDING		Team consultations		Train the trainers		Ongoing coaching of trainers		
		Ongoing: Training and leadership development sponsored by ChemPro & Corporate						
INSTITUTIONAL-IZATION OF VALUES FOR DIVERSITY		Special Workplace Chemistry Steering Team	People Team became sponsor					
		Ongoing: Staffing & promoting to build diversity; holding leaders accountable for supporting diversity; adding diversity-related criteria to formal work goals and performance evaluations						

FIGURE 1.6 Workplace Chemistry Initiative Timeline

organizational policies and approaches that would provide enduring systemic support for a diverse workforce.

Several components of the initiative were explicitly focused on diversity. The overall initiative began with an assessment of the diversity climate within the plant. During the first three months of our work, we conducted interviews with thirty-six individuals across the plant and then held feedback sessions with every unit.[2] This small-scale assessment was followed by a plantwide survey, the results of which were again shared with each unit. The issues identified included concern about a tight organizational culture (like "family") that made some people feel very included while others felt very marginal; significant amounts of racial and sexist razzing and teasing ("locker room culture"); daily interpersonal inequities or microinequities for women and people of color such as feeling ignored, unseen, not mentored; and a general sense that white men were unaware of the experiences of minorities within the plant. In addition, there was considerable concern on the part of many whites that "reverse discrimination" was leading to lower expectations and easier assignments for women and nonwhites. The goal of this assessment and feedback process was not just to identify diversity-related concerns but also to establish a shared baseline understanding of issues and goals. These initial efforts are described in more depth in chapter 2. The interviews were followed by a plantwide survey and a second round of feedback to broaden support for the initiative.

We then turned our attention to the development of plantwide diversity training. Using the initial assessment results as a foundation, we worked with organization members to design a training program specifically for ChemPro. We also developed a team of in-house diversity trainers and helped them enhance their presentation and group facilitation skills. We provided training for over 70 percent of the plant including employees from all levels and all departments. The training is described in more depth in chapter 3.

Although it was generally well received, the organization periodically had to put the training on hold while other pressing priorities dominated such as reorganizations, job redesign, and even downsizing. Periods with high overtime demands became difficult times to schedule training. During the breaks in the training, we worked with HR to keep the initiative alive through other activities such as team-based consultations, an interim training evaluation, and a follow-up plantwide survey.

A second set of parallel activities focused on general capacity building. Without focusing on diversity dynamics directly, these efforts fostered recognition that coworkers are highly interdependent: they depend on one another to get the work done successfully, and each person's contribution matters. Some of these activities were skill development workshops on topics ranging from communication skills to leadership development. In addition, our university-based group provided consultation to multiple intact workgroups. We worked with four of the five production units, both labs, and administrative staff over a five-year period conducting team-building workshops, facilitating strategic planning, and mediating conflict situations. These activities supported the diversity initiative by enhancing general teamwork and interpersonal skills even while having a less explicit "diversity" focus. The team consultations are described in chapter 4.

The third thread of activities focused on institutionalizing systemic supports for diversity within the organization, described in chapter 5. We considered it essential to weave a value for diversity into all aspects of organizational life, including the processes that guide selection, socialization, evaluation, and succession planning. Much of the work around organizational policies and procedures was driven directly by HR. The Human Resources Department affirmed hiring and promotion guidelines that placed a value on increased diversity among workers at all levels of the organization. We consulted with HR on how to incorporate performance criteria focused on working effectively with diverse coworkers. We also felt it was essential to have a broadly representative group within ChemPro feel a sense of "ownership" of the initiative. As will be described, we began with a steering team, but once the initiative was under way, we transferred sponsorship to a preexisting People Team.

In sum, the diversity-specific activities were designed to build a context-specific foundation of connection across differences, raise awareness of multiple realities among workers of different identity groups, and help workers to understand better their impact on others. The team-building activities emphasized the profound impact workers have on one another and sought to promote more inclusive and collaborative working relationships. The work around organizational policies, procedures, and sponsorship was designed to foster sustained commitment to these issues.

ecological reflections: anchoring organizational change in context

As the work with ChemPro began to unfold, lessons emerged that reflect broad dynamics of systems change and that have relevance beyond this particular organization. Peter Senge has counseled that understanding systems principles can help us move forward in creative ways:

> The challenges of profound change tend to be signals of hidden imperatives built into the organizational system. They arise from the "homeostatic forces" maintaining core elements of the traditional culture and functioning of industrial-age organizations. Though they may appear idiosyncratic to individual organizations, we believe most are near universal to all contemporary large enterprises. They can't be overcome through sheer brute force or willpower: rather, they require understanding and often counterintuitive strategies.[3]

When entering a new setting, it is useful to wonder about where the intervention and intervenor/s fit into the natural ecology of the organization. How has the history shaped its current circumstances? To what extent can the new goals blend into ongoing efforts with simple recalibrations, and to what extent are they disjunctures that will take the system in a whole new direction? What is the "fit" between the change agent (e.g., in terms of background, demographics, identity, and values) and the organizational ethos?

Initial groundwork involves exploring the current strengths, opportunities, and resources that exist within an organization before attempting to "ad-

minister" something new. Each organization has its own indigenous resources that provide the most respectful starting place. A new initiative will
be more successful if it is synergistic with—or at least cognizant of—other
current forces for change. Similarly, it is critical to work in ways that are
respectful of the current organizational culture and the organization's particular history and traditions. The ecological principles at play here are akin to the
observation that chemicals change form when heated or cooled. To do any lab
work, it is essential to understand the current state of the liquid as well as
whether the beaker is on a burner or on its way to the freezer. Each organization is unique in some basic ways, and interventions—even while guided by
"near universal" systems principles—need to be custom-designed with those
qualities in mind.

RECOGNIZING THE INDIGENOUS RESOURCES OF THE ORGANIZATION

When we first began working with ChemPro, the organization had already
established three critical elements for supporting workplace diversity. First,
it had a clearly articulated value for people as resources incorporated into
the company's motto, "People are Number One." This value was operational-
ized in several ways: an active cross-department People Team focused on
attending to and improving the quality of work life; an "open door" policy
that encouraged people to raise concerns at any level of the organization;
and numerous training sessions to enhance employees' interpersonal and
"people skills." Although there was not yet a *specific* focus on issues of race,
ethnicity, and/or gender, a clear value was communicated through ongoing
training and other initiatives about the importance of working effectively and
sensitively with other team members. An emphasis on valuing and respect-
ing diversity among workers was also backed up by the five newly codified
corporate values: respect for employee dignity, integrity, trust, credibility, and
continuous improvement.

Second, by the time we were invited into ChemPro, teamwork and "employee empowerment" were being promoted and rewarded. This spirit was
being fostered through self-managed work teams and cross-department
teams designed to address key organizational priority areas. As far back as
1985, owing to both the changing demands in the business environment and
the changing leadership, the organization had begun to work toward more
self-managed teams. In 1991, it moved to what was called "process-step"–
based teams, with manufacturing structured so as to support teams' control
over their own step in the manufacturing process.

Third, there was clear leadership support at top levels for making diversity a priority. The strong ideological commitment (based on personal experiences) of the director of HR (Keitha) was at the initiative's core. Although it took a little time for the issues to move up on the president's (Warren's) agenda, it was his pragmatic, yet also heartfelt, commitment that led ChemPro to contact me and my team and to establish a long-term and multilayered commitment to a workforce that could understand and foster diversity. The fact that corporate also had recently adopted a clearly articulated value for diversity was a huge bonus.

These elements—a value for diverse people as resources, a commitment to work teams, and leadership support—have been related to effective diversity in a range of other organizations.[4] In response to changes in the broader environment, ChemPro, in essence, had established an important foundation for supporting diversity. To ignore these indigenous assets would have been to invalidate our most valuable resources for change. The results of the initial assessment phase identified some significant barriers to diversity and highlighted the fact that articulated values and team structures were important but not sufficient to support diversity through all aspects of organizational life. Nonetheless, before moving ahead, it was essential to recognize the positive foundation provided by organizational practices in effect at the time. We worked to forge a partnership rooted in respect and to build on existing resources and momentum for change.

ATTENDING TO ORGANIZATIONAL MOMENTUM

An organizational change effort is not a beginning where everything starts anew. Instead, the first step in an initiative is more like jumping onto a moving train. An organization's history sets a certain trajectory—lays some tracks and supplies the engine with fuel. The organizational leaders, like engineers, have worked to establish the speed, style, and course. Workers have been taken along for the ride, even if they vary in their commitment to and enthusiasm for the journey. Such trains do not stop to let consultants on board; they keep moving, and you simply have to run and catch up. As one organization member commented, "Nothing ever stays the same around here." The organization is in motion, and, as a consultant, you have to be nimble on your feet and dance toward openings for change.

Given the constant movement, this story of organizational change is as much about the history and current motion of a particular organization as it is about the work of our consultation team. Any new initiative will be affected by other simultaneous organizational changes, and external consultants have to be cognizant of the ongoing work of organizational leaders. Done well, a consultation can be a catalyst that galvanizes other resources and positive interactions. As Trickett noted, "The spirit of ecologically based consultation is to contribute to the resourcefulness of the host environment by building on locally identified concerns to create processes which aid in empowering the environment to solve its own problems and plan its own development."[5] On the flip side, blinders to ongoing social and organizational trajectories can render a consultation seemingly inexplicably stuck. Consultants may find themselves stymied when strategies that have worked in other settings fall flat and/or generate considerable backlash, when in fact their approach is akin to asking the organizational train to jump tracks. If the approach is not grounded in the current realities of the specific organization, some resistance is not just understandable; it is almost inevitable.

The Workplace Chemistry Initiative could have been viewed as a distraction from all the challenges facing ChemPro—the pressures to compete worldwide, the changing expectations of managers, the increased demands on workers. Instead, given the nature of our partnership, our goals were in line with organizational priorities and were actually fueled by the sense of urgency Keitha and Warren felt about "attending to people issues." In reflecting back on our work together, Keitha said:

> There was a sense of urgency all around the edges. There were huge efforts going on; we were trying to stay in existence . . . Sometimes consultants have a hard time dealing with the amount of change that goes on in organizations, really being set on their final process. The partnership with UMass worked well, and your willingness to be flexible was a big part of that.

Ultimately, the consultant is only a bit player in a broader story of change. Understanding the job in this way is humbling yet it also underscores a tremendous responsibility to be attentive and respectful. Additionally, recognizing that organizational arrangements have evolved over time in reaction to multiple forces brings home the importance of a sustained effort. One-shot, one-dimensional interventions are neither powerful nor deep enough to ensure enduring change. The commitment to the process cannot be a "quick fix" approach to organizational priorities. It requires a serious, challenging, and long-term commitment that is synergistic with the ongoing work of the organization.

GETTING IN SYNC WITH THE ORGANIZATIONAL CULTURE

Once you are on board the moving train, you realize that the trajectory and motion are not as predictable as a train on a track. In many ways, it is more like entering a game of jump rope where the speed of the rope varies from day to day. Different people turn the ropes from month to month. Some days there is one rope, and some days two. The challenge is to sit back and watch the rhythm, discover the patterns, and experience the motion in order to join in ways that do not totally disrupt the game or, more dramatically, get you kicked off the playground.

An initial challenge was to introduce the project in a way that was compatible with ongoing organizational styles and priorities. One way we tried to honor ChemPro's particular instrumental, "if-you-can't-take-the-heat-get-out-of-the-kitchen, don't-just-talk-but-do" organizational culture was by adopting the mantle of "Workplace Chemistry Initiative." Our choice of project title (and the accompanying imagery) was in acknowledgment of what we understood to be the prevailing organizational culture described by Keitha as a "statistical culture." We were warned that words such as "understanding" and "supporting" would probably put people off and be dismissed by many workers as too "touchy-feely" or "soft." Such language would connote a less than "scientific" process to a group of predominantly male chemists, engineers, and production workers whose daily work tasks emphasized output over interpersonal processes. If attention to diversity was presented as based simply on being "nice" to one another or "being more understanding," we could have doomed the project from the beginning. Our play on the dual images of chemistry—the scientific and the interpersonal—plus our introduction of the topic as related to colliding elements, which can either combust or synergistically evolve into something exciting and new, became our call for action.

In addition to adopting a culturally compatible modus operandi for the initiative, I personally had to find my place as a consultant in this particular world of work. Class, race, and gender differences cannot be ignored as they shape differing worldviews and approaches. I am "like" the majority at ChemPro on several dimensions—white, heterosexual, able bodied. Perhaps these similarities made my entry smoother than it might have been otherwise. But as a professional brought up in a professional-class family, I had to find my footing in a blue-collar world. As a woman, I had to establish comfort working with male-dominated groups. As a white person, I had to earn the respect of the workers of color.

We all draw on the experiences that have shaped our identities vis-à-vis race, gender, and class. In my work, I could draw on my experience as a minority in my racially diverse high school; I could draw on my experiences as a majority in most other settings of my life. I could easily draw on my numerous experiences of being dismissed as a woman. I could go back to my summer job on an electronics assembly line and remember the palpable resentment of me as a "college kid." I could draw on my feeling out of sync at my elite college—the public school student who was disillusioned by the blind assumptions and sheltered lives of some of my very wealthy classmates. In reaching to appreciate life at ChemPro, it was essential for me to draw on all these experiences and more.

Perhaps the most striking challenge for me was to acknowledge some core differences in philosophies about work and work relationships. The old adage that "some people live to work, and others work to live" is appropriately descriptive of the differences I began to appreciate. My work defines me, and I feel validated by it. I have trouble asking to be paid for doing something I enjoy and find challenging. Yet I came to not just respect but in some ways envy the ability of many line workers to define themselves separately from their work. I grew to value their clarity about working to live. I could not be a partner in change if I were to assume they had the same relationship to work that I have—nor if I presumed my stance to be somehow superior. I firmly believe that you cannot work with people you do not genuinely respect. I knew that I needed to listen in deep ways to get a sense of and appreciation for the culture of ChemPro and the rhythm of the lives of ChemPro workers.

SYNTHESIS

Appreciating indigenous resources, understanding an organization's current trajectory, and working in ways that are in sync with a company's culture are all sensibilities grounded in an appreciation for organizations as living systems. These sensibilities build on ecological notions about interdependencies and person-environment adaptation. Change agents must recognize dynamics that Lewin has described as "equilibrium in motion."[6] There is both a natural momentum toward change and strong self-regulatory processes that continually press for a return to accepted ways of doing things. Change requires an understanding of and respect for the forces that shape the current organizational arrangements (i.e., a sense of *connection* and appreciation for current practices) combined with a concerted effort to challenge the forces that push against change (i.e., a willingness to *disrupt* the current equilibrium in order to move toward new patterns and new arrangements).

So what next? Where to from here? Our next challenge was to consider how to further set the stage for organizational change.

catalysts for change

SETTING THE STAGE FOR COLLABORATIVE ACTION

THE FIRST STAGE of organizational change initiatives often focuses on data gathering, but it is also an opportunity to generate "activation energy" for change—that is, the energy needed for initiating the desired chemical reactions. Thus, we designed an assessment process that would not only produce information but would also provide some momentum for change. We wanted to establish a collective understanding of the diversity challenge at ChemPro that would expand the then-current dominant story to incorporate multiple, and even conflicting, perspectives from people throughout the plant. As we sought a more inclusive view of life at ChemPro, we also needed to understand and attend to the varied forms of resistance to the initiative. Simultaneously, we started the process of bringing an ever broader group of organizational members on board as partners. With these goals in mind, the initial phase of our work with ChemPro involved developing a process that would foster partnerships while learning more about the experiences of workers and the issues facing ChemPro. Our hope was that all these activities would then become catalysts for ongoing collaborative action.

the assessment process

We chose a collaborative inquiry process because of our ecologically driven belief that organization members are in the best position to answer questions about their own setting and they are also the most knowledgeable about what questions to ask, how to ask the questions, and how to understand participants' responses.[1] Members of a system have unique knowledge. They are not only experts on their particular personal experience; they also have deep knowledge of organizational practices and the meaning of such practices for employees.

To facilitate such a participative process, we worked very closely with

Keitha and her staff. While we knew we ultimately needed to gain the trust of workers on the plant floor, leadership support was an essential starting place. After getting approval for the project from Warren, we reviewed the project with the unit managers. We then engaged workers from all hierarchical levels on a Steering Team and clarified the project mission with other preexisting groups such as a cross-department People Team. These meetings were followed by thirty-six in-depth interviews, participant observation of meetings, review of relevant company documents, and a series of feedback sessions. Each step in the process embodied the dual goals of gathering information and building partnerships.

LEADERSHIP SUPPORT

Many consultants recognize that leadership support is requisite for an organizational change effort.[2] This is particularly true when the initiative demands change not only in personal values but also in organizational practices. Learning how to interact differently across racial and gender differences can alter one's core sense of self by challenging many taken-for-granted assumptions at the organizational as well as personal level. We knew that the support of Warren would be essential if we had any hope that this would evolve into an effective initiative.

As the project unfolded, Warren was more than passively supportive. He understood that addressing issues of race and gender could be an emotional journey yet one that needed to be undertaken. In his message to the plant, he wrote, "For a while, this will be a painful experience, but don't let that stop us." He also expressed confidence that the plant would "rise to the occasion" and saw this as "an important opportunity." In reflecting on Warren's role, Rich said, "He started going around the plant and listening to people and then got some survey data. That's why he pushed the Workplace Chemistry Initiative and really endorsed that . . . he was really supportive of it."

Warren's investment was not merely strategic, as the following makes clear:

Rich: He grew up poor . . . I forget the whole story, but he grew up in the projects. So he always had a feeling for people that were in hard situations . . . The two main people that supported [the Workplace Chemistry Initiative] were Warren and Keitha. I don't think [some other managers] saw the value in it. I think some saw it as an add-on. "I just wanna make chemicals" and everything. But Warren saw past that. He thought if you keep your workforce happy and make it comfortable, it's the right thing to do. There is value. There's value in a couple ways. There's value in just the human aspect of value. And then there's the value of productivity, too.

Meg: So his commitment was both idealistic and pragmatic at the same time?

Rich: Right. It was also personal.

A testament to this commitment emerged when an interesting legal twist was raised by Corporate as we began our assessment process. Corporate recognized that if the company learned about ongoing discrimination or harassment, it would be obligated to address the problem. If it was not prepared to take action, it would put itself at risk for a lawsuit by the very act of asking. Even though the inquiry was university sponsored[3] and participants were assured confidentiality, the company needed to be clear about the depth of its commitment to take the results seriously before we moved forward. With full knowledge of the legal implications, Warren, backed by Corporate, gave the project his blessing, thereby publicly signaling his intention to take our findings seriously and to be ready to act on them.

STEERING TEAM OF THE WORKPLACE CHEMISTRY INITIATIVE

With this backing, we worked with Keitha to identify people to serve on a Workplace Chemistry Steering Team. About fifteen workers, who we felt could effectively inform and support the project, were invited to join this Steering Team. We sought partners who could help us see the issues from many vantage points—and who had the courage to speak out. Team members came from a wide range of departments, and they held positions at every level of the organization. Members represented diverse backgrounds with respect to gender, age, race, and physical disability. Of those who attended regularly, about half were people of color (black and Asian) and a little under half were women. This racial and gender diversity was essential; Keitha's involvement as a cofacilitator was invaluable.

Diversity was a new topic. There was not yet a shared language for talking about it. One manager actually came to the initial meeting thinking we were indeed talking about *chemistry* (having read the title on the invitation but not the fine print!), but he signed onto the goals of the initiative after he had time to adjust to the unexpected turn of the agenda. The Steering Team was invited to work with us to develop a shared vocabulary and an approach that would be in sync with the unique culture of ChemPro.

In the initial meeting, the team members reviewed the project goals and shared personal perceptions about work relations at ChemPro. It was a somewhat freewheeling discussion about both their general observations and their own individual experiences related to treatment that they felt was shaped by gender and/or race. Some team members shared examples of how the "worst is expected of people" based on their race, gender, and/or physical abilities. Some felt that the most pressing problem was "lack of trust" and an indirect organizational ethos: "Our culture is 'we talk *about* people not *to* people.'" Some pointed out that, with all the other demands on workers (reorganizations, automation, and the press for both higher quality and lower cost), "there is no time to consider people's differences." There was also some discussion about how the challenges differed from unit to unit. While the group agreed to work toward "creating an environment in which every individual is important," there was also very clear acknowledgment that the challenge facing us would not be simple. One of my students observed, "It seems there are so many issues at ChemPro that they just don't know where to begin." And yet our starting point of inviting participants to share a wide range of experiences and perceptions helped team members feel involved and validated. Grounding the work in participants' lived experiences within the organization is integral to working from a phenomenological perspective.

To move forward, we needed focus—a clear statement of purpose to guide the group and to rally others. So in the following meetings, we worked toward the development of a mission statement that we could share with the rest of the plant. Through a guided imagery process, I asked the group to imagine themselves ten years hence, "telling a friend about what a wonderful and diverse workplace ChemPro had become—a time when the chemistry was right." For example, "What would it be like to work at ChemPro? What would be different? How would they feel coming to work? How would conflicts be dealt with? What would they celebrate? How?" The process was designed to tap their hopes and their visions of a positive future in a way that got beyond any cynicism about the "real" likelihood of change and that did not get bogged down by focusing on all the potential barriers. After making notes about their personal vision, they then worked in dyads to suggest five to seven qualities of an ideally realized, well-functioning, diverse workplace. Encouraging individual writing as well as dyadic discussion helped to ensure input from all participants—even the quiet ones.

Several themes emerged as the dyads shared their ideas with the full group. It was a spirited discussion. They wanted trust, fairness, camaraderie, good communication, opportunity and inclusion, flexibility to change, and leadership through example and integrity. Building on these themes, the team collaboratively developed the following mission statement to focus the work:

> To create a work environment at ChemPro where every individual regardless of race, gender, and/or disability can work at their best by creating a culture of flexibility and sense of inclusion where all people feel wanted and appreciated.

With this statement as our guide, we moved to developing a strategy for getting out into the plant. We needed to firm up the initial assessment plan and interview questions. Concurrent with planning the start-up meeting of the Steering Team, our university team had conducted six preliminary individual interviews with volunteers from the Steering Team (two women/four men; two black/four white) to get an initial feeling for participants' varied experiences within the organization as well as to solicit reflections on how the organization was dealing with diversity in general. Based on the responses, we had drafted an interview outline. The full Steering Team helped to pilot this initial set of questions by using them to interview one another. This process had multiple purposes—it enhanced our understanding of the issues, it improved the interview guide, and it increased the sense of partnership with the Steering Team. As a full group, we discussed team members' reactions both to asking and to being asked the questions. They found some questions too vague and suggested we reword or give examples. They wanted the questions to "be more direct." They also had suggestions about new questions to add. And thus the final interview guide was born.

The Steering Team meetings were lively and engaged. Participants asked questions, challenged one another, and shared personal observations and experiences. Participants indicated that the process of the meetings was eye-opening: "I never thought about these issues before. We are more aware of issues around gender or race just by starting this team." Although there was always a dash of cautious cynicism, the team members were generally hopeful that the Workplace Chemistry Initiative would be helpful for others. This group became a core support for the overall initiative.

THE CHEMPRO "PEOPLE" TEAM

In this early phase, we also met with the organization's People Team to review the Workplace Chemistry Initiative mission and goals. This preexisting team was designed to be a place for the voices of workers to be heard, and it was critical to get support from this group before moving out to the full plant. The People Team consisted of nonmanagement representatives from every department (including Production, Labs, Facilities, and Administration). The exact makeup of the group varied slightly from meeting to meeting, and attendance at any given meeting ranged from twenty-five to thirty-five people. Approximately three-quarters of the members were white men. About three to five black men and five to seven white women typically attended. The group was charged with the responsibility for "people issues" throughout the organization and sponsored activities that ranged from identifying and addressing employee concerns to planning company-wide family celebrations.

When the Workplace Chemistry Initiative was introduced, the most vocal members of the People Team were white men who expressed the view that race and gender were nonissues at ChemPro ("It's all a matter of self-esteem and personality") or not relevant to their work ("People shouldn't bring their own personal problems to their jobs"). Some thought racism and sexism were often used as "excuses" for poor performance or lack of motivation. As consultants, we did not take issue with these views but rather listened and encouraged others to speak up; we trusted that alternative views existed within the group. Periodically Keitha, for example, would respectfully challenge these more blaming views by describing very specific instances of bias as well as statistics around performance.

As discussion unfolded, those who had experienced and observed biased treatment began to enlighten the others. A Caribbean-born black maintenance worker spoke about how he thought others assumed he was "dumb" based on his accent. A particularly powerful moment came when a white man shared his observations of prejudice within the plant. He gave an example of a black man on his unit. He had trained this man and knew he could do the job well, "but the other guys always questioned his work." He provided a detailed description and concluded, "now that's about race." He was a long-term, well-respected worker, and those who had initially denied the existence of problems seemed to listen. Looking back, we suspect that the clear endorsement of the initiative by management (in particular Warren and Keitha) combined with our nonjudgmental attitude helped give him the opening to cross a line and the support he needed to challenge his white coworkers.

Several other People Team members asked us pointed questions about our qualifications and our commitment to seeing the process through. In fact, one member confronted me about my personal commitment to stick with the process: "You can't come here and raise these issues then leave." He asked for and got my assurance that our team would not treat this as, in his words, "the flavor of the month." While this reaction could be viewed as resistance to the project, it also reflected the important gatekeeping function of the group. Once we addressed individuals' concerns directly and honestly, the intensity of the challenges seemed to dissipate. In essence, we understood their questions as expressing an understandable wariness about a project that had the potential to be quite disruptive. We neither took the challenge personally nor saw it as a lack of investment in the topic. Gaining the support of this group represented an important juncture for the project since the People Team was the primary structure for communicating information to and from workers and for sponsoring change initiatives within the organization. Working with such indigenous structures is part and parcel of a systemic approach.

INTERVIEWS

The next phase of the project involved the actual interviewing of a range of employees using the questions the Steering Team had helped to refine. When the expanded in-depth interviewing process began, our team of UML interviewers included two women graduate students (one white and one Latina) and me. Eighty employees, representing a cross section of roles, sexes, races, units, and physical abilities, were identified in collaboration with HR. Given the topic of interest, we oversampled women and people of color. The interviews were conducted on work time at a company-owned "Rec Hall" across the street from the main plant. To allow employees to freely choose whether to participate (without pressure or knowledge by the company), we sent letters inviting people to call us at the university to set up interviews. Twenty-four people responded, very few of whom were people of color (twenty-two, or 92 percent, were white). Women had the highest response rate of any race or gender group (50 percent).

The fact that so few people of color responded to the initial call for interviews was striking. When asked informally, some black employees expressed cynicism about whether the project could really have much impact. As one black man put it, "I've been black long enough to know nothing is going to change." Others indicated they were "scared" about the possibility that Keitha (the most visible and most senior black person in the plant) might be leaving ChemPro. It was public knowledge that she was contemplating an independent consultation practice. Some blacks feared that if issues were aired and then she left, no one would be around to represent and protect them. Both

TABLE 2.1 · CHARACTERISTICS OF INTERVIEWEES

	MEN	WOMEN	TOTAL
White	14 (39%)	12 (33%)	26 (72%)
Black	6 (17%)	1 (3%)	7 (20%)
Asian	2 (6%)		2 (6%)
Latina		1 (3%)	1 (3%)
Total	22 (61%)	14 (39%)	36 (100%)

the high response rate from women and the low initial response from people of color were probably also related to the fact that the interviewers were three women, and none of us belonged to the primary minority groups represented within the plant (i.e., black and Asian).

Given the underrepresentation of people of color, we put out a second call to all people of color on our initial list ($n = 27$), with Keitha also reassuring people that she was not on the brink of leaving. Through this encouragement, we were subsequently able to interview six more people, including two black men, two Asian men, one Hispanic woman, and one black woman (see table 2.1).

In total, we interviewed thirty-six people, including at least one person from each level of the organization and one from every unit. Everyone signed an Informed Consent form that spelled out the purpose of the interviews, the potential risks and benefits as well as the interviewees' rights to refuse to answer any question or terminate the interview at any time. We ceased interviewing when it appeared that, while we were continuing to get confirmation of observations from previous interviews, we were learning little new—a strategy compatible with generally accepted criteria for determining the size of a qualitative sample.[4]

Each interview took from one to one and a half hours. After asking for some general background information, we asked each participant to reflect on her/his own experience at ChemPro (e.g., How has ChemPro been as a place to work? What attracted you to ChemPro? What kinds of things have encouraged you to stay? If you have thought about leaving, what was going on?). We also asked participants to describe any times that they felt they were treated differently on the job because of their race and/or gender. Then we asked several questions about how they thought working at ChemPro might be experienced by various groups of people (i.e., women, people of color, people with disabilities, lesbians and gay men, heterosexual white men). In the final set of questions, participants were asked to describe the relationships within their work team, supports from supervisors, and unspoken rules or norms for appropriate interpersonal behavior in the plant. Although we offered the option to participate without taping, all but one of the thirty-six participants gave us their written permission to audiotape their interviews. All tapes were transcribed. The quotes included here are verbatim except where minor details needed to be changed to protect confidentiality.

The majority of respondents had very positive things to say about ChemPro as an employer. Many mentioned salary and benefits as the factors that both had attracted them to ChemPro and encouraged them to stay. Many talked about how they valued having close friends and family members working at the plant. The variety of job demands within each position was also mentioned as an attractive feature. However, the combination of long tenures and family/personal connections among employees seemed to have created a unique set of forces that worked both for and against effective diversity. For example, the "family" culture had helped to create a sense of loyalty and commitment to ChemPro. At the same time, the culture also appeared to intensify a press for homogeneity such that people who could not adapt to the dominant way of doing things were often considered deviant or personally defective in some way.

Women, people of color, and white men appeared to experience the organization quite differently from one another. Most of the white men we interviewed indicated that they saw no problems and/or inequities based on race and/or gender—except that some complained of reverse discrimination whereby blacks and women were not held to the same standards. In contrast, most women, many people of color, and a few white men described at least some instances of differential treatment. Black interviewees were very aware of being stereotyped and felt the accompanying low expectations were expressed in numerous formal and informal ways. As one black man said, "Around here blacks are perceived to be lazy. They are perceived to be always scheming, looking for the easy way out, and mainly, because of that, they are not given their just due." Some supervisors seemed to watch their black workers more closely, discount their complaints as excuses, and/or assume that absences were unwarranted. One black man described how unfair it felt when his supervisor hinted that his health problems could be cause for looking at him closely in downsizing, particularly since he saw a white man with similar problems being accommodated. Some other observations from black male production workers included:

When a black starts to complain, then they generally say, "Well, this guy—he's a troublemaker."

If a white person has a bad back, you will probably get maybe seventy percent of the group that thinks it's legit and would go out of their way to, you know, kind of chip in their help, or whatever, to make things easier for them. If the same situation arises, however, and it's a black person, then you get probably about 10%.

The negative stereotypes and low expectations led some blacks to conclude that "it doesn't matter what I do, so why work hard trying?" Any less-than-perfect performance or request for help could then be interpreted as *confirmation* that the individual was indeed shirking or not working to capacity. This self-fulfilling dynamic further intensified the situation whereby the black worker received relatively little support (of either an emotional or pragmatic nature). As one black worker said:

There were guys that started working entry-level with me that, academically, weren't, you know, anywhere near where I was. Job performance? They wasn't at the same level either, but I always got menial jobs . . . I would go to that area and I would see three guys in a control room, you know, sitting down having coffee with their feet on the table. The three hours that I was there, I was doing the work that they were supposed to be doing. And I'd tell my supervisor, "well, I don't think I should be going over there, because these people aren't being utilized properly." I'd get labeled as a troublemaker.

Another black man also reported doing substantial amounts of the work of his white coworkers, while feeling unable to discuss the situation with his white supervisor.

The dynamics that devalued and marginalized women appeared to be somewhat different. Women reported experiencing numerous microinequities that added up over time (such as being ignored or not taken seriously, having office work treated as if it was an easy job, having male colleagues change the topic of conversation when they walked through the door). As one white woman explained, "There's always that little something . . . you're not taken quite as seriously." A white woman in a business support role talked about how it had taken a long time before the men she worked for and with noticed her level of education and before they took her seriously. "They tend to be very patronizing even now." She was told by one male manager that "women don't belong in the workplace . . . [and] that he liked it when I wore high heels." Another woman who wanted to attend a professional women's meeting had her boss tell her, "Go ahead, have a good time at your hen party." Several women said they appreciated much of what the company did for them, but they had a vague, unsettling sense of being invisible. A woman who worked on the production floor talked about how it took six months to get a door put on the bathroom so she could use it: "It didn't sink in to him that I needed a door, and I said something, 'Think you could put a door in?' He said, 'Oh yeah, we'll get around to it.' It wasn't because they ignored me exactly it was just—I wasn't on his priority list." Many women ended up feeling that, in spite of some supportive acts on the part of the company, they were neither fully valued nor taken seriously enough to have influence over their workaday world.

In general, people responded favorably to the interview process. Some indicated that they found the simple presence of the Workplace Chemistry Initiative to be supportive. This type of comment was made most often by the women we interviewed who felt that gender had long been an invisible source of differential treatment at ChemPro. Several black and white male production workers who found the process hopeful recommended that coworkers call us to share concerns—some of whom did. Several interviewees said they had gained important insights as a result of participating in the interviews. A few managers indicated they would try to change their approach now that they had begun to consider how people of different races, genders, physical abilities, and sexual orientations might experience life at ChemPro.

FEEDBACK SESSIONS

We developed a summary of the themes that emerged from the interviews that revolved around the ways in which (1) the "family culture" had both positive and negative effects; (2) women, people of color, and white men experienced ChemPro quite differently from one another; (3) neither all blacks nor all women experienced the organization in the same way; (4) the message to women and minorities about what and who the organization valued was often filtered through how they saw *others* treated; and (5) many experienced contradictions between the openness promoted by management and their actual daily experience.

As a check on whether our interpretation of the interviews reflected a reality of relevance to members of the organization, we conducted a series of feedback sessions with employee groups. These sessions were also designed to solicit input about potential courses of action. We organized the feedback process by sharing our observations first with Warren and Keitha, second with the Workplace Chemistry Steering Team and the People Team, and then with workers on individual units.

Warren reacted to our results with interest, taking notes, highlighting sections of the report, and inviting a representative from Corporate to join a second conversation via conference call. He had thoughtful comments and ideas about how to begin addressing the concerns raised. He expressed his support by encouraging us to share results with employee groups throughout the plant and work with the Workplace Chemistry Steering Team to develop action recommendations to bring back to him. The representative from Corporate expressed enthusiasm and forwarded the written report to her Corporate HR team. We later heard that Corporate HR was not only supportive but felt that ChemPro was leading the way on diversity for the company.

The Steering Team thought the preliminary report was on target. However, we found it surprising that a project with such potential to disrupt the status quo had generated little gossip or comment throughout the plant. While it was comforting that a backlash was not emerging, the Steering Team expressed concern about whether the rest of the organization was taking the Workplace Chemistry Initiative seriously. It was curiously unsettling.

The meeting with the People Team was a pleasant surprise. While members of this group had initially had a challenging and skeptical reaction to the project, they were engaged as we shared our observations. Several felt validated by the content of our observations and impressed by the process. A particularly poignant moment occurred when we discussed what we perceived as the hesitant response from people of color. We acknowledged our concern that people of color may have been reluctant to respond without knowing how (and whether) the organization would take the feedback seriously. We also acknowledged the potential impact of our being a group of nonblack, non-Asian women. In response, one black man spoke quite openly about the wisdom he saw in keeping some distance from the project. His perspective was that others cannot be changed so things are often better left alone. He said, "You don't want to open more wounds or scars. You want to leave it like that, and live with it . . . deal with it." In contrast, a white man expressed hope for change, suggesting that if people throughout the plant heard about the interview results, they might begin to be more sensitive. The reaction of the overall group was enthusiastic; people agreed to consult with their individual units and arrange feedback meetings. Interestingly, the black man who had shared his worries about the project was one of the first to arrange for us to meet with his team.

The most striking aspect of the feedback sessions with the individual units was how varied the reactions were. In meetings with some of the non-production staff groups (e.g., purchasing, shipping, HR, business support—which were all fairly gender and somewhat racially diverse units), participants indicated feeling affirmed by the interview summary and hopeful that sharing observations would help others understand their experiences at Chem-Pro. In a sense, we named something they had been feeling yet did not know exactly how to describe. There was animated, thoughtful, and hopeful discussion of hopes for change.

In contrast, participants in meetings with other units said the issues raised simply did not apply to them or to their work group. For example, members of an environmental unit questioned the purpose and/or need for the Workplace Chemistry Project. Others pointed out that thirty-six interviews could not possibly capture the feelings of everyone in the plant. While these are important and valid concerns, they are also indicative of an important aspect of the diversity challenge at ChemPro. Many (mostly members of the majority race/gender group) did not see or feel the concerns being expressed by others (mostly members of minority race and gender groups). In a phenomenological sense, majority group members were largely unaware of the ways in which minority workers experienced life at ChemPro.

Some reactions to the feedback were more directly antagonistic—particularly from some of the production units. One sentiment was that if other people feel unhappy or marginalized, "It's not my problem." Many believed that looking out for oneself and maneuvering the system are simply "the American way." Comments made by members of the predominantly white male production unit, for example, included: "Racism is not my fault so why should I have to do anything about it?" "If you can't take a joke, it's *your* problem." "Sometimes blacks are more prejudiced than whites" (the implication being: so why should whites change?). The group, in essence, expressed the view that people should not have to be responsible for their impact on others—a paradigm in conflict with supporting diversity. Similar views surfaced in the session with the predominantly white male maintenance team.

The feedback process was enlightening. The ways in which the reactions to the feedback varied from audience to audience provided additional insights into the various subcultures within the organization. We heard more about sources of tension and learned about points of reactance. Through the feedback sessions, we were also signaling that a change process had begun.

emerging ecological portrait of diversity at chempro

From this initial assessment phase, a complex portrait of ChemPro's diversity began to take shape. It revolved around the following ecologically based themes: (1) the influential role of the organizational history and tradition in shaping current diversity dynamics, (2) the importance of understanding multiple realities, that is, how participants' *experiences* of events differed, (3) the power of informal organizational processes to shape daily experiences, and (4) the ways that dynamics within the organization were influenced by broader societal values.

INFLUENCE OF HISTORY

The particular history and traditions established at ChemPro had, over time, created a context that incorporated both a commitment to diverse people and some major barriers. For the organization as a whole, history and tradition established who had been hired and for what positions, and thereby shaped what types of people (by race and gender) had acquired positions of power and influence. Past traditions had also set the stage for the development of distinctive subcultures within the organization that differentially supported diversity.

Although company policy had shifted to encourage more diversified hiring, it was the hiring practices of the 1960s, '70s, and '80s that shaped the race and gender makeup of the plant in the 1990s because turnover was so low. As mentioned earlier, it was not uncommon for fathers, sons, and grandsons to have all worked at ChemPro. Working alongside siblings, cousins, and in-laws was part of the historical fabric. Even when fewer than half of current employees had relatives at ChemPro, the perception in the community continued to be that the main way to get a job at the plant was to know (and preferably be related to) someone already employed there.

Since the workforce had historically been white and male, this pattern was particularly evident among white men. However, family connections also appeared to be the main way blacks had historically obtained employment at ChemPro. One black employee told how "in those days it was more like they only hired black family folk . . . so if somebody was in, or whatever, you know you had a pretty good chance to get in. Anybody from the outside tended not to be able to come in."

There had also been noteworthy discrimination in hiring, and the barriers to hiring women and people of color were described by many interviewees. One black male interviewee related the story of how, back in the 1970s, his white wife called to inquire about openings at the company. She was told to send her husband right down because they were hiring. The black man showed up less than an hour later and was told there were no openings. He described how he eventually got the NAACP to intervene and secure him a job. Such experiences reinforced the prevailing belief that unless you did something extraordinary, the only way into the organization was through family. Given there were so few blacks to begin with, this hiring tradition ensured that the ratio of blacks to whites remained low.

Historically based traditions not only played a role in establishing membership in the organization as a whole; they had also been forces in establishing how different types of people were distributed across the organization (i.e., in what departments, and in what types of jobs, and where in the hierarchy). Not surprisingly, there was a long history of women being clustered in office jobs, while production had been dominated by men—undoubtedly shaped by gender-stereotypic expectations. More unusual, perhaps, is the way segregation *within* production (i.e., among the five production units) was established and maintained by the distinctive histories and evolved subcultures of the different units.

Processing, the production unit with over 90 percent white male workers, had a history of excluding women that the men felt was "justified" because the work required greater physical strength (i.e., lifting large filters and cleaning huge kettles). The group had developed a sense of superiority that came with having the most physically demanding job in the plant. As one man described the attitude, "In my department, it is a male-dominated, men's world . . . it's great. Sorry girls, it is great we don't have you here." At one point when a woman was hired onto this unit, lunchroom conversation reportedly included statements like "Women don't belong here" and discussions about how men were not going to let their unit become "all girls" like the Drying unit next door.

The history of the Processing unit seemed to have fostered an exclusiveness among members that went beyond their sense that women didn't belong there. The subculture evolved in such a way as to be less tolerant of *any* people outside their norm—including people of color. Racially and ethnically tinged banter and teasing were intense and justified with comments like, "Slavery is not my fault . . . so why should *I* have to walk on egg shells?"

The work of this unit had become more mechanized, and the monitoring of the work was increasingly computerized. These changes had eliminated many of the barriers for people with less physical strength. Yet the unit continued to have a reputation for being inhospitable to women and people of color. Changes in the organizational culture and power structure did not keep pace with the changes in technical procedures.

Drying, the production unit with the highest percentage of women (39.1 percent), was only somewhat less physically demanding yet had always been more inclusive of women than the other production units. This unit had historically been the entry point for new employees of both sexes. The men generally moved on to other units (usually higher-status units) while the women remained. Although they still comprised more than half the workforce in Drying, male workers complained that they were teased about working in "the women's unit" and told their jobs were easier than others. The work in this unit even had a lower job grade than other production jobs in spite of the facts that the tasks in Drying were more specialized than most and that a mistake by this unit could be more costly than one made at another point (i.e., since it was at the end of the production process). The prevailing criteria for job grade did not take such factors into account but rather focused on one's flexibility to do a variety of jobs—arguably a form of institutionalized bias where cross-training and heavy lifting (with most opportunities available to male workers) were more valued than specialization and precision (the "women's" unit). Additionally, the unit had the reputation within the company for being fairly quiet and reluctant to raise concerns or problems in public settings.

In short, historical trends simultaneously shaped the demographics of the Drying unit and rendered it less respected. Until the Workplace Chemistry Initiative supported calls for reevaluation, that lack of respect was embodied in a lower pay grade. This dynamic of devaluation parallels trends observed in the broader U.S. workforce, where there is a long history of positions/professions losing pay and status when they become more populated with women (e.g., bank tellers, restaurant staff, and, more recently, computer-based jobs).[5]

The most racially diverse unit, Prepping, was historically (and informally) the unit where "problem" employees were sent. It was physically the farthest away from the management offices ("the hill") and had always had a somewhat more marginal identity and somewhat more adversarial relationship with management. It developed a reputation as a difficult place to work but a place where people of color who did not fit elsewhere could go. Women were still a very small minority there.

As these descriptions illustrate, the histories of particular units intersected with race and gender distribution to create distinctive subcultures within Production that affected ongoing support for diversity. As often happens, reality may change while the way we make sense of it lags behind. That is, even when actual job requirements and hiring patterns changed, the legacy of those historical patterns continued to influence life for diverse peoples at ChemPro.

MULTIPLE REALITIES

When considering the issue of diversity within an organization, it is important to recognize that women, people of color, and white men can experience the same organization or event quite differently.[6] This was indeed the case at ChemPro.

As expressed in the following quotes, most of the white men we interviewed saw few problems or inequities based on race or gender:

> Overall, I think it's a good place for a woman to work. I think they're more respected than in other industries.

> I always felt that I had a job to do and if you do the best possible job, okay, nobody is going to treat you different. I don't care if you're black, pink, purple, okay. If you do a good job, nobody is going to treat you different. That's the way I feel.

> Individually, individual people in this place might have done things like that [harassment], but . . . especially in the last 10 or 15 years, those things aren't happening.

When conceding that problems might exist, they tended to downplay the significance:

> I never think about it [gender issues] in terms of day-to-day life . . . I can't think of any [problems for women in this company] unless they in fact are intimidated by the white male presence. But it's not really an issue with me.

> I'm not aware that any of them [women] ever left, if you will, as a result of discrimination or harassment or anything. I know we've lost a lot of what I consider to be good, promising people. They *chose* to leave and I never really understood the root cause. I mean, it always seemed to be related to spousal movement or better opportunity or something.

The most common concerns for white male participants were their perceptions that blacks were not held to the same standards and that women were given easier jobs than white men. This is summed up by one white man who said:

> In general here, some minorities are taken care of better. I mean if they did something wrong, their punishment might be less severe than for a non-minority . . . I think girls or females, whichever, tend to be favored by not asking them to do anything that is really laborious or maybe extremely dirty. They will take a male operator off the machine to put a female on it so the male operator can go do something that is physical or mechanical.

Several thought blacks were not being held to the same standards as others because managers feared being called racist. In contrast, most women and people of color described at least some experience of being more closely supervised, having more attention paid to mistakes, being more heavily hazed by coworkers, being excluded from conversations, or being overlooked for promotion opportunities.

There were also striking differences among the black employees based largely on the region and racial context of their youth. Most reported experiencing some inequitable treatment or racist comments at ChemPro, and yet the depth to which it angered or frustrated them varied considerably. All had, no doubt, experienced prejudice while living in the United States. However, the blacks from the southern part of the United States described a humiliating racism that left scars that deeply affected how they responded to current events. As one black man who grew up in the South in the '40s and '50s said:

> I been a Nigger all my life . . . my father died "a boy" . . . if you came up in the South where you have so much racial hate, the last thought that would come to your mind is to have anything to do with anybody white.

The blacks we interviewed from the northern part of the United States (who all grew up near large urban black communities) seemed a bit more philosophical or resigned—maybe even somewhat protective of their white coworkers. They indicated that while they saw racism at ChemPro, it was "no worse than elsewhere" and therefore not something they focused on much. As one northern black man said, "It [being the only black on his team] didn't bother me because I've been the only black since we lived in [this northern city]."

The feeling seemed to be that some bias and discrimination are a given so why not make the best of it—particularly when you have a fairly well-paying job relative to what else is available.

The black workers from the Caribbean indicated that growing up in a country where blacks are the majority provided them with a perspective and reservoir of support for coping with bias and slights. As one man said:

> I probably don't feel the race issue as much because I wasn't exposed to a lot of the same things that the normal black American has been exposed to . . . Where I come from, you know, people interact with one another. [My island] is a tourist attraction. We get to see people from all different walks of life, all different races. And one of the things these people say about the island and the islanders is that they are very friendly people. I just can't relate or understand the way that people around here treat you based on race.

Thus, the interviews revealed, first, that various groups experienced the workplace differently and, secondly, that the groups were differentially aware of one another's experiences. As one white woman said, "Even though they [male coworkers] heard the same words, they didn't interpret it the same way and lots of times it's really small things that blow up into huge things here." One white male manager indicated in his interview that he would be shocked if anyone had trouble talking to him—especially about issues of race and gender. However, the next female interviewee who worked for him felt quite strongly that he did not take her seriously—particularly when she had raised concerns about gender harassment.

INFORMAL ORGANIZATIONAL PROCESSES

At ChemPro, even though there were formal policies designed to make the workplace broadly inclusive, the informal processes served as fairly subtle, yet powerful, barriers to achieving that goal. This dynamic can be traced to some striking contradictions between the stated policies and the informal norms of the organization. Two interrelated organizational processes at Chem-Pro involved access to informal influence networks and more general access to settings for voicing concerns and attaining power. The informal dynamics that regulated access to such networks and settings worked to create an organizational culture that reinforced sameness and marginalized those who did not fit the norm.

In spite of team structures and "open-door" policies, employees described

ChemPro as navigated primarily through an "old boys' network." Numerous interviewees indicated that people were more likely to achieve what they wanted (from shift assignment to positive performance appraisals) through these informal connections and alliances than through formal channels. Many interviewees talked about frustration with favoritism. One black man said, "you have a certain chemistry with a boss and you suck up, and when you suck up, you know, you become favorable." Others were more colorful and talked about "kissing butt" as the modus operandi at ChemPro. As one black man put it, "kissing butt, it's rampant in this place . . . You get ahead if you're a butt kisser." He described telling his boss, "'If you want a kiss ass, you better go somewhere else' and you know what he told me? 'Kiss ass is not a bad thing.' And I'll never forget that and right away I saw where he came from." One black woman jokingly referred to PAs (performance appraisals) as "Personality Appraisals."

While concerns about the informal networks were expressed by people of varied races and genders, the exclusion of most women and people of color from these networks was particularly noteworthy. As one white woman said:

> They move men up the ladder. Like, they get buddy-buddy with another male manager and they're pulled up, you know, politically . . . There's a white male who my [white male] boss is trying to pull up through the system. He's not going to give it to me because he's concentrating on pulling this guy up.

Other white women described frustration and a sense of learned helplessness that there was no one in power to talk with about problems or concerns. Another described:

> There was a man who also reported to him [her boss] . . . When I first came here, he and the guy would go out to ball game and go to the bar and drink and talk, and I'm not invited. So, I mean, I'm used to this.

Blacks described similar experiences. A black man talked about his feelings as the only black on his shift:

> I feel like I am in isolation . . . when these Caucasians, they get ready for their breaks or get ready for their lunches; these three people are together. I am alone out there. And, it makes for a very long 12 hours . . . black basically stick with black, and white basically stick with white as a whole. You know, then I am left out.

He went on to describe how a fellow worker, a white, played golf with a foreman who "took care of him . . . they were going over to each other's house. They were socializing is what I'm trying to say. So how in the hell do a person like me compete with this?"

As discussed above, the exclusion of women and people of color was, in part, rooted in traditions and family connections that were the historical backbone of the sense of community at ChemPro (i.e., most employees with long family roots at ChemPro were white men). However, the exclusion had also become embedded in the operating culture of the current influence networks—requiring a style that was described as countercultural for many blacks and women. Ogbu and others have described the deep adaptation dilemma that emerges for members of involuntary/subjugated minority groups (e.g., African Americans), particularly when it appears that adopting dominant approaches will contradict coping strategies developed over decades of oppression.[7] As one black interviewee put it more succinctly, "Sucking up is not African American."

One woman talked about the pressure to actively advocate for herself and her group: "I'm not as aggressive as some other people, so . . . unless you're really pushing yourself and the work that you're doing and so forth, you're perceived as not doing anything . . . particularly as a woman." Given her discomfort with self-advocacy, she had been less able to work the subtle influence networks. This dynamic tends to be gendered in that many women are socialized toward fostering relationships and interdependence while males tend to be better socialized for self-promotion.[8] As another woman put it, "I tend to look at things differently . . . in terms of a process by which things happen and focus on that as opposed to looking at the individuals involved . . . I don't view myself as being territorial."

While both women and people of color described themselves as being outside the informal influence networks, the interpersonal dynamics that marginalized blacks seemed to differ from those that marginalized women. These differences, then, seemed to create differential requirements for systemic supports. Stereotypes about blacks (particularly U.S. mainland blacks) limited their opportunities, shaped how others interpreted most of their behavior, and, in somewhat insidious ways, became self-fulfilling prophecies. The women simply felt invisible. Interestingly, much of what really angered women was less their own treatment at ChemPro than their view of the treatment of other women. At ChemPro, two central female role models (the sole white woman on the leadership team and Keitha, the African American director of HR) were widely viewed as treated more poorly than male counterparts (i.e., expected to hold multiple positions, treated as "junior members" of the management team, given the same work with less status and pay than men). Keitha was not included on the Leadership Team until a couple years after she became head of Human Resources. The buzz was that Keitha was doing her African American male predecessor's job without either his status or his salary. In referring to the only woman on the Leadership Team, another woman said, "She's the least recognized and most overworked . . . that sends a message to me that I have to work three times as hard as a man." It was other women, not the women in leadership roles themselves, who articulated the criticisms of their treatment. This observation is consistent with Clayton and Crosby's finding that women are often better at noticing the unfair treatment of others than they are at seeing or pleading their own case.[9] Many people see their own treatment as a unique or individual case rather than as representative of broader issues. Thus the person discriminated against is often not the best witness on her own behalf. It is also consistent with Michelle Fine's discussion of the problems with self-reporting when claims of no discrimination often simply mean, "I am coping."[10] In general, respondents indicated that the daily microinequities, taken together with the treatment of the most visible women, sent the message to all women that they were second-class citizens at ChemPro.

The real nature of the influence process was further mystified by contradictions between the openness promoted by management (formal policies) and employees' perceptions of the "real" contingencies of the organizational culture (informal processes). For example, in spite of an open-door policy that allowed all workers to raise concerns with people at any level of the organization, many respondents indicated that they did not really feel free to talk openly. In response to an interview question about the unwritten rules for behavior at ChemPro, respondents said: "Work hard, don't complain"; "It's unacceptable to raise criticisms"; "Don't express a criticism unless you have a solution"; and "If you raise a concern, you are seen as making an excuse." Some workers even cynically referred to the policy as the "open door, out the door" policy. As one white male put it, "What they want to hear is that ChemPro is doing well . . . you don't say any of the problems." In particular, there was considerable feeling that reporting injuries was detrimental to minorities and women. Some described how the system that was established to make the work environment safer and better for employees worked against them. A black man described his experience as follows: "If you're injured you almost don't want to say anything. You're almost, you know . . . if you're injured and you report it, there's that label [that blacks are lazy, trying to avoid work]."

Informal processes that serve as barriers to raising concerns function as supports for the status quo vis-à-vis the relations among gender and diverse racial groups—particularly when there is the illusion that organizational mechanisms exist for discussing problems. While it was not always clear what was expected, it was evident that people felt they were supposed to work hard and not complain. These organizational messages were particularly relevant to diversity at ChemPro in that when concerns about race and gender were raised, they were often viewed as excuses for not working harder.

The sense of marginalization among women and people of color was also generated, and then reinforced, by being in the minority. The relatively low numbers of women and people of color in management positions and the perceived poor treatment of those who were in highly visible positions communicated strong messages to all the women and people of color in the plant.

BROADER CULTURAL CONTEXT

Individual, group, and organizational dynamics at ChemPro have been shaped by institutions and practices in the larger U.S. society. Most obviously, it was the U.S. context that placed white men in the majority by virtue of their overall favored position in the workforce.[11] Predominant societal beliefs about gender and gender roles undoubtedly influenced the placement of women in business support and men in production roles. It is also interesting to note that in almost every setting at ChemPro where we shared the interview summaries, someone in the group reacted by saying, "Well, isn't this just the way it is in society?" or "It's all related to how people are brought up"—as if these comments both explained difficulties with diversity *and* eliminated responsibility for making any changes. These types of comments reflect particular perspectives prevalent in the United States regarding both what is considered normative *and* what is considered possible.

Within the United States the strong historical value for individualism and the cultural belief in the survival of the fittest are strong influences in how people view the diversity challenge. As described above, in spite of the organizationally articulated value for teamwork at ChemPro, most influence was garnered individually through informal networks. Even teams lacked influence unless they were self-promoting. Yet the inherent contradictions and tensions between the individualism of self-advocacy and the communalism of teamwork were not apparent to many workers—or even leaders. In fact, looking out for oneself and working the informal systems of power were considered by some (primarily white men) to be an obviously superior stance. The hegemonic nature of this point of view tended to go unnoticed by the dominant group. For example, when the process of the old boys' network was discussed with the predominantly male production group, one white man responded by saying, "isn't sucking up just part of the American way?"— which stands as an interesting contrast to the "sucking up is not African American" comment by a black worker mentioned earlier.

The focus on individual rights over communal responsibility is clearly rooted in Western cultural beliefs. However, the belief that an individual is neither responsible for his/her impact on coworkers nor primarily accountable to the group is a major barrier to creating a setting that is supportive of people with diverse approaches, perspectives, and histories. These beliefs support the silencing of alternative points of view. At ChemPro, people who did not easily adapt to the dominant way of doing things were considered deviant or *personally* defective in some way (e.g., "If you can't take a joke, *you* have a problem"), and the onus for adaptation was placed on the person already feeling marginal (e.g., "Why should I have to work harder [to be sensitive], if he's the one who's unhappy"). For example, people who did not enjoy the banter common in many production units (which often included teasing about ethnic backgrounds, gender, and/or physical abilities) were told to "develop thicker skins." If people found the banter offensive, they were told, "don't take it so personally."

Some reactions to diversity in general, and to the Workplace Chemistry Initiative in particular, seem rooted in an assumption that all groups have (and have always had) equal access to resources. People who did not fit were considered to be making an informed decision (e.g., "It all goes back to everybody has got their own choice") or simply making an excuse for not taking advantage of opportunities open to them (e.g., "I think if somebody's looking for an excuse, you can always find one . . . through your life it's so much easier to be the victim and say, excuse my language, 'life has dealt me such a shit hand what am I going to do?' as opposed to just doing"). The starting point for such perspectives is the individualistic belief that anyone can have access to the "American Dream" by just working hard and long enough.

Thus, the demographics of the United States combined with pervasive national ideology about individual rights and equality provided a particular context for the dynamics at ChemPro. In many interrelated ways, the case example illustrates how the prevailing U.S. ethos can create a less-than-ideal context for supporting the diverse workplace.

ecological reflections: recognizing assessment as an opportunity to create energy for change

In chemistry, a catalyst is something that allows a reaction to proceed more quickly or with less resistance—it reduces the amount of activation energy needed to make things happen. We hoped that the initial process of inquiry and feedback would be such a catalyst by beginning to shift organizational sensitivities.[12] While this was essentially an "assessment phase," it became clear that the mere presence of the Workplace Chemistry Initiative was an intervention that began to create some energy by raising awareness of (and worries about) diversity dynamics. We were deliberate in our desire to conduct the initial interviews in a manner that would help set the stage for continued collaborative action. In this entry phase, we faced process challenges with regard to developing a shared understanding that would incorporate multiple voices, put resistance into context, and broaden the bases of support for the change process.

INCORPORATING MULTIPLE VOICES

The crux of the issue for creating settings that are supportive of diversity is that when the varied experiences among groups go unacknowledged, the resulting organizational culture will be dominated by the views and values of the majority group. Through the interviews, we heard divergent perspectives on life at ChemPro. We considered it particularly important to solicit and then help give voice to those experiences that had previously been ignored. There are numerous dilemmas built into the task of developing an ecological portrait of an organization that incorporates previously silent voices, validates diversified views, and can, thus, form a platform for collaborative action.

It was apparent that most males were relatively unaware of women's experiences of the organization. Most white males were additionally unaware of the barriers experienced by people of color. These findings parallel observations made both in clinical settings[13] and in other organizational settings[14] that those with greater access to power and resources are not as likely—nor as compelled—to understand the particular experiences of those with less status. In their research, Fiske and her colleagues have found that those with greater organizational power (i.e., control over others' outcomes) are prone to stereotyping the less powerful groups. In contrast, people with less power tend to be keenly aware of unique individual characteristics of those of higher status; they pay closer attention to subtle differences presumably because of the impact the more powerful can have on their own access to resources. "People may have less concern and less need to be accurate about those considered relatively insignificant to their own outcomes."[15]

The dynamic was additionally reinforced at ChemPro by the fact that many people who cared about diversity issues did not feel free to share their observations, which then shielded the majority from hearing about their concerns. For example, in one feedback session, a few vocal participants were firm in their belief that although the issues we raised might be relevant to some in the organization, they were clearly not of concern to people on their own unit. To support this belief, they put forth the claim that no one from their unit had been included in the interviews—when in fact three people in the room during that very discussion had indeed been interviewed. The interview participants had shared many of the concerns summarized; however, they obviously had not made their concerns public, nor did they choose to divulge their identity during that feedback session. It is also worth noting that women and people of color in general seemed particular reticent during the feedback sessions when they were a lone representative of their gender or race group. Several came up to us after the meetings, however, to share reactions and thank us for summarizing their concerns. When varied views are not expressed, they are not easily incorporated into the prevailing organizational culture. In essence, a certain myopia is reinforced by the same dynamics that silence the relatively powerless members of the organization.

A significant aspect of this challenge to incorporate minority experiences is developing a process that truly invites, accepts, and embraces a wide range of voices. Our experience with these initial interviews brought home the fact that both who the researchers or consultants are and how the work is conducted can determine what they are invited to hear and witness. This observation resonates with the ecological notion that investigator and setting have significant effects on each other during all phases of our work, and it pushes us further to attend to power relations.[16] Reinharz cautions, "Before researchers can expect to hear suppressed voices, they will have to examine the power dynamics of the social location they are studying and their role in it."[17] As three women interviewers, we had to work overtime to hear from men of color. As representatives of academia, we had to listen carefully to hear the experiences of the hourly workers who face the grit of manufacturing on a daily basis.

In order to validate the full range of experiences, we did not try to reconcile seemingly "contradictory" information. Rather we fed back all the varied views to the organization as legitimate "realities," phenomenologically honest expressions of people's experiences. Listening to people can aid in their empowerment;[18] additionally, articulating the shared experiences to a broader audience can add to the impact of the new voices. Many people felt that they had expressed opinions held by no one else. After one meeting, an individual reflecting on the feedback we had shared with her team commented that a point we had made was obviously based on her interview. Another member of that informal gathering then laughed and said that he too thought it was based on his comments. They had both felt that they were the only one to express the concern, when in fact they were merely two among several.

As an outside group, we were in the unique position of being able to put forth the previously unspoken with a force of authority (and data) behind us. As we took the interview feedback to the plant unit by unit for reaction and discussion, many women and employees of color shared with us how validating this process felt and how relieved they were that the top levels of management were taking the concerns seriously. We were shedding light on invisible experiences and labeling the previously unseen with the goal of incorporating multiple voices into the dominant organizational story. At the same time, we were offering to those who felt invisible an opportunity to see how others reacted when faced with this new information (i.e., giving a preview of potential reactions). Perhaps most importantly, we were able to help the people who were feeling relatively marginal find some community in the process.

It is also significant that we did not push a hegemonic or absolute interpretation of work life at ChemPro. To elevate and incorporate previously silenced voices, we needed to resist the press to present a neatly packaged analysis of what was "really" happening. In each meeting, we acknowledged that there were multiple perspectives and varied experiences within the organization. ChemPro was such a small community that people assumed that they knew their coworkers better than they did. People presumed that they knew who had expressed what, when in fact they did not. As we shared results, we described constraints (including organizational, societal, and historical issues as well as our own races and gender) that could make it hard for some people to share their experiences as openly as others. As we acknowledged that there remained much to learn, some of those previously untapped perspectives were shared. In essence, we tried to heed the call from

Trickett, Watts, and Birman for work on human diversity to utilize methods that are "congruent with the value assumptions underlying the diversity concept . . . methods that can appreciate diversity from the inside out and . . . those kinds of collaborations that empower rather than objectify the people we wish to understand."[19]

PUTTING RESISTANCE INTO CONTEXT

The responses during the feedback sessions underscored the complexity of reactions to addressing diversity at ChemPro. Some employees felt validated by the Workplace Chemistry Initiative and hopeful that their work and perspectives would be taken more seriously. Others expressed varying degrees of indifference and/or resistance,—for example, considering the Workplace Chemistry Initiative unnecessary ("doesn't happen on my unit"), an annoyance ("it's not my problem"), or too unsettling ("it's opening up issues we can't solve anyway").

The majority view among white male workers at the beginning was that there were no race or gender-related problems or concerns. Many of these workers saw the attention to diversity as, at best, a lot of fuss about nothing and, at worst, reverse discrimination. These majority group members also expressed the view that even if there was a real need, there was no potential for change anyway. There was considerable cynicism about the organization's ability to sustain commitment to issues over time, which resulted in the worry that diversity would be just another passing fad. These white male employees were not alone in their reluctance to address relations among diverse workers.

There was wide recognition that talking about race and gender would make the issues more salient. Not surprisingly, some worried that discussing diversity concerns would overemphasize differences and make things worse. This fear was initially raised in the People Team meeting. A black man worried that we were "opening up a Pandora's box." While he was also a member of the Steering Team and supported the initiative in spirit, he remained wary and maintained some distance from it. Although workers of color could clearly describe discriminatory treatment by management and coworkers, for some the fear that it could get worse instead of better was more salient. Several said, in essence, "The known is easier than the unknown. We have learned how to cope with these injustices, so let's just leave well enough alone."

Similar fears surfaced again strongly in the production unit with the largest percentage of people of color. After our feedback session with this unit, some white workers apparently asked a black manager if it would still be acceptable to joke around with black coworkers. I supported him in trying to walk the fine line between raising awareness of one's impact and making people too nervous to say anything at all. Clearly, while increased visibility of the issues can be an important first step toward addressing diversity concerns, it can also signal an uncomfortable disruption of the status quo. The message people were hearing was that the rules would be changing. What the new rules would be and what changes would really be required on a daily basis, however, remained unclear.

Rather than seeing these forms of reluctance as emanating from resistant individuals or groups, we sought a more contextualized, ecological understanding. Majority group members are often shielded from experiences that would allow them access to experiences of women and people of color. Not only are there power dynamics that render such awareness "unnecessary," as discussed previously, but the organizational culture may also prescribe what is heard and acknowledged, and what is to be left unspoken. There are often strong norms that preclude any challenge to the dominant view that "there's no problem here." This can be compounded by the sense of an uncertain future. When a problem is first identified, there is often no clear understanding of what an alternative approach might look and feel like. Majority group members confronted with the possibility that the power relations among groups might shift are often left to worry that the only alternative to being the oppressor is to be the oppressed. These are understandable fears that are shaped not just by the individual psyche but also by team dynamics, organizational arrangements, and societal constraints. In fact, what we call "resistance" or "backlash" can be viewed as a healthy reaction to demands for change and the uncertainty that the changes signal.

We tried to approach these types of reactance with care and respect by emphasizing the gradual development of the project and very explicitly grounding it in workers' expressed concerns. It was particularly important to allow the project to evolve gradually. We started with interviews, then moved to a plantwide survey, and only in the third year entered a training phase. Given the organization's sustained commitment, we were able to let each phase evolve out of the increased awareness fostered in the prior stage. It was also essential to acknowledge that diversity initiatives *would* accentuate differences that had been previously ignored. This did not, however, have to be accompanied by a search for someone or something to blame. We had a commitment that even though the diversity initiative would primarily focus on reducing barriers for members of minority groups, our work would not ignore the disruption felt by members of the majority groups.

BROADENING THE SUPPORT BASE

To have any hope of changing the organizational culture, we knew that it was important to get as many people "on board" as possible. Our dialogues with HR, the president, the Steering Team, and the People Team brought an ever-widening circle of organization members into the process. They informed us; they advised us; they challenged us—and became deeply engaged in the Workplace Chemistry mission as a result.

In approaching our goal to broaden the support base, we recognized that there is a reciprocal relationship between the process of gathering information about the experiences in an organization and the act of shaping participants' understandings of those experiences. Our work with the Steering Team and with the People Team not only guided the project but also raised awareness among members and brought them into the shared agenda. The interviews were data-gathering tools *and* interventions that spurred participants to think about new issues. The feedback sessions, which were designed partly as consciousness-raising settings, were important sources of information about the subcultures within the plant. In any inquiry process that allows one to get close enough to learn about the intricacies of human interactions, the line between inquiry and intervention becomes blurred. In fact, the value of drawing such a line is questionable. If we had not worked so closely with the participants at ChemPro during this assessment phase, it would have substantially weakened our ability to observe and understand the internal dynamics of the organization.

It became apparent that a participative and self-critical process of assessment could help facilitate broader support.[20] Potential action steps were generated during all the feedback sessions. We shared these with the Steering Team and then brainstormed additional action items organized into four themes: (1) emphasizing commonalities among employees, (2) appreciating and supporting differences among employees, (3) establishing and rewarding fairness, and (4) paying attention to "hot" spots. The Steering Team recommendations were shared with the president and the Leadership Team. Some recommendations were to be implemented by our university team and others by HR, the People Team, and/or the president himself. At the end of the first year, as the action plans were being collaboratively fine-tuned, we all agreed to shift the sponsorship of the Workplace Chemistry Initiative from its own Steering Team to the People Team—representing a step toward institutionalizing the value for diversity by joining with an ongoing, preexisting group to champion the initiative.

As the initiative evolved, we also developed symbols to acknowledge all those who had signed onto the goals of the project, which then served as a reminder of the commitment to diversity even when no activities were under way. For example, a banner with the mission of the initiative and personal signatures of all those who had completed the training spanned the company's main meeting hall. It was the only such banner of its type in the facility, and employees had to pass under it on their way to the majority of plant meetings. It was interesting that when we were out at the plant years later to administer a follow-up survey, several workers pointed out the banner with some pride to the students who came with me.

At ChemPro, where team processes were woven into all levels of the work, the benefits of collaborative inquiry were, perhaps, more easily realized than might be the case in other organizations. In some sense, participation "fit" with the existing organizational culture. Yet the dilemma we experienced on this front as we got further out into the plant was how to engage reluctant partners when some saw no need for change and others saw the need but feared possible negative outcomes. We could not *force* people to be partners— but, rather, it behooved us to seek multifaceted, multilayered ways to understand and address the barriers to partnerships.

It is useful to understand that organizational consultants are often asking people to be partners in dismantling a world that makes sense to them. Many white, male, long-term employees—in particular—had really known of no other way for manufacturing teams to operate. Additionally, as we moved further from those in leadership roles (with formal position power) and/or line workers who were involved in crosscutting teams (with informal collective power), we were asking those with relatively less influence to trust in an organizational change process they were not sure was in their best interest. This sense was probably intensified at ChemPro by the fact that the Workplace Chemistry Initiative was simultaneous with other restructuring and organizational change processes—all of which signaled further disruption to daily life—and with the fact that there was no collective body like a union specifically designed to advocate for workers. Recognizing these constraints did not deter us or make us reluctant to act, but we did need to factor them into our work.

SYNTHESIS

The challenges at this stage revolved around how to approach the assessment process in ways that brought people together—ways that raised previously silenced voices yet did not blame or distance others (i.e., connected and disruptive). The process at ChemPro underscored the fact that an outsider cannot enter an organizational system without in some way affecting and altering the ecology of that setting.[21] Thus, what may be labeled an "assessment" is, nonetheless, also an intervention. As Prilleltensky and Nelson argue, "problem definition is not just a professional act, but a political one as well."[22]

We felt it was important to adopt a conceptual framework for understanding issues that avoided finger-pointing or shaming individual organizational members. By placing organizational issues into historical and societal perspective, we sought to emphasize that many of the problematic dynamics had been set into motion and reinforced by forces beyond the local cast of characters. At the same time, in revealing the stories of injustice that had not previously been visible, we sought to awaken the workforce to the need for change in current practices. We wanted to help energize the current leadership to take action, and gradually help workers experience the initiative as in tune with other changes they would welcome (e.g., enhanced working relationships, increased team effectiveness, improved quality of work life).

During this phase, we were largely successful in creating catalysts for change. People were now both curious and unsettled. The next step was to corral the emerging energy for change—and redirect the sense of disruption—in order to move in positive directions.

formulas for action

DEVELOPING AND DELIVERING THE TRAINING

AS A RESULT OF THE INTERVIEWS and the feedback process, awareness of issues was beginning to emerge in various corners of the plant. We had created the spark to initiate some action; now we needed to generate broader sources of energy to keep it going. We had the organization's attention. We had some committed partners, but we did not necessarily have widespread consensus or endorsement. Our challenges at this juncture were to unveil the broader range of experiences within the organization and to increase people's ability to make sense of the differing experiences in a manner that would move our work forward. In other words, we were cognizant of the need to shift the collective paradigm from "people or groups with complaints" to "the development of an organizational culture of inclusion." We wanted to increase *what* people saw and also shift *how* they made sense of it.

setting the stage for training

To move in this direction required that additional groundwork be laid before moving forward with plantwide training. We decided to take the assessment beyond the initial thirty-six interviews (described in chapter 2) to hear from a much broader cross section of organization members through a plantwide survey. Given the culture of the plant, we saw that an additional benefit could be adding "hard data" (i.e., number ratings on surveys) to the qualitative interview responses. In addition, in order to help the organization adapt a non-blaming, inclusive, multilayered interpretation of the expanded assessment, we wanted to enhance the sophistication about diversity of a core group of organization members—that is, develop an expanded cadre of ambassadors who could promote the shifting focus. So, two efforts were initiated to set the stage for broader change initiatives: (1) a plantwide survey and (2) in-depth training for a core group.

A PLANTWIDE SURVEY

While sharing the initial interview results, several people urged input from a greater number of people throughout the plant. Concurrently, HR wanted to assess employee opinions on a variety of other personnel-related matters. HR's interest provided an opportunity for our next stage of assessment to be integrated in an organic way with ongoing organizational efforts. We worked with the onsite nurse, as the designated HR point person for the survey, and the People Team to design a survey that included sections on diversity-related concerns (e.g., personal attitudes and beliefs about dealing with differences; assessments of the organizational climate with respect to inclusion of diverse groups; and observations of harassment, discrimination, and unfair treatment); overall quality of work life (e.g., work satisfaction, peer and supervisor supports); the structure of work (e.g., shift preferences, overtime concerns); and general quality of life (e.g., health and well-being, child care needs, and benefits questions/requests.) By addressing a wide range of personnel issues (shift preferences, overtime concerns, child care needs) alongside the assessment of harassment, discrimination, and diversity climate, we sought to send a message about the place of diversity in the web of organizational life, that is, central and connected to other issues. Diversity was woven into the full HR agenda—not a "special" initiative off to the side and not a mere footnote relegated to an affirmative action officer or outside consulting group. Including it in such a comprehensive tool sent an important message.[1]

Although the questionnaires were distributed to all employees with the help of the People Team, we asked participants to return them directly to the university. We hoped that the use of an external address would help reassure people that their participation was voluntary and that their responses would be held in confidence. We received responses from 141 people out of the 210 full-time employees, which represented a response rate of about 67 percent. This was an impressive response, particularly when you consider that the survey was ten pages long! We heard from at least one person on every unit and someone at every level of organization. About 18.6 percent of the respondents were women, and 15.6 percent were people of color—percentages that signify slightly higher response rates from people in these groups since the workforce was 17.1 percent women and 14.2 percent people of color. This was a clear sign of progress over the initial response to our call for interviews. With this broad response, we could move forward with the confidence that we were hearing about a wide range of experiences throughout the organization.

The survey results reinforced many of the themes that emerged from the interviews.[2] Respondents indicated that they felt basically satisfied and some-what successful in their work. Most respondents reported low- to midrange stress levels associated with their efforts to balance work and family life. How-ever, men generally felt more satisfied and more successful at work than women; women felt less respected and experienced more stress than men. Re-spondents generally agreed that management was serious about wanting to treat people of both genders and all races equally. Yet men described management as more serious in these regards than did women, and most respondents—of both genders and all races—thought that a white man was still more likely to get a new leadership position than either a woman or a person of color.

People overall reported moderate levels of support from supervisors and a generally positive sense of community, yet women experienced the organiza-tion as less supportive than did the men. They described less support from peers, less openness to new ideas, less sense of community, less sense of fair-ness, and less support for their advancement. There were somewhat different patterns for people of different races. People of color, in comparison to whites, reported less support for the advancement of nonwhite workers but also a *greater* sense of ChemPro as open to new ideas. There were also some differences between departments with respect to feeling supported by supervisors and believing that supervisors were supportive of diversity, with ratings by workers in Facilities being significantly lower than for workers in other departments.

In terms of diversity-related attitudes, people indicated that they general-ly felt OK both about adapting personally and about having the organization adapt to varied worker needs, such as being asked to accommodate to cowork-ers who may have different needs based on race, religion, disability, sexual orientation, gender, or family responsibilities. Workers tended to disagree with the view that people of color and women should work harder "to fit in with how things are done at ChemPro." However, whites, men, and techni-cians working on the plant floor tended to endorse more conservative beliefs about how to deal with diversity. For example, they more strongly endorsed the view that "we have gone too far in pushing equal rights in this country" than did women and people of color.

The most common experiences of harassment were based on race, gen-der, and family responsibility. Perhaps the most striking finding was that about 62 percent of the 21 respondents of color indicated that they had expe-rienced some form of harassment and/or discrimination based on their race, and 61.5 percent of the women ($n = 26$) indicated that they had experienced some form of harassment and/or discrimination based on their gender.

About 38 percent of the people of color also reported some harassment based on language or accent, probably reflecting the experiences of the Caribbean blacks and the Asian-born workers. Almost 31 percent of the women and 13.3 percent of the men reported biases based on family responsibilities. A few workers also reported harassment or discrimination related to health/disability and sexual orientation. Reports of age-based discrimination were hard to decipher, since some felt they were discriminated against for being too old and some for being too young. In addition to documenting personal experiences of discrimination and harassment, the survey revealed that workers of color were significantly more aware of discrimination against other people of color in the organization than were whites. Women personally experienced significantly more sexual harassment than did men and also observed significantly more discrimination against both other women and people of color than men did.

The initial interviews had provided a qualitative accounting. The subsequent survey added quantitative data that documented the widespread nature of the concerns. The portrait that emerged from both assessments was one of an organization that meant well but did not always succeed. There existed both a general appreciation for the organization and widespread experiences of differential and biased treatment.

Again, we summarized the results in a manner that would preserve confidentiality and headed out to the plant floor to share the findings. We could now use the numerical results to expand on the issues we had presented earlier. Reactions were more subdued and discussions less animated than they had been during our rounds with interview feedback. It seemed there was a combination of acceptance, appreciation, and, perhaps, some resignation that the Workplace Chemistry Initiative was really moving forward. The discussions this time revolved more around *what* we were going to do rather than *whether* action was needed. The language of numbers was powerful in garnering broader recognition that there was indeed an issue here that needed to be grappled with. Actual percentages were less debatable, less deniable, and less dismissible—particularly in this organizational culture, which valued measurable indicators and clear documentation. We could now build on the survey results to propose an action agenda.

DEVELOPING AMBASSADORS

While we knew that we would eventually want to roll out a training program for all organization members, we wanted to begin by enhancing the sophistication and skills of a strategically selected core group. In our effort to establish a broad support base, we had been endorsed and guided by our Steering Team and were about to shift sponsorship of the Workplace Chemistry Initiative to the People Team. However, we also wanted to establish a larger cadre of organization members with particular *expertise* in fostering a more inclusive organizational culture. We wanted to move the expertise from a specialized project group and begin to infuse it throughout the organization. An approach most organic to the organization would be to expand our work to include the group at ChemPro that was already most interested in interpersonal issues—the People Team—as well as any managers who expressed interest.

It occurred to us that a unique opportunity we could make available, given our connection with a university, would be to offer a course for college credit. This seemed an exciting opportunity to put the university's resources at the service of the region—a central aspect of our state university's mission. We arranged to offer a course, "Workplace Diversity," through the UML Office of Continuing Education on-site at the ChemPro plant. Keitha and I invited the members of our Steering Team and the People Team to participate. Since I personally did not have time at this juncture to teach such a course, I arranged for the university to contract with an experienced instructor, and ChemPro offered to cover tuition costs for any interested workers. The course ran with about twelve students who attended on paid work time. We set it up with differential course requirements for undergraduate and graduate students to increase its appeal to workers at different educational levels.

I initially thought this idea quite brilliant, but it actually provided a humbling lesson on how little I understood the community of workers at ChemPro. After the course got under way, I was to learn that no one opted to take it for university credit! A bit incredulous that people would pass up what I saw—wearing my professorial hat—as an "incredible opportunity," I inquired as to why. I learned that a few university credits were basically irrelevant to most workers' lives. Those who had not gone to college had no intention of completing a whole course of study—so three credits were not particularly useful to them. Those with degrees already had enough education to qualify for their jobs and felt no need for additional credentials. Clearly, I was functioning with some class blinders and had misjudged the value that university credit might hold. This was an important reminder for me to keep my attention on understanding ChemPro as experienced from the inside—versus looking in from my academic perch on the outside.

Despite the flop of the college-credit-as-incentive idea, the course was generally well received. This semester-long course gave additional legitimacy to "diversity" as a serious topic. At the same time, it deepened the collective organizational knowledge base about race, gender, and the dynamics of oppression. Some of this preliminary work can be likened to the art of building a campfire. You want to stack the twigs and logs so that you can start the fire with a spark rather than a blowtorch and so that you can keep it going with only minor tending rather than needing to periodically start over from scratch. The survey and the initial course helped to set the stage for rolling a training program out to the full plant. Or in chemical terms, these activities provided additional "activation energy" to fuel the plantwide chemical reaction.

DESIGNING THE WORKPLACE CHEMISTRY WORKSHOPS

Ecological principles about system change guided the process of developing and delivering the plantwide training. Tailoring a program that spoke to the specific challenges at ChemPro was foremost in our minds. To ground the workshops in the experiences of people actually working in the plant, we built on the results of the initial assessment and also recruited a diverse team to design and pilot the training program with us. The design team included staff and students from UMass Lowell as well as workers from ChemPro. The initial group included Rich (a white male), Byron (an African American male production worker), and Linda (an African American woman from production). At this point in time, Rich was relatively new to his position as a training coordinator in HR. He was also new to the topic of diversity yet approached it with a thoughtfulness and openness that we grew to rely on. Even while fully engaging the goals of the training, he gave voice—and humanity—to the perspectives of white men who had spent years working in the plant. The two African American workers were a bit reserved at first but gradually opened up to provide critical examples and insights that greatly enhanced the training. Keitha often joined our planning meetings offering input, feedback, and examples. I suspect that the mutually respectful yet blunt and down-to-earth nature of our discussions was the essential element that enabled this sharing.

The UMass Lowell side of the partnership included a racially and gender diverse group of staff and graduate students. Robin Toof, a white woman from the UML Center for Family, Work and Community, brought her expertise in experiential learning and was a very active partner in both the development and delivery of the training. The students involved in the earliest stages included a Latina, two Asian Indian women, a white woman, and a white man.[3]

The emphasis of the Workplace Chemistry Workshops was not on presenting "information" about diverse race, ethnic, or gender groups, but rather on addressing personal perspectives that support diversity as well as on interpersonal, team, and organizational dynamics that are related to diversity.[4] In essence, our hope was that we could help participants understand the world in more ecological terms—that is, recognize the ways in which people's experiences of the world differ greatly depending on membership in identity groups (phenomenological attitude); appreciate the ways in which all members of a system are interconnected and how what each one of us does can affect the quality of life for others (interdependencies); and understand that there are individual, team, and organizational issues that influence the organization's ability to welcome and support diverse groups of workers (multiple levels of analysis).

Our fundamental guiding assumption was that a collective appreciation for—and enactment of—these principles would shift the organizational culture in critical ways. These aspirations were articulated as the three main training goals shared with participants: (1) to increase attention to context and understanding of how factors at multiple levels are all important to diversity dynamics in organizations (i.e., factors such as individual skills, team dynamics, and organizational culture—including exploring how privilege affects one's reactions and one's impact on others), (2) to increase awareness of multiple "realities" and appreciation for factors that influence the experiences of diverse people, and (3) to promote accountability for one's *impact* in interpersonal interactions at work and to do all of this in such a way that it would promote a culture of connection.

In promoting attention to context, we were working to get away from the notion of blame by increasing understanding of how individual, team, and organizational factors are all important to diversity (challenging the stance of "I just need to look out for myself"). The overall idea was the development of a nonblaming, systemic, connected approach to challenging unquestioned privilege and the status quo. In addressing multiple realities, we sought to increase empathy and awareness that people may experience the world quite differently based on their race, ethnicity, gender, and other identities that embody power differentials. We developed some training activities that addressed this directly, but we also developed a process that would promote sharing throughout the training so that participants could enlighten one another. We talked about the challenge of accepting that divergent experiences can coexist as a "both/and" perspective. Addressing the topic of ac-

TABLE 3.1 · OUTLINE OF TRAINING

Day #1: Introduction: Getting people on board

GOALS:
to establish a training environment that is safe, honest, and respectful
to illustrate the importance of attending to workplace diversity

TOPICS:
 · Welcome and Setting the Stage
 · Review of Issues at ChemPro
 · Experiencing Another Culture
 · Guiding Model and Basic Assumptions

Day #2: Points of view: Making room for both/and

GOAL:
to increase awareness of multiple "realities"

TOPICS:
 · Exploring One's Own Point of View
 · Empathy: Skills for Understanding Others' Points of View
 · Adopting a Both/And Perspective

Day #3: Interpersonal dynamics: Moving from intent to impact

GOAL:
to promote accountability for one's impact

TOPICS:
 · Dynamics of Stereotyping and Prejudice
 · Recognizing Privilege
 · Intent vs. Impact
 · Accountability for Impact

Day #4: Team and organizational cultures: Institutionalizing change

---

GOALS:
to enhance understanding of how team dynamics affect diverse members
to increase attention to organizational factors that promote or inhibit diversity

TOPICS:
 · Elements of Effective Teams
 · Building a Multicultural Organization
 · Celebrating Participants' Heritage

---

countability for impact involved promoting awareness of (and responsibility for) workers' effect on one another. The notion of accountability builds on awareness of interdependencies and the way interpersonal actions radiate throughout a system. It embodies a value stance that having good intentions is not enough. It also involves exploring the role of privilege both in determining people's impact and in blinding them to the effects of their behavior. We worked from the observation that people in the majority group are typically less aware of their impact on those in the minority—not only because they often have less contact with minority group members but also because people in nondominant groups tend to be less assured that they can speak their minds free from negative consequences.

After establishing some basic training goals, our planning team met about ten times over the following five months. We began by reviewing the survey results and brainstorming topics. Early on we discussed guiding frameworks—building on ecological notions but working to develop language for the principles that were syntonic with ChemPro's (and Corporate's) other training programs. We worked from there to articulate goals for five training modules and to brainstorm training activities that would address each goal (see table 3.1). We drew on our past experiences as trainers; our ChemPro partners drew on their knowledge of their coworkers and the dynamics within the plant. Together we worked to develop exercises and examples specific to the history and current work circumstances in the plant. We reviewed a mountain of diversity manuals purchased by Keitha and previewed numerous training videos. We sought feedback on training ideas from others in the plant and tried out each activity on our own group.

To pilot the first draft of the training package, we invited members of our original Steering Team and interested members of the People Team to participate in an initial run. At the end of each training day we asked for feedback on the design and, at the conclusion, revised the training outline to address their recommendations. What evolved was a four-day training workshop that was highly participative and activity based with group discussions, simulations, films, case analyses, personal sharing, and individual reflection and, most importantly, that was grounded in the specifics of life as a worker at ChemPro.

the workplace chemistry curriculum

DAY 1
The first day was primarily devoted to setting the stage and establishing a comfortable, respectful training environment—getting people on board. We knew we needed to acknowledge participants' worries and hesitations about addressing diversity. We were aware that even as we had a growing cadre of partners, there was some increased resistance as people recognized that this initiative was moving ahead—including requiring four full days of training for *all* workers.

We began with a welcome and introductions, but then quickly got people into an exercise about the nature of the world's population that demonstrated how hard it is to know about the diversity in the world when many of us live in fairly homogeneous communities and are surrounded by people like ourselves. We discussed the ways in which this is particularly true for majority group members whose peers at work and those with authority in other daily transactions are likely to mirror their race and gender. During the first morning, we also engaged the group in defining what it means to support diversity and outlined common approaches to diversity. The morning was structured to provide opportunities for participants to connect with one another by working in dyads, while, at the same time, engaging in the topic at hand.

With both seriousness and a bit of humor, we used comics to illustrate the wide range of concerns that people have about addressing issues of race and gender. We labeled the worries about opening up Pandora's box; making a bigger deal out of things by talking about them; and people getting blamed, bashed, and/or ridiculed. Relevant comic strips abound and can be extremely useful in helping trainers make these points because they can be both poignant and lighthearted at the same time. We wanted to step outside the stereotype of "politically correct" trainers who take themselves too seriously, and also establish ourselves as down-to-earth and direct.

We took care to allow time, but not *too* much time, for the discussion of worries. We wanted to acknowledge people's concerns, but we did not want to debate them or even dwell on them to a great extent. Rather, we moved fairly quickly into what training would and would not do and laid out the following assurances:

- We will start with establishing some ground rules to make this a safe place to explore diversity.
- We begin with an assumption that we learn most about working effectively with others when we are aware of *both* similarities *and* differences—we cannot afford to ignore either one.
- We believe blaming is unproductive and senseless; we will look at individual, group, work team, and organizational factors that all contribute to the diversity challenges at work.
- We will emphasize the importance for all of us to take responsibility for our *impact* on others; we assume that the vast majority of bias and stereotyping is not done on purpose.
- We will not focus on what is "politically correct," but rather on what is respectful and makes for an inclusive environment.

It was only after we had spent some time introducing the topic and recognizing some of the common concerns that we asked participants to share their hopes for the training and to establish some ground rules for the group. Our rationale for beginning with worries was that we have found that it can be difficult to step into hopes when the concerns loom large. The temptation can be to follow each hope with a "but . . ." Simple acknowledgment can be helpful at keeping the concerns at bay, at least for a while. Minimally, participants learn, first, that they are not alone in their worries and, second, that we as trainers take those worries to heart.

The setting of ground rules was also helpful in establishing the climate for training. We typically began by suggesting some basic rules about the value of participation, listening before responding, speaking for oneself, and avoiding casting blame on others. In addition, the "pass rule" (allowing people to opt out of an exercise) is an important way to communicate that no one will be forced to share or be put on the spot in uncomfortable ways. After suggesting some basics, we invited the group to add their own ground rules, listing each one on newsprint, then asked each participant to sign the list to indicate agreement. These rules were hung on the wall for all four days of training.

We had three goals for the afternoon of the first day: to ground the training in the specifics of ChemPro, to anchor the training in an experiential understanding of what it feels like to be "different," and to review the model and assumptions that guided the training. Even though many participants had heard the survey feedback on their unit, we reviewed highlights of the findings, emphasizing that the training grew out of what they had told us. With this real-life data as a backdrop, we then engaged people in a cross-cultural simulation game called BafáBafá, which creates two new "cultures."[5] The simulation package is designed to create feelings among participants that are similar to those one encounters when finding oneself in a foreign culture unaware of the accepted practices and "rules" for appropriate behavior. BafáBafá is a very structured, prepackaged exercise. While the goals of BafáBafá are quite serious, the enacting of the new cultures generates a lot of laughter. The simulation allows participants to be very playful as they learn a silly language or play out rigid rules for interpersonal communication. The debriefing discussion can also be a bit playful as members of each culture caricature the other group, yet we returned to the serious by asking the group to make connections between the game dynamics and work at ChemPro and to reflect on how it might feel to be a worker outside the majority group, culture, or gender.

We wanted to end the day with something that would both leave people with a sense of validation and connection and, at the same time, embody the serious and substantive spirit of the training. Using the imagery of the inter-connected elements of a mobile, we discussed the principles guiding the training, then invited the whole group to collectively design and build an actual mobile using wire, fishing line, and pictures we had taken of each person at the start of the day. They needed to work together to attach and arrange their pictures so that the structure was in balance. These somewhat makeshift but highly personalized creations then hung in the room for the next three days of training to visually anchor the ecological notions of inter-dependence and connection.

DAY 2

The theme for the second day of training was "Points of View: Making Room for Both/And." Our goal for the day was to anchor the notion of "multiple realities," first by exploring the factors that shape a person's own point of view and then by challenging the notion that there is only one "right" way to think, feel, interpret, and act. We worked with the participants to move away from "either/or" thinking and to embrace "both/and" thinking.

Each day, we sought to anchor the training in participants' own experi-ences. Thus, the morning of Day 2 began with several exercises that asked participants to reflect on lessons learned during their lives about race and gender. Easing them into it with an exercise called "cultural affirmations," we asked participants to form a circle. We then read a long list of characteristics, pausing after each one to invite participants to step inside the circle if the characteristic read by the trainers applied to them. This exercise highlighted the sources of diversity within the group, many of which were not evident from looking at one another and unknown even to those who had worked side by side for years. For example, they learned that the Chinese man with a very thick accent spoke five different languages, which shifted his image in the group dramatically—from one who "had difficulty with English" to "a master of many languages." The affirmations exercise allowed people to "tell" one another more about themselves without much verbal exchange.

However, once they were warmed up, we did ask them to engage in dyadic conversations about early lessons around diversity (e.g., talk about when they had first noticed differences and what lessons they learned about the mean-ing of differences at that time). The goal of both the affirmations exercise and the circle of sharing was to enhance their appreciation for how their identity and past experiences shaped how they thought, felt, and interpreted events.

At the same time, this was an opportunity for them to enhance their connection to one another by learning more about the diverse personal experiences of those within the training group.

With this foundation, we turned to the topic of empathy. This is not an easy concept to teach, as the notion draws on many skills and assumptions. It is critical to distinguish it from sympathy (which implies a more hierarchical "feeling sorry for") and from agreement (which is both more cognitive and implies that you would feel or think similarly in the same situation). It is also not built on the "Golden Rule" of "Do unto others as you would have them do unto you." While kind, the Golden Rule is applied from one's own frame of reference without regard for the values, traditions, and preferences of the other. By emphasizing empathy, we wanted to push participants to get inside what others might experience or feel without letting go of their own experiences. Empathy involves an awareness that another's experience might be quite different or even in opposition to one's own yet can be understood and "accepted" from what we refer to as a "both/and" perspective. Perhaps there is a revised Golden Rule here: Do unto others as you would have them do unto you *if* you were in their shoes.

To explore and illustrate the "both/and" challenge, we used video clips that present a situation from various participant's perspectives—somewhat like the classic play *Rashomon*.[6] After viewing clips that showed the identical dialogue from the perspective of two different actors in the scenario, we asked people to reflect on how each perspective might be shaped by the player's cultural background, group identities and gender roles, social and occupational roles, self-concept, as well as physical condition. The facilitation challenge is to keep the discussion focused on how *each* participant's perspective is "understandable" when the temptation of many participants is to determine whose interpretation is "right." We were asking people to step outside of "right versus wrong" thinking and into "both/and" thinking.

To move the discussion to situations faced on a daily basis in the plant, we developed several scenarios that directly reflected situations at ChemPro. We asked small groups to work through a set of questions about a scenario that required them to articulate an understanding of the situation from various perspectives. Finally, they were to develop a stance where they could accept *both* perspectives as simultaneously "true." For example:

You are a white employee who has many family traditions about how you spend your time on President's Day. You have a black co-worker who feels the company should consider Martin Luther King's birthday as a holiday instead of President's Day. Your co-worker is going to suggest this change to management, and you are quite upset.

You are an African American who grew up in the South and you still have many family members living there. Your aunt died and you ask for 2 days off to go to the funeral in Alabama. A white co-worker complains to your supervisor since he only got one day off when his uncle died. This is upsetting to you.

You are a woman on a predominantly male unit. Whenever you enter the lunchroom, it seems to you that the conversation stops. You feel like everyone is staring at you, and you feel very self-conscious. You are becoming increasingly angry and frustrated that these guys do not treat you like you are welcome there.

You are a man on a predominantly male unit. Two new women were just hired onto your shift and you are upset that management is pushing so hard to get women into your unit. You are worried that these women are going to slow you down. You try to help them out, but they do not seem to be learning the job very fast. They keep saying they do not feel very welcome on your unit, and you are afraid you might get labeled a harasser so you try not to say much at all to them.

Small groups were each assigned one of the scenarios and asked to write down four perspectives: (1) the stance of the main character in the scenario is understandable, (2) the stance of the other in the scenario is understandable, (3) there is merit in both views, and (4) it does not ultimately matter who is "right" or who is "wrong." Large group discussion followed to further develop the notion that there are multiple legitimate, understandable perspectives on touchy situations.

Asking the trainees to embrace a view that it does not matter who is "right" or "wrong" was probably the most unsettling aspect of this exercise. This was one of the many junctures where we asked participants to set aside familiar ways of making sense of the world. Looking at the situation from another point of view can indeed be challenging, but suggesting that no one has to reconcile the differing views or judge one as superior to the other is downright radical. While initially disconcerting, the shift to both/and can also be freeing—the realization that you do not have to give up your own view or consider yourself "wrong" in order to step into someone else's shoes and understand how s/he might have a very different vantage point opens up wonderful possibilities. We talked some about what can render certain views invisible. However, we waited until Day 3 to fully incorporate the layer of power—how the dynamics of privilege shape which views tend to be dominant and which perspectives are most valued within a group or organization.

To recap the issues covered on this second day, we ended with a discussion regarding how easy it is to misperceive others. We wanted to complement the focus on empathy with a challenge to avoid making assumptions. After discussing common sources of perceptual biases, we showed some pictures of faces with ambiguous expressions. This typically became a spirited and somewhat playful discussion as the group generated numerous possible interpretations of what the person in the picture might be thinking and feeling.

DAY 3

The third day of the training was the most intense. It was essential that the first two days had set the stage and fostered the trust necessary for the group to engage with the topics introduced here. We started the morning with exercises about stereotyping—asking people to reflect on common stereotypes and on the ways in which stereotypes affect the targets. Then we shifted to the topic of privilege.

The centerpiece for our discussions about privilege was a movie called *The Color of Fear*, which chronicles a group of men on a retreat to discuss experiences of race.[7] As described by one of the cast members in the film, "TCOF is highly emotional and provokes intense thoughts and discussion among viewers as they witness the men in the film struggling with issues of identity, white privilege, inter-group relations, and the building of cross-cultural alliances. The filmmakers documented some of the most highly charged discussions, experiences, and feelings that exist about racism, situations that often lead to further racial divisions between people of color and whites, but in this case showed how people from diverse backgrounds can build powerful and positive relations."[8] Indeed, the movie provoked some intense reactions. One of the men featured in the movie is a white man named David, who articulates a fairly privileged perspective on race that is not unlike that held by many white men at ChemPro. Some colleagues have been surprised to learn that we used this film with a predominantly white male group of production workers. On the surface, it would seem much too provocative—as David's blinders are heavily confronted by others in the film and these emotionally charged challenges are a primary focus of the film. Rich guided us here. Rather than allowing us academics to treat participants with "white gloves" or to fear potentially regressive reactions, he assured us that our viewers could—and would—engage the topic in useful ways. He was right.

The discussion that followed the movie was structured to allow first for dyadic conversations so that everyone—even the very shy—would have the opportunity to share some reactions. Then we opened it up to a full group discussion. We asked participants to reflect on what they saw as messages about privilege in the movie and what sorts of things made it hard for participants to recognize their own privilege. Many did see themselves in David and saw him as well meaning, but rather than treating him as misunderstood or the victim of unfair and harsh critiques, we were able to shift discussion to how easy it is to be blind to one's own sources of privilege. Perhaps David's being a "boss" rather than a "worker" kept most of our participants from fully identifying with him—allowing them the insights without taking the critique of David personally and helping them to both appreciate David's humanity *and* see his blinders. Many participants continued these conversations over lunch.

Following lunch, we wanted to give participants another perspective on privilege and did so using an exercise called "the race."[9] All participants lined up outside along a line we drew in the parking lot. This was the starting line, and a finish line was visible about 100 feet across the lot. We introduced the exercise by telling participants they were going to have a race: "You have all been gathered here so we can determine who among you is most worthy. We decided that a race is the best test since you all have two feet and can move in a forward motion. That seems fair enough, don't you think? This is the race of life. But before we begin, it is important to know something about your background. The kinds of resources you have had access to will affect where and how you will begin this race."

After this setup, we read a list of privileges. Participants were invited to take one step forward for each statement that applied to them (e.g., take one step forward if: both of your parents graduated from high school; there were fifty or more books in your house when you were growing up; you can shop in a fancy store and rarely, if ever, worry that you might be followed; most of the trusted professionals you have dealt with were the same gender as you; you never wondered if your sexual orientation was normal or not)—or one step backward for situations that signaled a lack of privilege (e.g., take one step back if: you ever feared being raped; English is a second language for you; a parent was partly or fully illiterate; you had to keep your sexual orientation a secret; a family member had ever had to sell or pawn something to pay for necessities). Once we were done with all the questions, participants were asked to look around and take stock of where they now stood relative to others. Then we signaled the start of the "race," with the three making their way to the finishing line first receiving a prize.

This exercise is designed to help people understand that, in our society, we do not all start out with equal access to the resources we need to "win" or "succeed." The game makes explicit some relatively invisible sources of privilege as well as the types of experience that hinder success for many members of our present society. Further, the game seeks to dispel the myth that privilege and oppression have not had an effect on the participants as individuals. All are affected. The exercise does not just challenge the belief that "everyone could just pull themselves up by their bootstraps if they worked hard enough" but rather clarifies that the footrace is made easier or more difficult by the ways in which privilege has shaped every person's life. You can still win if you start farther back, but you have to be exceptionally fast to overtake those who start out several paces in front of you.

Although not *all* the white men stood out in front, inevitably those who had moved the farthest forward were white men, and those who still stood closest to the original starting line were the men of color. The women, mostly white, tended to be in the middle. It was striking to use the race exercise with this particular group of workers—the majority of whom were techs and operators who had never before in their lives felt the least bit privileged. In fact, in many ways they were not—being, for example, hourly workers with relatively little control over their schedules and vulnerable to layoffs. Most people were not surprised when managers emerged at the front of the pack, but when the folks who worked on the plant floor found themselves out there, they were generally shocked.

Facilitators debriefed small groups to help participants identify those sorts of experiences they might have assumed everyone shares (e.g., that most people on their shift grew up like they did; that the conversation in the lunchroom is on topics of interest to everyone; that all coworkers feel comfortable joining conversations around the watercooler/coffeepot, or that they feel equally safe driving home after a late-night shift). We wanted to highlight how easy it is to make unfair assumptions or judgments about others if we fail to recognize how privilege has shaped experience. We also felt it was important to clarify that recognizing privilege does not mean that people are undeserving of their jobs, their pay, or their promotions. Rich, in particular, helped us to pay attention to the fear that acknowledging privilege would feel like admitting to cheating and suggested we frame our questions to provide some reassurance—for example, "Given that you have worked hard for what you have gotten, what helped you be able to earn it?" To make the point that privilege is not something people should feel "ashamed of," we asked participants to consider, What makes privilege hard to see or be aware of? What makes it hard to talk about? We also asked them to reflect on what it is like when someone sees them as "more privileged" (e.g., How do you think others' assumptions about you affect your relationship or interaction? What barriers or distance result? What can you *not* say? How do you deal with it?).

To emphasize the importance of getting beyond blame to action, we ended the day by asking each participant to share what they had learned about privilege by completing this sentence: "It's not anybody's fault but ____" and commit to some action step by continuing the sentence ". . . and therefore, I will ____."

DAY 4

The main goal of the fourth day was consolidation of learning. The first topic was team functioning, building on the many themes introduced in Days 1–3. Through two simulation-type activities we encouraged participants to reflect on how diversity might affect team functioning and how they could work with this diversity constructively.

The first simulation involved asking two small groups to each build one end of a bridge over a river (using Legos and other modeling supplies)—with half the group working from one "riverbank" and half working from the other. The catch was that the groups could not observe each other's work; they could only hear about it from representatives who attend "high-level planning meetings" in some neutral place. Additionally, within each small group we gave individual participants cards with "cultural dictates" or beliefs that shaped how they worked in groups and what materials they valued (e.g., "your culture favors blue," "you have been brought up to believe that to promote harmony in the universe, we should avoid the use of straight lines as much as possible," "you believe all decisions should be made by consensus"). Participants needed to collaborate not only within their building groups but also between groups if they had any hope that the two halves would ultimately connect. Throughout the process, they had to negotiate the various "culturally based" values and preferences of team members.

There was typically a good laugh at the end, when the groups moved their bridges to the same location to see if they actually would meet in the middle, but the debriefing was quite serious. We asked about what issues had arisen that illustrated the challenges and the benefits of working with diverse people. We asked about the impact of the cultural dictates on the process. Some groups had outright rejected the concerns about straight lines because they felt the person promoting them was simply impeding the process. Groups were often annoyed with the member who wanted blue. Groups rarely uncovered the reasons behind members' different preferences. However, when the issues were framed as culturally based during our debriefing, they felt they could have been more understanding. We asked them about effective communication strategies within and between groups, and how they might get a deeper understanding of differences among coworkers. We then asked them to reflect on any similarities to or differences from their real-life teams and lessons learned about ways they could personally enhance the positive aspects of diversity and minimize potential negatives.

This activity set the stage nicely for engaging the theme of accountability. We defined accountability as including three main expectations: (1) that team members will look out for their impact on the team, (2) that team members will be responsive to one another, and (3) that team members will do what they say they will do. These are simple yet profound challenges. Facilitators pulled out examples from the building exercise of times when team members held one another accountable and times when they could have but didn't. We asked: What did you or others do to hold teammates accountable? What worked and why? What did not work? How did team members' personal or cultural beliefs shape their impact on the group? What did you find yourself *not* saying? Why? Then, turning to daily applications in the plant: What do you do on your team now to give one another direct feedback and hold each other accountable to group expectations? We wrapped this discussion up by rehearsing communication skills for giving honest feedback and talking about strategies for fostering accountable teams.

The emphasis throughout the day was on the attitude of "we are in this together," and on making links to how accountability to the group and organization builds on ChemPro's core values of respect for employee dignity, integrity, trust, credibility, and continuous improvement. The final afternoon began with a fun exercise about learning organizational rules. A subgroup learned a complicated interactive sequence of hand movements, which they then set into motion as a group. Newcomers were invited to join the group and tried to enter the system without being directly taught the rules. Some sat back and tried to learn through observation; others jumped right in trying to learn through trial and error. Since the groups' movements were interconnected, each misstep by a newcomer had a reverberating effect on others "down the line." We usually ended the exercise by collapsing into chaos and laughter. A discussion of organizational culture and unspoken norms followed.

The most moving aspect of the whole four days was the final sharing. All participants were encouraged to bring a "symbol of their heritage" to share. We encouraged people to think broadly about how they defined "heritage"—it could be cultural, regional, religious, or simply unique family traditions. People brought food—sometimes traditional foods of their cultural heritage, sometimes treats that held childhood memories. Others brought symbols, tools, or artifacts—a cricket paddle from Barbados, a shoeshine box inherited from a father and used as youth employment (before the widespread popularity of sneakers), a key chain with the logo from a family-owned business, a handwoven shawl from "the old country," and a baseball cap from a youth team. While the specific objects were quite diverse, they all carried memories of significant life influences. The process of sharing brought tears to many eyes as participants not only shared a slice of their past but also reflected on the lessons learned from four days of sharing aspects of themselves they had rarely reflected on, let alone opened up to others. Along with the sharing of their symbols, every participant was asked to make a commitment to take action on what they had learned in the training. They were asked to reflect on what they would take away from the training and how they could use the lessons learned to move the organization in a positive direction.

DELIVERY

We offered eight rounds of training and, for each, we recruited a group of approximately 15–20 people who varied in terms of race, gender, job level, and department. Each session involved two full days one week and two the following week. In all, 91 people were able to attend a training workshop during an initial round and 50 more about a year later, bringing the total to 141. The training was done in two phases, the break in the middle being the result of cutbacks in overtime that prevented people from attending (since other workers would have to be paid overtime to cover their shifts).

Rich summarized the flow of the training as follows:

On the first day, people didn't want to be there; they didn't know why they were there: "I'm not a racist; I don't need to be here." "You should have the people that have problems in here, not me." And that's like a day one attitude. Day two would be a little bit more breakthrough. You'd have a little bit more discussion, a little bit more fun. Still though a little bit of confusion at the midpoint of day two. But people started to come around, and they were getting into the conversations, learning a little bit more about each other. By the end of day two, I think people—most people—were looking forward to day three. It was always a week away, but I think most people were looking forward to it. They had started to get into it a little bit. Day three—tough day. That's the day we were hit with the movie 'Color of Fear' . . . a lot of . . . little bit of tension and everything. By the end of day three I think people are pretty well mentally stressed out. And then day four, they came back together and started to see where everything fit together as far as teamwork. And that it's okay to be different and, that we need to work as a team, and you need to accept the differences. And I think that message got out. It probably didn't get out to everybody, but I think we got to a lot of people.

ORGANIZATIONAL SUPPORTS

Two other aspects of the training deserve highlighting: the role of the president and the involvement of the ChemPro cotrainers. Warren was visibly supportive of the plantwide training effort. In Rich's words:

He totally supported it. He came down a few times and sat there and listened. It sent the message that the company was serious about achieving the workplace where everyone felt comfortable. He'd pop in and out when he had some time. He'd ask people how the training was going. He was busy, so he didn't stay for the whole sessions but he would pop in and out. I think he did that to let people know that he was on board with this . . . It wasn't just saying he believed in it. There was something more than that. There was passion there.

This type of management support—from Warren, Keitha, *and* Rich—was clearly essential. On a more bottom-line note, it was also Warren who supported the financial investment that this effort required. As university-based trainers, the cost of our contract was minimal. However, the full cost of the training—in terms of both time and money—was not insignificant, since all participants were paid for each day they attended the workshop and their units had to bring others in on overtime to cover their shifts for four full days.

For each round of training, we had from five to seven trainers. Rich and I were the constants involved in every step and in every training session; Robin Toof was involved in the majority of the sessions. Numerous UMass students cycled through our team as the project evolved, and our ChemPro partners shifted with promotions and turnover in the plant. At various stages, our team of ChemPro trainers expanded to include a white female electrician and three other African Americans who worked in production—two men and one woman. Even with the periodic changes in staffing, we were able to work with a diverse group from the development stage through all phases of the actual delivery of the training. Rich, as the co–lead trainer, and the ChemPro workers, as assistant trainers, were magic ingredients. The university side of the partnership could provide the conceptual structure, and we could facilitate and contain any intense or difficult discussions. However, there could be no replacement for the real-world examples and genuine connection to the issues provided by our in-house partners.

training evaluation

EVALUATION PROCESS

It is no easy task to assess the impact of this type of training. Some of the effects are visible; some dimensions, however, are issues of awareness and sensitivity and thus both less visible and more difficult to measure. Nonetheless, we set out to assess reactions to the training as well as the impact that the training might have had on participants. We felt we could consider the training successful if participants, first, felt engaged and interested; second, felt they had learned some things they could use in their daily lives when interacting with diverse coworkers; and, third, felt that the lessons of the training had radiated out to have a positive impact on interactions among coworkers on their team and/or on the quality of their work lives. In other words, our goals ranged from the modest hope that participants would simply take the training seriously to the more expansive hope that it would change the culture of ChemPro.

To assess reactions to training, participants completed daily feedback forms. We developed an *Images and Insights* questionnaire to use each day to ask participants to reflect on what they found most and least valuable as well as to identify any issues they wished to explore further. At the conclusion of the full workshop, we used a *Training Satisfaction Questionnaire* to ask participants to rate the various elements of the training. During a hiatus between the two phases of training during Year 4, we were able to conduct *individual interviews* with workers who had participated in the training a year earlier. Two interviewers who were not among the original trainers asked participants about their reactions to training.[10]

The Year 4 interviews also probed the impact of training beyond the classroom, including the effects of the training on work relationships. This information complemented the results of a series of *pre-post questionnaires* that we gave to those who attended training in Year 5 to assess changes in participants' self-assessments of such dimensions as empathy, attitudes toward diversity, and beliefs about adapting to differences. We also asked about general work life issues such as job satisfaction and work climate among peers and with supervisors. All these formal assessments were supplemented with process notes and on-site observations.

REACTIONS TO WORKPLACE CHEMISTRY TRAINING

The results of questionnaires and the reflections shared during the 1999 interviews provided a mix of quantitative and qualitative information about reactions to the training workshops. The Training Satisfaction Questionnaire asked participants to rate seventeen topics and twelve training activities.[11] Overall satisfaction with the training received a mean rating of 4.40 (s.d. = .67) on a 5-point scale. Most topics and activities received mean ratings above 4.0 on a 5-point scale, and no topic or activity received a mean rating lower than 3.5. The most highly rated topic overall was "How workers from different racial and ethnic backgrounds might experience ChemPro differently from one another." Most other topics received positive ratings (means ranged from 4.13 to 4.38); however, in each case at least one person did not find the topic useful at all. Training activities that received mean ratings over 4.0 (and that were also mentioned as memorable in the interviews) were ones that explored issues of racial identity, privilege, stereotyping, and viewing issues from others' perspectives. Many people found it quite moving on the final day when participants shared some aspect of their own heritage. Participants found the movie that profiled a group of men exploring issues of race and privilege during a weekend retreat particularly compelling (Color of Fear X = 4.66, s.d. = .81). Given that each group was fairly small, we could not ask about participants' race or gender without compromising the anonymous nature of these evaluations. Thus, we were not able to do comparisons by gender or race.

The Year 4 interviews were conducted with twenty-four training participants and three cotrainers to ask them about their reflections on the training they had experienced a year earlier (i.e., about a quarter of the ninety-one who had completed the training to that date). We wanted to know what they liked about it, what they learned, and what they felt could be improved. We sought to identify interviewees who varied in terms of race and gender, but we also deliberately oversampled women and people of color, since we deemed it critical to assess the reactions of workers in demographic minority groups. Because we wanted to hear a diversity of views, we invited both people who had, from our own observations, seemed to enjoy the training and those who had not. The interviewees included seven white women, one woman of color, ten men of color, and six white men. During the interviews, participants shared a wide range of perspectives about both the process and the content of the training. The elements they felt were most important to the success of the training were the accepting atmosphere, the humanizing of coworkers, and the enhanced understanding of privilege.

Accepting Atmosphere. The initial expectations of many participants were that the training would put people on the spot, be adversarial, and include uncomfortable confrontations. However, most found the training nonblaming and constructive.

> Went over there with a chip on my shoulder . . . how dare you think I need this. But didn't take long to realize that it was, it really was great training. I got a hell of a lot out of it . . . I was saddened that they didn't continue it for everyone last year. I thought it was well worth it. (white male)

> These guys are, "We don't need it" . . . Then this one guy sent out a note—about how he felt after the diversity [training] and it was real positive. And it blew me away, because this is a guy that initially would say, "It's a waste of time." He has said that . . . As a matter of fact, I think one time he refused to meet with Meg. After he went, this guy sent a note out to the whole plant complimenting the program and the training. So, I said, "Wow. Something did click finally." So, that was positive. (black male)

> I mean, the whole process was an eye-opener. I mean, everything that they did. I mean, it opened a lot of eyes. (white male)

> I think the whole design of it was just laid out to a point where it was— you took an uncomfortable bunch of people and gradually dropped

their fears and inhibitions and got to be a working group . . . The fact
that I had to be open and honest with how I felt . . . it made me—she
[Meg] made me stop and think about why these other people were like
they are. (black male)

A critical factor that interviewees felt made the training constructive was
that people felt welcomed but not forced to participate.

The first day there were some people with some attitudes, and there
were attitudes. But [the trainers] made everyone very comfortable with
it. No one was forced to do things that they didn't want to do. Quite
a bit of levity was going on, which was good, between folks. I didn't
see anyone put in a position that they were made to feel terribly
uncomfortable . . . No, I think it was just a feeling that we were a
group; we were in this for four days. (white male)

I thought they were very good in just the way that they did things, period.
I think they were very professional about it. They didn't force anything
on you. It was something you wanted to bring out in the first place.
(white male)

The sharing wasn't limited to the formal training time. There were
exchanges during breaks that were often just as valuable as the discussion
during the structured exercises. For example, one of our UMass trainers from
India connected with a manager named Leland who was originally from a
Caribbean island with a similar history of British colonization. Their long and
involved discussions about cricket over lunch baffled many of the rest of us,
but the two of them shared a unique cultural experience. On the final day
when participants each brought a symbol of their heritage, Leland brought a
cricket ball, which he then gave to Raji as a thank-you gift.

Humanizing Coworkers. Many interviewees indicated that the most compelling aspect of the training was the way that it humanized coworkers
through the opportunity to see people outside their work roles. Some felt the
training increased their empathy for others by enhancing their appreciation
and understanding of alternative perspectives.

I have been in a minority for my whole life and in situations where it's
been like that . . . But when the shoe was on the other foot, some of the
people—I guess they didn't realize how it could be like that. I guess it
was a wake-up call for some of the people. (black male)

It made people real to me, people that were just people I worked with. It gave them an identity which they really didn't have before. And in this environment, you don't have time—I mean, there are days over [in the plant] there that you just fly all day long. So you don't have time to get to know anyone . . . there's not enough of us. . . . And the training gave a chance to personalize it and to see people as they are. And it opened some eyes to the culture and the backgrounds and the differences. (white male)

A lot of us came to tears at certain points in different discussions . . . we sat in a group, and we had to explain to each other about our background . . . it explained a lot. I mean, people have such tough lives. You come to work and you think you just do your job. But people come with a lot of history . . . I'm like wow. If I was set up in life with those disadvantages, how would I interact? So it helped to really hit home about different aspects of people. (white female)

I'd say from the whole week, what stands out is people's feelings from all walks of life. Everybody has feelings and they are sensitive to the pressure—and I'm not just talking about ChemPro. I'm talking about everything like the pressure of prejudice. I'll have to say that's what stands out. And I think that week helped me understand how people feel. (white male)

That people of different backgrounds, color, creed could get together and talk about their lives and how they see the world. I think that was an eye-opener, because you hear things you wouldn't under normal circumstances. You wouldn't be fortunate enough to be in that environment to hear people talk about their personal stuff or where they come from. I think that was pretty enlightening. (black male)

Attention to Privilege. The training also uncovered common misunderstandings through exploring concrete examples where people's *intent* did not match their *impact* on others. And several participants indicated that the training enhanced their understanding of how the dynamics of privilege shape people's impact on one another.

One of the exercises I think, where how many people in this room own a computer? How many people in this room have gone to the twelfth grade? And just step forward. How many people grew up with two parents in the home? And it was amazing. By the time we were done, it showed how advantaged the white American was to other people . . . And then you say wow, that's unbelievable. You mean, you didn't have this and you didn't have that? And we take for granted that maybe everyone did. (white male)

And I felt like I'd been pampered after all that, and it was a real eye-opener to listen. I think one of the things that really stuck with me was the feeling that we—that we as white people—feel that people that are different from us ought to change to be like us . . . I guess you just assume that they would want to change to be like you. And it really made me start thinking differently about their culture is right for them, and my culture may be right for me. And I need to understand their culture, as opposed to expecting them be part of my culture . . . to take a little less for granted. (white female)

Other Reflections. Other aspects that interviewees felt contributed to the success of the training included the actual diversity within the training groups, without which the opening up of new perspectives could not have happened. People noted the importance of the mix of ChemPro and external trainers, which made the training feel more organic to their lives. Many also commented on the simulations and activities where there could be both serious discussion and a sense of playfulness and levity. Based on her work in Italy, Donata Francescato notes that "joy is a powerful change agent" and that "empowerment comes from laughter not pain."[12] Interviewees remembered the silliness of some of our training exercises with what sounded like fondness.

Not all interviewees, however, were positive about the training, and several were concerned that it had only limited impact on their work group and the organization as a whole.

Being at the training, then actually day in and day out seeing that this detachment was still there. They left there with a lot of people not really getting it. They still had that detachment. (black male)

It didn't help, or didn't deter what I thought or felt . . . My mind was already geared toward most of this. I mean, it wasn't like it was anything that really made me change my way of thinking. (white female)

That movie raised some hard feelings, the movie with the, I think it was a black and a white, about six people in it . . . I mean, it was an atmosphere we're not used to. Most of us haven't sat in a classroom in years. So it was different. (white male)

Some felt that the goals should be to work with only those people who "have problems with diversity"—even though they also recognized the value of working on changes in organizational culture.

BEHAVIOR AND ATTITUDE CHANGE

Newly acquired behaviors and/or shifts in attitudes were assessed through both the pre-post questionnaires and the Year 4 interviews. There were forty-eight people who completed the pre-post questionnaires (96 percent of the fifty who participated in the second phase of training). Their ratings indicated some changes in individual values and attitudes immediately following the training. Participants became more open to adapting for the sake of others, and there was some increase in their self-reported empathy. There was not, however, much change in the endorsement of conservative beliefs about diversity. We also asked them to rate the general quality of their work lives. While there was only a slight change in overall job satisfaction, there was a significant increase in people's sense of being respected in their work and some increase in their ratings of peer cohesion (see figure 3.1).

These results suggest that the training may have influenced attitudes specific to working in the ChemPro context (e.g., willingness to adapt, feeling respected, and a sense of connection with peers), while having less impact on the immediate conditions of work (i.e., satisfaction) or on deeply held beliefs (i.e., endorsement of conservative attitudes). The numbers of women ($n = 7$) and people of color ($n = 9$) who completed these questionnaires were quite small, so statistical comparisons are difficult. However, looking at these ratings more closely reveals some other interesting patterns.[13]

While endorsement of conservative views remained at about the same level if you summarize across all groups, people of color actually reported slightly *more* conservative beliefs at the end of training than they had at the beginning. Their mean scores post-training were still considerably less conservative than whites' scores (whose ratings changed very little from pre to post), but what had been a statistically significant difference between groups disappeared after training. Empathy ratings went up for whites and men; people of color, whites, and men all reported some decrease in concerns about adapting to differences at work after completing the training. However, mean self-reports of empathy actually reduced somewhat for women and

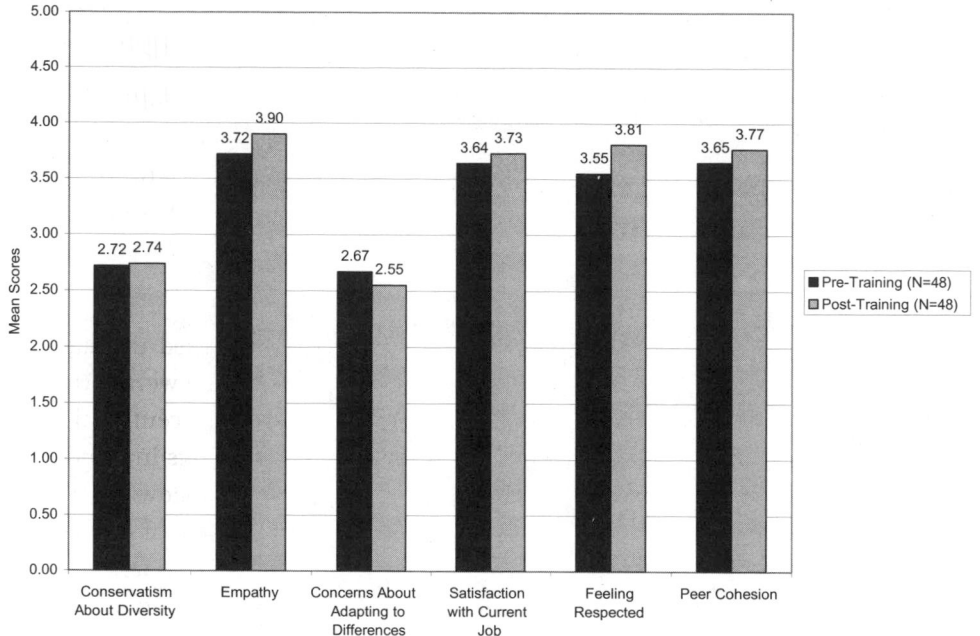

FIGURE 3.1 Changes from Pre- to Post-training: Individual Values and Quality of Work Life

people of color. Although not significantly different, women felt the least satisfied and respected while people of color felt the most satisfied and respected in comparison to the other demographic groups. The subgroups that reported the largest increases in feeling respected were whites and men, while people of color reported some increase in job satisfaction and women reported some decrease in feeling respected. While most subgroups experienced some positive changes in their sense of peer cohesion, the mean ratings for women actually decreased post-training.

While it looks like whites and men (overlapping groups) generally experienced changes in the hoped-for directions, the results for women and people of color were more mixed. As a group, women seemed to feel less assured of being accepted and respected by their peer groups and simultaneously concerned about being asked to adapt to coworkers. Some caution is needed here in interpreting these results. Just because mean ratings either increased or decreased for a particular group does not indicate that *all* members of that group responded in the same way. Nonetheless, the patterns are windows into questions we should ask ourselves about how the training may have affected members of different demographically defined groups differently.

The adoption of new behaviors was also assessed through interview questions such as: How have you been able to make use of the training? What gets in the way? What helps? Examples of specific ways interview participants reported changing their behavior at work after the training included stopping to think before reacting, refusing to participate in racist or sexist bantering and jokes, watching one's own language, being more considerate of others, and working to compromise more in groups.

> It brought me up to another level as far as feeling and watching what I say and how I approach a person. I got that out of [the training]. (black male)

> You find out that almost everybody is prejudiced in certain ways, you know. And I think that finding that out kind of bothered me. I found myself wanting to listen more to people . . . it was a hard thing to find out, but I think it was a good thing. I think I'm better for it today. I think I listen more. You know, I try and concentrate on what people are saying. (white male)

> I might be a little bit more vocal now for other people. Say well hey, think about what you're saying. Before I would probably just walk away, and not deal with it. Let the next person take care of it . . . I just felt bad for some people, hearing their stories. And they didn't have anybody to stand up for them. They didn't know how to stand up for themselves. So sometimes you just don't realize how people are really taking things . . . [like when] people are joking around at a break table, or they're discussing different nationalities, which we do a lot of around here. (white female)

> I think it helped to just wake me up, and remind me that back in the sixties when people were burning down cities, we were angry. For years, things have been comfortable, and I think I've just gotten kind of lazy about my thinking. And I think that just seeing some of those films, and talking to people really helped raise my awareness. (white female)

Although most did not comment on the impact of the training on their lives outside work, some indicated that they carried the general lessons beyond the workplace. Some transferred the training to their relationships with partners and other family members.

Outside of work I don't see a lot of people of color. I see a few a day, a couple of people of color a day, but not a lot. So my kids don't know a lot of people of color . . . but I'm raising them not to be prejudiced at all. So I don't let any of that kind of stuff enter my house because of some of the things we talked about. (white male)

I'm trying to work on [my relationship with my wife] a little bit, you know. So the training made me think that maybe some of the things I was doing weren't correct. So after the training, I said well, gee maybe I should be a little more, think about her more. (white male)

Even among those who felt very positive about the training, there was discussion about barriers to transferring learning beyond the classroom. Some were concerned that not everyone was motivated or able to understand the content of the course (i.e., concerned about individual-level barriers). Some felt the training was unnecessary because it covered material they were already familiar with. Others felt the training would not change people's actual behavior at work until supervisors took the lead and department and organizational cultures were more supportive and empowering of workers (i.e., concerned about addressing organizational-level barriers). Along the same lines, some people emphasized the importance of backing up the training with organizational policies and felt that ChemPro's "zero tolerance" stance was helpful support for these changes.

ecological reflections: connecting training to everyday life

The qualities that participants felt made the training successful—fostering an atmosphere that was accepting, humanizing, and attentive to the role of privilege—all flow from the guiding ecological framework. The lessons that emerged during this phase revolve around the need to ground the training in the specific context and everyday experiences of participants. For example, stories from people's daily lives were the primary resource for humanizing "the other." As we sought to create awareness of the dynamics of privilege, we needed to be sensitive to the fact that most did not *experience* a sense of privilege day in and day out. Additionally, we needed to be cognizant of the *daily* context into which participants had to take the workshop lessons, and the ways in which ongoing team dynamics sometimes made the transfer of learning challenging.

INTEGRATING NEW "REALITIES" THROUGH STORYTELLING

The training was less about the coverage of particular topics or techniques than about introducing new ways of thinking about and experiencing difference. The workshops provided a safe context for participants to tell stories about personal experiences. Sharing across differences became an integral part of the training process and was at the heart of what participants told us they valued most. Creating settings where members of more marginalized groups are able to "name" their experience—and where others will really listen—is critical in opening up a group to the inclusion of diverse members.[14]

Some of the most powerful training moments were when people of color described experiences previously invisible to their white coworkers. For example, during one workshop, Carlos described a situation where he was asked by a fellow patron to serve up a refill on coffee at a local restaurant. He felt his distinctly "Latin look" was the reason he was mistaken for "the help." Stanley, a gentle, religious black man talked about a time when he was pulled over by police and questioned about how he got his car. Because he is black and was driving a Cadillac in the middle of the night, the assumption seemed to be that he was a pimp or drug dealer rather than a skilled technician going home from a late-night shift. Another African American man who grew up with many of his white coworkers talked about how even though he was voted "most popular" by his senior class in high school, he could not go to the prom because there were no black girls in his school to be his date. In several workshops, women shared experiences of feeling invisible. For example, Mary Lou described frequently making suggestions that were attributed to male coworkers. Lillian described being asked to do some repair work that she struggled with because she had not been given all the information she needed. When another mechanic (male) stepped in and did the repair in ten minutes, she felt humiliated and undercut. Still other examples from both on and off the job were shared.

The very matter-of-fact way in which these stories were told made them even more compelling. The tone conveyed an ordinariness or everydayness of these events in the lives of the women and people of color.[15] Other participants were disbelieving after one example, but unsettled after hearing the collection. They could no longer go on believing that "we are really all alike." Through examples from people they had worked with side by side for years, participants could not avoid the fact that life in a different-color skin or as the opposite gender *is* different in many daily yet profound ways. The unsettling aspect for some was that they could no longer just assume that their experience of events was the only or right one. It became clear that many had been missing hidden stories that were obvious to others.

Part of the power of hearing personal stories is the humanizing of others. A coworker of a different race or gender could no longer be just "a guy from Prepping" or "a 'gal' from the hill." They gained names and faces . . . and depth. Interpersonal distance is maintained by assuming that members of an outgroup are all like one another yet profoundly different from one's own ingroup. The sharing made it more difficult to engage in stereotyping by turning coworkers into real people with unique experiences and circumstances. It is much harder to generalize about "blacks" or "women" when you know more about the lives of Carlos, Eddie, Mary Lou, and Lillian—accentuating the humanity that workers have in common as well as underscoring how poorly generalizations actually fit any individual's circumstances. Social psychologists write about the "contact hypothesis," and the process of "decategorization" that can accompany personal exchanges that increase knowledge of more intimate information about members of other groups.[16]

This process of telling stories may also free up possibilities for redefining what Rappaport has referred to as the "community narrative."[17] The dynamics of privilege function such that the stories of the less dominant groups are not the ones told in the lunchroom or on the plant floor. The examples shared within the training were not revelations that the women would make to men in daily conversation. They were not stories the people of color would share with white coworkers except under very safe conditions. Thus, this alternative set of experiences of life had not regularly entered into the white workers' understanding of their coworkers of color. In an important sense, the public sharing during the training made these new "realities" accessible to be integrated into the organization's "narrative" or way of understanding life at ChemPro. Our hope was that the sharing would help shift the organizational culture by reshaping this new collective narrative.

It is important to remember that, from the perspective of members of marginalized groups, the opportunity to share one's stories or "reality" and to entrust members of the more dominant group with feedback about their impact does not come without some wariness and cynicism. The benefit is that in sharing one's experience, it is named; and in having it witnessed by others, it is validated. However, there is also considerable risk inherent in going public and, in essence, abandoning effective coping strategies that one has developed over time to adapt to particular organizational circumstances. So while storytelling was a critical element of the training, the ChemPro-based trainers expressed some concern that people of color and women carried the bulk of the burden for enlightening their coworkers. Indeed, the major awakenings during the training were not primarily for the women or people of color but rather for the white men. Without parallel sharing from the white men, there is a risk that issues can get defined as "minority problems." Although some women and people of color did tell us that the workshops opened their eyes to privilege dynamics, there was not the parallel introduction of completely new worlds. This may well be appropriate, as such "minority" views are typically the ones that were previously absent from the collective narrative, and it is the more powerful groups that tend to have been lacking access to experiences beyond their own.[18] The value for members of nondominant groups may be in the telling and being heard, while the value for the dominant group is in the listening and discovering new perspectives. The differentiated goals have a solid rationale, yet the uneven sharing can also mark differential levels of vulnerability—and associated costs.

This dynamic may help explain some of the results of the pre-post questionnaires where there was enhanced empathy and tolerance among men and whites—but actually some *decrease* in empathy among women and people of color. Learning that your coworkers have been unaware of your world may not be an entirely good thing. I was particularly left to wonder whether some women, in unique ways, took unfortunate lessons away from the training. Was there some increased alienation from their male coworkers reflected in their reduced ratings of "peer cohesion"? Did the bonding within the training occur more for the men—possibly at the expense of at least some women's sense of belonging? Surely, the historical and current dynamics of privilege can obscure important alternative "realities" even when there are initial invitations for sharing. The challenge for trainers is to stay attuned to the potential costs for those who open themselves up within the training setting.

ADDRESSING PRIVILEGE IN A GROUP THAT DOES NOT FEEL PRIVILEGED

The discussion of privilege is always difficult, but with a group that in many ways does not feel privileged, it can be particularly unsettling. During the training, we defined "privilege" as "a special advantage, immunity, permission, right, or benefit granted to or enjoyed by an individual, class or caste."[19] This definition incorporates the notion that privilege is a set of advantages that one gets without asking for them, circumstances that make life easier, resources that make success more attainable. From inside the skins of the white men working in line positions, the worry was that it meant that somehow they had not earned their jobs, their hours, their pay levels—that some-how they had gotten more than they "deserved." "Privilege" has become a pejorative term. Feeling saddled with the implication that somehow they have "cheated" can easily fill people with either tremendous guilt or anger. For the production operator who punches a clock, who is vulnerable to his boss's whims, who has little say over his daily workload, and who sees very few alter-natives, it can be downright discombobulating. From this vantage point, look-ing at the privileges one might have is not a mantle that can be easily or grace-fully donned without deconstructing it rigorously.

We found it critical—yet very challenging—to decouple the notion of privi-lege from blame. It is not anyone's fault—nor a fault of character—if some-one has had some advantages in life that have opened doors simply because of that person's sex, skin color, heritage, sexual orientation, disability status, and/or language. This message, however, is nuanced, and can easily get lost in the subtleties. We worked to clarify that having privilege need not be a part of one's core identity even if it is a central part of one's context. It does not define you, but it can help you. Privilege is something a person *has*—not something a person *is*.

While it can be a trap to talk about relative *deprivation* (i.e., trying to decide who is more oppressed than whom does little to address the problem of op-pression as a whole), it may be worth acknowledging gradations in levels of *privi-lege*. There are certain privileges that come with just being in the mainstream—for example, your experiences, feelings, thoughts, preferences, aspirations, and so forth are considered normative, while others are deemed deviant by merely being different from you and your cohort. In reflecting on racial privilege, Michelle Fine writes, "whiteness accrues privilege and status; gets itself surrounded by protective pillows of resources and/or benefits of the doubt . . . whiteness repels gossip and voyeurism and instead demands dig-nity."[20] At the same time, being just a middle-class "white guy" who has a steady job feels qualitatively different from having access to a prep school, an elite college, and/or a million-dollar bank account. When understood as something external to the individual that some people have more access to than others, privilege can be seen as a powerful aspect of the ecology of life that exerts an influence on all types of workplace interactions. It is not something you either have or don't have—it is, to varying degrees, a factor that affects your impact on others, your degree of influence on outcomes, your ability to take action, and your opportunities to make things happen. As such, it is part of the contextual field surrounding all interpersonal interactions, and the issue is not who has more or less privilege but, rather, what are the radiating effects of one's level of access to privilege.

Therefore, the challenge within an organizational change effort becomes how to make it visible, how to acknowledge its influence on work relations, and how to hold people accountable for attending to the ways it shapes their impact on others. In some ways, this work is akin to teaching people to be social critics. When my son was in first grade, he showed me a bookmark with a quote on it: "The whole world opens up to he who reads books." He declared, "Mom, this is awful." Hoping he got the message about the joy of reading, I was a bit confused until he clarified what he saw as "awful": "It says 'he.' It should say 'people.'" I quickly dumped the lecture forming in my head about the value of books and instead celebrated his budding ability to analyze his social world. We cannot get rid of privilege or shield a workplace (or even a child) from its influence—we cannot make it go away. But we *can* help people see it, and thereby lessen its hold through critique.[21]

We were not suggesting that those with some degree of privilege should feel bad about it. In fact, most of us seek to gain advantages and do what we can to help our children and other loved ones gain access to opportunities that will help them along in life. If it was a totally "bad" thing, we probably would not want it for those we care most about. However, when people are unaware of how their mere membership in some demographic group has garnered them access to unique opportunities, it blinds them to the experiences of others and can contribute to victim blaming.

MANAGING THE TENSION BETWEEN INDIVIDUAL AWARENESS AND TEAM CULTURES

Many of the participants who were pleased with the training and found it validating and enlightening also related stories of returning to their unit and being "invited"—even directly pressured—to trash the training. They were offered sympathy for having been required to attend, and they were pressed to tell stories about how the training had been a waste of time. While some resisted the pull, others described feeling caught in a loyalty bind where they risked being ridiculed if they revealed what they had learned or even shared the sentiment that there might be some value in addressing diversity-related issues. Participants complained that it was hard to change their own behavior if their coworkers did not understand the issues (e.g., around racist or sexist banter). The transfer of learning from the training to daily life was clearly being hindered by existing team cultures. The insights and awareness triggered by the training were indeed disruptive and demanded new behavior from people who were reasonably comfortable with current arrangements. The simple existence of the Workplace Chemistry Initiative was still seen by some as an implicit condemnation of white men. In ecological terms, the context was exerting a pull on participants to return to business as usual. There was, in essence, pressure on workers to maintain loyalty to the status quo.

These team dynamics emphasize the courage and the critical role of the cotrainers. In particular, the African American man from the power plant and the woman electrician were going against the grain of their own teams' cultures—against the peers with whom they still had to work side by side when they were not helping with the training. The need to support and buoy them was essential. We could do that in part during joint lunches on training days and in debriefing meetings both at the end of each training day and during special meetings between training sessions. These were wonderfully authentic settings where we all let down and shared our reactions. However, probably the most important support they received was from the participants themselves, many of whom directly expressed their admiration for the work of these cotrainers. In some ways, those who had gone through the training became a community of support for one another.

In addressing the pull for team loyalty, we found that some of our greatest critics could become our best allies. One white man, who had previously refused to meet with me when I had been asked to consult with his team, came to the training clearly upset and unhappy to be there. As a worker, he was very well respected by his peers for his technical competence (from his over thirty years as an operator), for his sharp and articulate critiques of management, and for his advocacy for coworkers. On the morning of the first day of training, he openly voiced his belief that this entire initiative was a waste of time. He was vigilant, asking pointed questions, pressing us to be very specific, and challenging each definition and rationale. The good news was that he was clearly engaged.

We invited him to talk about his concerns, figuring they represented questions others shared but were not articulating. I think he was surprised and a bit perplexed by our attempts to acknowledge and address his concerns directly and by our unwillingness to cast blame or put anyone in the hot seat. By the second day, he was actively participating, laughing, and having some fun. On the third day, after an intense discussion of white privilege, he pulled me aside to explain (and apologize for) his past refusal to work with me. He shared that he was impressed. While he figured he and I were miles apart on many value issues and politics, he said he appreciated the nonjudgmental and respectful stance of the training process. At the end of the fourth and final day, he wrote an e-mail to the entire plant thanking us for the "eye-opening experience." Most wonderfully in this plantwide communication, he commented on the courage of the cotrainers to engage the issue in such a constructive manner. He was a strong opinion leader largely because of his cynicism, and this message went far beyond anything we could have planned in opening up possibilities for others to claim the training as valuable.

Interestingly, while some of the other participants were reluctant to become advocates of change within their own work units, they did become partners in pressing for the training to continue. People who had been through the workshops began urging both our consulting group and the Human Resources Department to ensure that everyone would be required to take the training, and they wanted us to be quick about it. They acknowledged that it would be much easier to work with what they were learning if their coworkers were also on board, and they urged our help with that. We forged ahead and trained about 70 percent of the plant; we also worked directly with individual teams.

SYNTHESIS

The training seemed to increase awareness of interpersonal dynamics related to diversity, enhance empathy for others, and open participants to new perspectives on discrimination and privilege. We heard stories of remarkable transformations. Yet the dilemmas surrounding training were manifold, and there were barriers to fully integrating the new insights. We worked to create a culture of connection by inviting personal sharing both during and around the edges of the training. The trust that developed enabled participants to share personal aspects of their lives, which rendered them more human to coworkers who may have previously judged them only by their physical appearance, race, and/or gender. Through these new connections, people were introduced to new "realities" and were, as a result, invited to hold multiple realities. However, we were also aware that the the conundrum created by differential privilege had to be navigated along the way. The emphasis on accountability was the antidote to complacency—it was the disruptive element that emphasized responsibility for ensuring that personal actions did not further contribute to inequities. In other words, we worked to pair *connection* with *disruption*.

As time went on, the organization had difficulty sustaining its commitment to training on a regular basis. The stresses of everyday life often made it difficult. Also, some Corporate-directed reorganizations that were seen as necessary for the company's survival periodically placed the training on the back burner. Consulting in the real world of organizational life demands creative solutions at times like this. Proclaiming from one's high horse about the ideal way to approach an ongoing initiative simply would not have been workable. The leadership at ChemPro expressed interest in continuing to support diversity, but we had to devise ways to keep the issues alive when the time and budget for the current training model were simply not there. We used some of the "lulls" between training to do interviews (Year 4), conduct a follow-up survey (Year 6), and facilitate workshops with managers (Year 7), all of which helped to keep a serious focus on diversity. Also, over the many years at ChemPro, we consulted with individual units about team building. We saw in these natural settings an opportunity to carry the Workplace Chemistry Initiative deeper into the organization.

4 out of the laboratory

WORKING WITH TEAM DYNAMICS

WORKING TOWARD CHANGE in the controlled "laboratory" of the training workshops was a valuable starting place. The workshops offered a foundation for organizational change by providing moments outside the organizational routine where everyday contingencies were on hold and a safe environment where participants could try on new attitudes and approaches. Individual sensitivity to diversity is an important building block toward a more inclusive organization. It is helpful when a person becomes cognizant that the sex, race, and ethnicity of all coworkers shape what they experience and how organizational events affect them. It is useful when an individual worker takes stock of her/his impact on coworkers and on the functioning of the team. It is vital that each team member understand that effective functioning involves more than a collection of disconnected individual members. However, individual awareness of these issues is not enough.

The training workshops created windows to new ways of operating, but they did not, in and of themselves, move from the laboratory to the "real" world. Transferring the workshop lessons over to the workaday routine requires more effective and inclusive team dynamics and organizational arrangements. Enabling workers to make use of the insights provided by training requires a collective effort and organizational supports for that effort. This is consistent with the ecological requirement to look beyond individual change to also change the context within which people operate—including interactional patterns, group dynamics, and any work patterns or policies that support old values.

Thus, we complemented the training workshops with consultation with intact workgroups. Our goal was to foster team functioning that embodied the values for diversity promoted during the training: increased sensitivity to *multiple "realities,"* accountability for one's *impact* on the team, and attention to how *multilayered factors* (including individual skills, team dynamics, and organizational culture) affect team functioning. Over the course of five years, my colleagues and I facilitated team development work within almost every major unit at ChemPro—including Maintenance, Security, Prepping, Washing, Processing, Drying, and both the Research and Development and Quality Control Labs. We also did a short consultation with administrative support staff to address some interpersonal conflicts and a lack of clarity about the division of work tasks.

We preferred to work with units where the manager actively sought our consultation. Keitha played a pivotal role in encouraging various units to confer with us; thus the consultations were not always driven by managers alone. However, we were also clear that it would not be useful to *impose* our services. Compelling individuals to attend plantwide training workshops has the advantage of introducing new ideas that participants may not seek out on their own. Some may resent it, but if handled well, the training group tends to bring the reluctant members along or, at least, move along for all but the most resistant individuals. Team consultations, in contrast, cannot proceed without the commitment of a leader to champion the work and to ensure continuous team building beyond our time-limited efforts. I facilitated some consultations in collaboration with Keitha, some with university-based colleagues, and some alone.

building diverse teams through shared vision

Although the overall Workplace Chemistry Initiative was concerned with addressing issues of equity and improving relations across differences, the work with teams did not need to revolve *explicitly* around "diversity" in order to contribute to the overarching effort. It did not matter that some team members had participated in the Workplace Chemistry Training and some had not. Rather, the consultations were focused on establishing a team vision and reinforcing the sense that members had both the capacity and the responsibility to work collectively to achieve that vision. Within that context, the goal for all our consultations was to support the development of team cultures that would promote meaningful inclusion of all members toward a shared end. The workers did not need to become friends; they did not need to spend time together outside work; they did not even need to like each other. However, they *did* need to figure out how to encourage all team members to contribute their utmost in order to accomplish their shared goals.

Focusing on collective team visions to achieve support for diversity may, at first glance, seem a bit counterintuitive. It may not be immediately clear what having shared goals has to do with diversity. In fact, can't such a focus actually pull for conformity and place a priority on sameness? Conceivably, focusing on what group members have in common could devalue, or at least mask, differences. However, as summarized in the introduction of this book, the research tells us that while homogeneous groups tend to be more cohesive, diverse groups have the capacity for greater creativity and more effective problem solving than homogeneous groups *when* members of the group are all pulling in the same direction. Thus, we built our work with teams on the premise that they needed to be clear about what ultimately bound them together in order to fully appreciate and access the benefits of the rich diversity among members. Establishing common ground through a shared vision provided a rationale for why they should care about whether or not their team was supportive of the diversity among group members and, in this way, established a foundation from which we could promote greater inclusion and equity as team members worked toward achieving their goals.

ASSESSING TEAM ISSUES

Each consultation was designed specifically for the unit in question and thus started with interviews of team members to develop an understanding of their unique challenges. Most manufacturing departments were set up with twelve-hour shifts, and workers were on a "two-on-two-off" schedule—working two days, then taking two days off. With this type of schedule, four groups of workers (two groups on day shifts and two groups on night shifts) could keep the plant functioning on a 24/7 basis. Thus, the assessment process for most departments required at least two trips to the plant during a block of time around shift change (7:00 A.M. or 7:00 P.M.) that would span two of the four teams per visit. The interview protocol varied a bit from unit to unit to allow flexibility to probe issues specific to that unit, but it typically followed a fairly straightforward outline asking workers to reflect on what they liked best about their jobs, what they saw as the strengths of their team, what they saw as areas for improvement, and what recommendations they had for change.

My goals with assessment interviews were generally threefold. The first goal was to begin to develop personal connections with team members by learning about them as individuals and listening to their concerns. This goal is rooted in the belief that developing some connection based on respect and recognition of existing competencies is essential before challenging a group toward change. The second goal was to build an understanding of the team dynamics that would synthesize the varied, and sometimes contradictory, views into a coherent picture. I strove to develop a picture that acknowledged the existence of multiple "realities," by raising awareness of the minority voices typically missing from the teams' narratives about themselves. The framework for developing this community narrative or team portrait was shaped by a conceptual grounding in the ecological priorities for a phenomenological approach that incorporates a multileveled analysis of contributing factors. The third goal was to identify openings for change. Building on strengths and past successes can provide important momentum; identifying strategic opportunities helps focus where that momentum can most effectively lead.

Developing a feedback summary that incorporates this spirit involves a balance between being *nonblaming* (i.e., validating the diverse "realities" of team members; looking beyond targeting "defective" individuals to understanding the broader context and system dynamics; and including organizational policies, structure, values, and organizational trajectories such as reorganizations and downsizing in the analysis) and being *challenging* (i.e., emphasizing the opportunities and importance of change and holding team members accountable for taking action). When effectively done, this approach is another manifestation of the stance of *connected disruption.*

Honoring multiple realities in the assessment summaries is more an art than a science. I worked to make visible and to validate the range of experiences among workers. If different workers reported different interpretations of the same events, I worked to describe the variability as legitimate. Rather than trying to reconcile different interpretations and present a "professional" analysis of what was "*really* going on," I presented the existence of variation among experiences as the *substance* of the analysis. For example, rather than trying to discern whether the solo woman on a unit was indeed isolated by her male coworkers, our summary simply juxtaposed her description of feeling alienated and unsupported with her male coworkers' description of feeling "we are a tight group" and "everyone knows what's going on." On another unit, rather than judging whether team members felt free to express concerns, my summary described how some members (primarily white) felt that their team was very open and functioned smoothly while the African American members felt there were favorites and rarely spoke up, because they felt it was important to avoid making waves.

Elevating the previously silent voices and laying the divergent views side by side is not a dismissal of either view, but it *is* a challenge to the hegemonic nature of the dominant "reality." In other words, the assessment summaries sought to render the views of the majority group as *a* perspective but not the *only* perspective and, in doing so, to challenge the power of the dominant group to define the "team reality" for all members. What we give attention to grows, and simply noting disparities between the views and experiences of dominant groups and those of minority groups can help to begin to shift the power dynamic. Articulating the multiple realities and offering them up for the team to see rendered them catalysts for rethinking some assumptions strongly held by the majority team members. Including previously hidden perspectives as part of the portrait of a team can shake up their sense of equanimity yet do so without making team members "wrong." This approach makes space to challenge the status quo, without activating as much resistance as approaches that directly dismiss the dominant view.

Remembering the image of the mobile used in the training workshops, the assessment summaries, while emphasizing the ecological theme of multiple levels, often included formulas or diagrams of interactions among multilayered factors. For example, one assessment report outlined ways that changing demands (industry and organizational level) were interacting with varied reaction styles (individual level) and the lack of times and procedures for addressing problems (team level) to produce tensions within the team: Changing Demands × Varied Reactions × Lack of Problem-Solving Mechanisms → Team Tensions.

Building on the ecological theme of interdependencies, summaries also often emphasized that problems emerge from the dynamics *between* people rather than from isolated problematic individuals. Identifying problematic interpersonal patterns can open up the possibility of understanding participants in a conflict as well intended even if their actions have negative consequences for others. The primary focus of the assessment summaries was on *eeect*. An analysis that can honor intention, even while critiquing effect, can diminish the sense of blame and free up more energy for change. For example, while a wide range of individual reactions to changing work demands may all be understandable, some (e.g., constructive critique and problem solving) have a more positive effect on the team than others (e.g., complaining to coworkers).

It is also important for an assessment summary to emphasize the positive possibilities and opportunities that would greet a more inclusive team. An approach that only emphasizes problems can create anxiety and uncertainty about the future, and thereby undermine a group's collective motivation to change. In the acknowledgment of the positives, the challenges facing teams are framed less as static "deficiencies" and more as "barriers" to overcome in order to be the more inclusive team they have the potential to become. The recognition of strengths allows an affirmation of how team members are connected to—and dependent on—one another.

THE VISIONING PROCESS

As part of each consultation, we summarized the assessment and developed an intervention plan in consultation with the manager, working with Keitha to address personnel policy issues as needed. In most cases, after formulating a plan with the manager, we brought the team together to share the feedback and to set the stage for addressing the emergent issues. Before digging into problem solving, we engaged most groups in a team visioning process. In other words, we shared our observations about the current situation, engaged the team in filling out that portrayal, and then asked the team to develop a picture of their ideal team. To formulate the ideal, we asked participants the "miracle question"—which was to imagine waking up one morning six months hence to find that their group had miraculously become the effective team they had always wanted.[1] They were then asked to jot down the characteristics of this imagined team by describing how they would notice their enhanced effectiveness as they went about a day of work, including how they would feel, how they would act, and how others would be acting and feeling.

The purpose of this visioning process was to help the team collectively articulate their values around positive team functioning and then to publicly commit to working toward that shared vision. To generate a plan in which all participants felt some stake, it was essential to adopt a consultation process that engaged everyone in some way. Thus, we were quite deliberate in asking participants to articulate their vision first individually—writing down their personal responses to the miracle question—and then in dyads to select their top seven to ten elements of a shared team vision. Requiring both individual reflection and dyadic discussion makes space for even the quietest, most reluctant team members to contribute. Following the dyadic work, the full team worked together to pull out themes across the contributions from all dyads. The facilitation challenge for this type of process is to help the group identify the themes that run through all their hopes for the future of the team and to articulate them in such a way that the team becomes energized for action. It is useful to help the members of the group use their own language to describe the elements of their team vision while at the same time encouraging them to frame the elements as positive qualities to strive toward (e.g., "treating each other with respect") rather than as negative states they hope to avoid (e.g., "no infighting").

Across the various ChemPro units, the team visions had some common dimensions yet also some interesting distinctiveness. For example, the workers in Maintenance described their team vision as including respect for personal differences, interpersonal openness and honesty, good communication, acceptance of responsibility, shared workload, management support and backup, and planned workloads. Security's version incorporated a positive attitude toward work, personal and friendly relationships with one another, dealing with today (giving immediate attention to problems), professional image, neatness, support for one another, appreciation and respect, communication at shift change, and acting as team players. Drying wanted to strive toward a team where members helped each other, shared a strong work ethic, had a sense of equality, engaged in more two-way communication, respected one another, had a positive attitude toward work, had stress-free relationships, and effectively managed external influences. All the team visions incorporated some aspects of support, improved communication, and community building, yet each also had elements unique to its subculture. As the stories unfold, it will become clear why the vision for Maintenance included "management support," Security included "neatness" and "professional image," and Drying included "managing external influences."

team consultations

Once the members of a group had collectively articulated the elements of their envisioned team, the consultation turned toward analyzing what was needed to move from their current state to their desired state. Before outlining specific action steps, the process typically engaged the group in considering both the resources (or driving forces) that the team could draw on to reach their vision and the various barriers (or restraining forces) that could make it difficult. This type of process has been written about in many ways. Kurt Lewin referred to this as "force field analysis"; others describe a similar process as a SWOT analysis (Strengths, Weaknesses, Opportunities, and Threats);[2] still others utilize a related "logic model."[3] The reason similar processes come by so many different descriptors probably owes to the appeal of analyses that are firmly rooted in both the current situation of the team and a hoped-for outcome or vision.

Lewin's conceptualization in particular, by assessing forces within the environment that can influence the movement toward or away from a team vision, places the process into a systemic framework. The force field analysis is much more than a list of pros and cons or strengths and weaknesses; it is an analysis of the preexisting context—including competencies, resources, structures, contingencies, and trends—both within an organization and outside, in the broader social and economic environment. Lewin notes that the study of the conditions for change must begin with an analysis of the conditions for "no change," because "to bring about any change, the balance between the forces which maintain the social regulation at a given level has to be upset," then "hand-in-hand with the destruction of forces maintaining the old equilibrium must go the establishment (or liberation) of forces toward a new equilibrium"[4]—i.e., the social processes that push for the status quo (i.e., support the current state of affairs) need to be upset. Considering forces that exist at multiple levels that either help create momentum toward desired team functioning or push against change embodies the ecological spirit of contextual analysis and understanding. In our work with ChemPro, we could move from this analysis to develop action plans that would enhance driving forces (e.g., capitalize on cross-training as an opportunity for job growth) and/or address restraining forces (e.g., reduce confusion about job tasks and/or worry about the future).

Although there were some commonalities across consultations, it is the differences that are most instructive. For some teams, we facilitated a review and analysis of individuals' contributions to the team; for others we focused on specific interpersonal or organizational barriers to more effective teamwork. Still other teams were ready to move more quickly into collective problem solving about how to become a more cooperative and inclusive team. There my role was simply one of facilitator, keeping the group focused on problem solving, ensuring that decisions represented a true consensus of the group, and recording the proposed action steps.

Some aspects of the consultations were similar to the four-day training. Early in each consultation, we would engage the group in establishing guidelines or agreements about rules for participation in the team-building sessions. Some ground rules typically revolved around communication agreements (e.g., listen carefully before responding, speak for and about yourself, look at your *own* role in the team), while other agreements addressed broader issues (e.g., everyone's concerns are legitimate, everyone needs to participate to make this useful, or the "pass rule" that no one has to say anything s/he is uncomfortable sharing). Although we would often suggest some basic rules, it was important to invite each group to "personalize" them—alter and add rules to fit the specific dynamics and circumstances of that team. After discussion and reaching consensus, we would ask each participant to sign the newsprint that contained the summary list. The signatures signaled both a commitment to the agreements and authorization for the facilitator to hold the group to the rules.

These types of agreements serve multiple purposes. First, the mere act of establishing them can be an early success experience for a team, as it requires working collaboratively to make important decisions. Second, the rules provide a useful guide if discussion becomes contentious. Referring back to the agreements on the rules can help to rein in discussions that wander toward the nonproductive and/or negative. Third, working from group agreements that embody values for respect and shared participation can help the groups begin enacting the desired goal—in our case the culture change that was at the core of the Workplace Chemistry Initiative.[5]

Three consultations (with Maintenance, Security, and Drying) are illustrative of our work to foster diverse teams through the visioning process. The *Maintenance Unit* could be characterized as a sheltered enclave where the demographic homogeneity gave rise to a myopia that ignored experiences outside those of the dominant white male group. In this unit, there was a particular blindness to the experiences of women (i.e., "multiple realities"). *Security* was a small, racially diverse group of men whose interpersonal tensions had subtle racial overtones, and team-building challenges revolved around the recognition of interdependencies and team members' impacts on one another. *Drying* was stigmatized as "the women's unit," and the team-building work had to address their collective sense of being devalued by the rest of the plant.

MAINTENANCE: THE MALE ENCLAVE

The Maintenance Unit included twenty-one people, all but two of whom were white men (one white female electrician, one white female supply clerk). I was initially invited by Brian, the Facilities Department manager, to work with the Electrical Team (a group within the Maintenance Unit of the Facilities Department) because there was brewing unrest that he felt needed to be addressed before working with the full unit. The all-white electrical team (one female and five male electricians) was led by Jack, the white male Maintenance Unit supervisor. Between the work with the Electrical Team and the

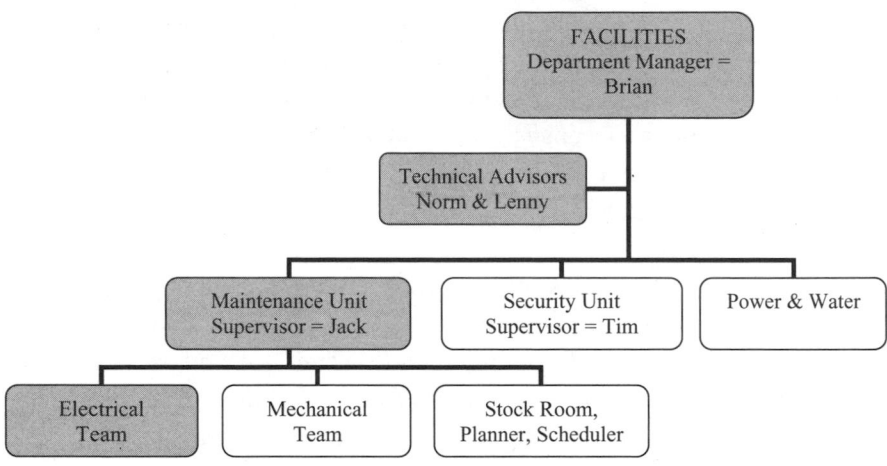

FIGURE 4.1 Organizational Chart of Facilities Department

full Maintenance Unit, I facilitated five days of group team building over about a year and a half and consulted regularly with managers along the way. See figure 4.1 for an organizational chart (the shaded areas were involved in the consultations).

Electrical Team. From my initial interviews, it was apparent that the electrical group was dealing with an intense interpersonal quagmire produced by a mix of historical events (e.g., shifts in managerial responsibilities and the structure of jobs), differences in job emphasis among workers (e.g., code enforcers vs. those who felt "close enough is good enough"), and assumptions about others that were often off base (e.g., social awkwardness being read as haughty and judgmental). What I wrote in my process notes at the time, however, was: "What is most noteworthy about the group is not the complexity of the problems. Many groups have a history of conflict and changing roles. What is truly striking is how entrenched or stuck the group seems." Team members were concerned about their collective inability to address conflict situations, and most were pessimistic about the possibilities for change in the group's dynamics. As the consultation progressed, it became clear that the informal leadership style of the supervisor, the homogeneity of the group, and the white male culture of the trades had combined to play a role in the sense of being "stuck." Issues both internal and external to the organization were forces against change.

The most apparent tensions revolved around the electricians' relationships with two white male technical advisers who were also considered part of the team (i.e., providing expert guidance but no hands-on technical work). Norm had been a licensed electrician for over twenty years; Lenny had over fifteen years with ChemPro and several prior years at Corporate. Both had at one point been supervisors but had subsequently been moved into "individual contributor" jobs—basically lateral moves but also signals of company dissatisfaction with their supervisory skills. On the other hand, Jack, the current supervisor, had about twenty years of experience in production but no skilled trades or technical background. I was told he was made a manager because of his effectiveness in getting tasks done and his "easy-to-get-along-with" managerial style. The unclear accountability structure, which included a supervisor with no specialized training in the trades plus two advisers with technical expertise but no supervisory authority, clearly contributed to the tensions. I facilitated a couple of meetings with just the department manager (Brian), Maintenance supervisor (Jack), and the two advisers (Norm and Lenny) to clarify their roles vis-à-vis one another. Further work to clarify who was accountable to whom and for what was woven throughout the consultation.

Norm, in particular, was at the center of much of the tension within the Electrical Team. A nasty interpersonal pattern had developed wherein Norm's investment in high standards led him to pay close attention to the work of the electricians—particularly given his concern that Jack lacked technical expertise. Norm would comment whenever he felt there could be improvement but rarely when the work was done well. As a result, the electricians felt he was overly critical and actively avoided him. The more Norm felt they were avoiding him, the more he felt his technical knowledge was not valued, and thus the more he felt compelled to demonstrate his expertise through critique— and thus the more the electricians felt he was "out to get them" and had to be circumvented in any way possible. The pattern was self-perpetuating and had intensified over time.

After developing a shared team vision, we looked at barriers to change within the group. It quickly became clear that the sequence was being fueled by many less-than-useful assumptions about one another's intentions. Anger and reactivity was spurred by these erroneous assumptions. We decided to explore the theme of intent versus impact as a way to disrupt the problematic interpersonal patterns. One particularly effective exercise involved asking each person to fill out a two-by-two grid. Along one dimension was "strengths and contributions" and "areas for growth" and along the other "how would you describe yourself?" and "how do you think others would describe you?" (see figure 4.2). Our hope was that if we could facilitate honest feedback, we could both

	HOW WOULD YOU DESCRIBE YOURSELF?	HOW DO YOU THINK OTHERS WOULD DESCRIBE YOU?
STRENGTHS AND CONTRIBUTIONS		
AREAS FOR GROWTH		

FIGURE 4.2 Team Contributions Exercise

increase awareness of each team member's impact on others and directly challenge the blaming assumptions that were fueling the problematic dynamics.[6]

Given the small size of the group, we were able to devote time for everyone to share what they had on their own grid and for each person to hear feedback from teammates. This structure provided powerful openings to contrast people's intent with their impact. For example, Norm learned that his focus on strict code enforcement was experienced by others as scolding and demeaning—and the electricians heard for the first time how much Norm wanted to earn their respect and thought that he needed to do so by demonstrating he had expertise to share with them. It was particularly instructive for Norm to learn that the impact that he had on others was not at all what he intended. It was also eye-opening for those describing the negative impact to begin to understand that the intentions behind his actions were not malicious but rather misguided—not the result so much of arrogance as a desire to be needed and accepted.

The initial portion of the consultation was organized to address the tensions between Norm (and to a lesser extent Lenny) and the other electricians. However, also embedded in the team-building work was a focus on the marginality of the lone female. Taking time to review the team contributions of each person provided an opportunity to review her contributions to the team. This increased her visibility and gave her an opportunity to hear coworkers' reflections on her contributions. In the discussion of her two-by-two grid, Nancy was recognized as "being a team player," "willing to take on responsibility," and "interested in her own continuous growth" (she was working on her master's license as an electrician). Her teammates urged her to talk more and bring up issues that might "stress her out." In this context, she was able to raise the concern that the others sought out fellow male electricians for backup, ignoring her even when she was available. She did not feel included in the team and lacked information that the others shared with each other informally, and thus she felt she was not able to contribute as much to the group or to further develop her individual skills.

Raising her issues directly within the group represented an important shift in team dynamics. Giving voice to her perceptions was not something Nancy did without prodding, but publicly speaking the previously unacknowledged made it harder for the group to perpetuate her exclusion behind the scenes. As Catharine MacKinnon notes in her pathbreaking analysis of the harassment of women, "lacking a term to express it, sexual harassment was literally unspeakable, which made a generalized, shared and social definition of it inaccessible. The unnamed [however] should not be mistaken for the nonexistent."[7] Nancy's exclusion was not really news to her teammates. In fact, in private, at least one coworker had expressed the feeling that Nancy was "not fully one of us," and the intensity of sexist comments among team members had led another coworker to express worry about Nancy's safety. However, these concerns had not been spoken publicly. After the team discussion, however, the men could no longer pretend that Nancy was unaware of their tendency to avoid or work around her. When the issue was finally publicly named, it could no longer be mistaken for nonexistent.

The sharing based on each person's two-by-two grid created openings for participants to acknowledge the different styles and priorities among team members without engendering a lot of defensiveness. While the process did not "resolve" the tensions in any ultimate way, it did shake things up enough to help the group get "unstuck" and entertain some ways to move beyond the interpersonal tensions. Separating intent from impact is not a matter of letting people off the hook because they tell you they mean well, but rather is a process of setting aside intention (and all the blame and defensiveness that it generates) and focusing on what needs to change so that the impact on the team can be more positive. It is critical to pair the opening up of new ways of understanding one another's behavior with clear expectations that emphasize team members' accountability for their effects on one another. Thus the remainder of the consultation focused on clarifying accountability structures and establishing ongoing settings for giving and getting feedback (and fostering the requisite communication skills to use these settings effectively).

It was also useful to understand the team tensions within the context of changing organizational expectations. As Norm said in a memo to me after our first team meeting,

I have a new appreciation for the need to work hard at improving and maintaining relationships. Prior to the meeting with you, I did not appreciate or value the need for interpersonal skills. ChemPro only expected me to fine-tune my technical skills and stay "state of the art" in my field. This was a big mistake for me, but one I think I can rectify.

Brian, his boss, was encouraged when, after the consultation, Norm met with each of the electricians one-on-one to ask what he could personally do to improve the relationship. I continued to coach Norm individually for a few months to help him find new ways to uphold the standards he held dear without the other electricians feeling belittled. Unfortunately, the other workers were slow to cut him much slack. As the department manager described it, "Norm was hopeful for an exchanged commitment from them, but they are not that far yet." Without this reciprocity, it was difficult for Norm to act on his new insights, but his efforts were nonetheless commendable.

What became evident over time was that the shunning of Norm and the isolation of Nancy were connected in important ways. They were both victims of a strong hegemonic culture that tolerated little outside the homogeneous inner circle. One person even referred to their ingroup/outgroup dynamics as "ChemPro communism," a comment on the rejection of those who did not conform to the ingroup expectations. This conformity pressure was intensified, even if inadvertently, by the style of the Maintenance supervisor. Most of the "guys" liked Jack's low-key style; they felt he was supportive and an effective advocate. Most agreed, however, that he tended to deal with problems informally and indirectly. Jack saw himself as a "peacemaker," and some indeed experienced his work behind the scenes in this light. However, those outside the inner circle experienced it very differently. They felt it involved "playing favorites" and saying one thing in public but doing something altogether different in private. Norm worried that he was being "belittled and ridiculed" behind his back. Nancy, in her understated, matter-of-fact way, simply described Jack as "not big on communication" but acknowledged that he did talk with workers he considered friends, just not with the full team.

Once again, varied experiences of the same behaviors existed side by side. Intent and impact did not line up. In efforts to make "peace," Jack actually contributed to a divided team; those in a very homogeneous inner group felt that they belonged, and those who did not fit for various reasons were a "problem." The outsiders were left dangling (as Norm put it, he felt he was in "a nowhere land"). The group dynamics I had initially described as "stuck" emerged as being related to the team's strong norms for conformity supported by the informal network that had been formed to adapt to conflict alongside a lack of clear systems of accountability. These conformity norms were stronger within Maintenance than in most of the rest of the plant. I strongly suspect that this dynamic was buoyed by the general culture of the trades, where "loyalty" is highly valued and where women and people of color are often treated as outsiders.[8]

Norm may have been a white man, but in his style he had nonetheless violated the informal norms of the dominant group. In addition, as I learned later, he had been the person who had hired Nancy and developed her apprentice program to achieve the on-the-job hours as well as classroom training necessary for her to complete her journeyman rating. While Norm had done this for others as well, he had a particular investment in Nancy as the first woman electrician hired by the plant. He took it very personally that the team had not supported and mentored her development more actively. What he did not fully appreciate was that he had, in effect, defied the ethos of the group when he invited in this person who disrupted the predictable—and homogeneously male—environment that had always existed. The problem was not really the individual team members' rejection of Norm (or Nancy), but the lack of accountability and collective ways of operating that had not yet made room for diversity and could not easily accommodate approaches outside their current practices. Within this context, Norm's decision to encourage Nancy had been added to his long list of transgressions against the culture of the unit and further contributed to his treatment as a misfit.

The team-building work with the Electrical Team was successful in providing some new understandings and giving voice to some important minority experiences. While there was only limited change in the enduring team culture, the complacency of the team was challenged, and some shifts in ways of relating began to emerge.

The Full Maintenance Unit. With the pockets of tension in the Electrical Team somewhat more contained, we began our work with the full Maintenance Unit. Given that this was a larger group, I invited a colleague (Robin Toof) and student (Steven Lockney) to cofacilitate these meetings. As with the other units, we brainstormed, then outlined the elements of a shared vision for teamwork. The group then refined that vision to be "to work together and help each other in a respectful and fun manner in order to draw upon each team member's expertise so that the total team is seen as a resource for keeping production going to allow the company to meet its goals." After generating a shared team vision, we facilitated a force field analysis to list, on the one hand, the resources and forces available to move the team in the desired direction toward their vision and, on the other hand, the constraints, barriers, and forces that could make the vision more difficult to achieve. The dynamics within the full Maintenance Unit, while less visibly conflictual, mirrored those of the smaller Electrical Team. In many of the discussions, there were a few very vocal spokespeople with firm convictions about "how things are done around here." We actively worked to make space for alternative perspectives to emerge in that large setting, however, the most vocal participants were rarely challenged by their coworkers without our invitation.

How can work with a totally white (and almost entirely male) group be construed as diversity related? In some ways it cannot, since there is little racial or gender diversity to work with. It was abundantly clear that there were limitations to what could be accomplished when working with a group where there was minimal demographic diversity and a lack of supervisory resolve to change this. There is no substitute for hiring to achieve gender and racial diversity that might disrupt the exclusivity of a white male enclave. In other ways, however, our work with this unit was critical to diversity goals. The consultation helped to bring broader team attention to the lack of support for the lone female. Further, with more long-term change in mind, our work focused on shifting the culture in ways that we hoped would eventually make more space for people who did not conform to the dominant ethos. When reviewing the day, one person indicated that what had surprised him most was learning "how some people felt left out and not valued." Another talked about how the team had a habit of avoiding differences and difficult issues, but during the consultation he was struck by how "we can get together as a group and get a lot of issues out on the table, get honest answers, and still go home feeling good." These were hopeful insights.

SECURITY: RACIAL OVERTONES

The team building with the Security Unit, while also incorporating the development of a team vision, took several turns that were quite different from the work with Maintenance. The Security team was a small group of six people who divided up shifts. They worked in a small shed from which they could monitor who came into and went from the plant twenty-four hours a day; they were also on call to venture into the plant to deal with any emerging security concerns. Even though each person generally worked alone on a shift, these were tight, shared living quarters that presented different interpersonal challenges than, for example, work on the plant floor cleaning kettles or providing plant upkeep. Thus, my work with this group focused heavily on helping them develop constructive communication, problem-solving, and conflict resolution strategies. We met approximately once every two months over the course of a year, and I consulted informally with the team supervisor in between. The all-male group included three white men, two African American men, and one Caribbean-born black man. The supervisor was a white man.

The initial interviews identified many team strengths, including their shared commitment to their jobs and their desire for better working relationships. They also collectively acknowledged that the team members brought diverse competencies that could potentially complement one another. They had a supervisor, Tim, whom they saw as sincerely committed to supporting their team and who provided clear expectations regarding performance goals. The issues they saw as barriers to teamwork included not recognizing the ways they were dependent on one another, few times or spaces set aside for resolving conflicts, worry about being criticized by one another, and tension around day/night pay differentials. In their words, they did not "see themselves as a team" and were functioning in parallel but disconnected ways that allowed plenty of room for misunderstandings and little room to address them.

The differences the team grappled with explicitly were differences in standards of cleanliness, approaches to record keeping, and accountability for follow-through on work projects. While the personalities involved and the structure of the job may have been enough to set the stage for interpersonal conflict, there were additional tensions that had racial and cultural dimensions. Roy, one of the African American men, was meticulous—not only in his personal hygiene but also in his detailed record keeping. This created some conflict with his black Caribbean teammate, who was much more casual. Manny was often more than a few minutes late, arrived with shirt untucked, and did not log the same level of detail. Roy's conflict was most intense, however, with his longtime white coworker Pete, whom he did not always trust to follow through on promised work or even to return personal loans. The style differences of these three coworkers had at least some roots in racial and cultural differences. Manny projected a more laid-back "island" approach to life fitting the stereotype of his Caribbean background, which stood in contrast to Roy's more urban, religious, disciplined style. Pete, on the other hand, projected the sense that he was immune to the same requirements as others and, even if indirectly, communicated the expectation that people around him would make allowances for him—a sort of casual expression of privilege that was probably reinforced by going through life as a white man.

Other conflicts were more explicitly race related. For example, the two men who regularly worked nights—and thus were paid more—were Roy and Manny. The fact that they were both black gave rise to some grumbling by the white men who worked days about reverse discrimination and some questioning of the rationale for the pay differential (i.e., why should night shifts be paid more than day?). There was also some racial subtext to the reluctance of the white day shift workers to raise their concerns directly. The comment of one older white male coworker who said he was "afraid of the guys on nights" certainly could be interpreted as having racial underpinnings. Keitha and HR were charged with addressing the pay differential issue through formal personnel channels, whereas my consultation challenge was to address the latent racial stereotyping while helping to strengthen the team.

The team-building work had two main components: to establish systems of accountability from shift to shift and to build trust across the interpersonal differences. So one aspect of the work involved helping the group develop shared standards for their work (e.g., from record keeping to housekeeping) and procedures to monitor and support follow-through (e.g., checklists for closing out a shift). Toward this end, we devoted consultation time to articulating, then gaining consensus on, specific standards and procedures.

The other, more challenging aspect of the consultation was to build bridges across the differences. Not unlike the plantwide training, part of the process was to offer opportunities for team members to get to know one another outside their roles in the security shed (i.e., to "humanize the other"). With such a small group, this might seem a more manageable task than for larger teams, and in fact simply gathering all six individuals in one room at the same time was a profound intervention. However, some of the problems had long, mangled, and deeply personal histories. Many of the tensions grew out of assumptions the coworkers had made about one another—their feelings, their attitudes, their intentions—and were maintained by the fact that there were limited opportunities for experiences that might challenge or counter the worst-case interpretations. Providing a facilitated environment to raise issues and address them was essential.

Following the development of a team vision and an analysis of supports and barriers to teamwork, we devoted consultation time to establishing a more constructive approach to problem solving within the team to help bridge specific conflicts. We worked to define a structure for dealing with emergent differences and interpersonal problems (e.g., shift changes and monthly meetings), agreed on some ground rules for dealing with future conflicts, and began to practice using a win-win conflict resolution approach. The win-win framework has some elements that are very compatible with the conceptual base of the Workplace Chemistry Initiative. The first few steps involve identifying the problem, agreeing on a mutually comfortable time and place to meet, and then describing the problem and individual needs using "I statements." The formula for such statements is to present a problem description in behavioral terms and pair it with a description of the *impact* of those behaviors on the individual, on the team, and on the organization. These steps lay the groundwork for moving forward—no arguments about intentions, no blaming about ill motives, and no discussion of who is at fault. The next two steps dovetail nicely with the other Workplace Chemistry work. Step 4 is "consider your partner's point of view," and Step 5 is "establish common goals," followed by Steps 6 and 7, "negotiate a solution" and "follow up." While this phase of consultation had a strong focus on individual skill building, it embodied an ecological spirit by incorporating sensitivity to other's points of view and by placing any conflict in the broader context of the team and shared goals. By engaging everyone in the development of a team vision and providing opportunities for the voices of all team members to be heard in these conversations, we were providing an alternative to the ways in which interpersonal power differences had previously allowed some views to dominate without question.

As with the Electrical Team, we devoted considerable time to exploring a shift in team values, from a focus on intent to a focus on impact. Building on the elements of their vision that emphasized respect and interdependence (i.e., dealing immediately with issues, fostering appreciation and respect, being team players), I likened their job to playing catch with an egg—you have to be very aware of both how you throw *and* how you catch the egg in order to avoid a messy outcome. If your shared goal is to pass the egg intact, a classy-looking throw is useless unless it is easy for the receiver to catch. Simulations can be tremendously useful to get members of a group to think about how they work together in this regard. For example, during one session, I engaged them in a two-part task where they worked in teams, first to dismantle a tower of blocks without it tumbling down and then to build it up again as high as possible. They were to take turns to add or subtract blocks and were told that their primary responsibility was to ensure that the person who followed them did not topple the structure. These building tasks were selected because they mirrored the structure of their job. One at a time they staffed the Security shed, and it was what they left behind at the end of the shift that most affected their working relationships.

We used the debriefing time to draw parallels and generate agreements about how to improve teamwork. The basic framework for debriefing that I follow involves first asking the group what they observed (What happened? What did you notice?), then how they made sense of what happened (What struck you? What were your reactions?), and finally how their observations related to their daily world of work (What lessons will you take away from this?). In other words, what did you *see*? What do you *think* about what you saw? And what will you *do* based on these observations? With the building simulation, we would also periodically stop action and ask participants to reflect on what they were noticing about the process and whether they wanted to shift strategies in any way. After engaging in the group task, shaping observations, and reflecting on the process, the group generated a series of lessons and action steps related to enhancing their collective commitment to focus on impact, address issues directly, and actively value their personal connections with their teammates (see table 4.1).

The consultation needed to both emphasize the connection among team members and establish some commitments to change. On the connection side of this equation, we punctuated the consultation with opportunities for them to get to know one another better outside the focal problems. For example, in one exercise we asked them to engage in a series of dyadic conversations with each teammate in order to identify at least three things that they were previously unaware that they had in common. Other exercises were less verbal, like pounding out a rhythm as small groups, then as a full team. A word of warning, however: Too often trainers do "fun" exercises just because they are fun. In these exercises it is essential to be thoughtful not only about the possibilities for deepening workers' connections with one another but also about the group dynamics brought forth in the process, that is, to link the exercises to the themes of the team-building work *and* to their real lives as workers at ChemPro, and to use the exercises to enact new ways of working together. For example, in another activity we asked each person to share two truths and a lie, and then asked the group to try to identify the lie. In this exercise, my own list included: I was on my high school gymnastics team; my house burned down when I was twelve years old; and I learned to read at the age of four. Gymnastics was not a common high school sport in the 1960s, nor does my aging body look like it could still wrap itself around

TABLE 4.1 · LESSONS OUTLINED BY THE SECURITY TEAM

Value connections/support the team
· Remember the importance of negotiating differences · Be open to benefit from other people's experience · Remember the plant sees Security as a team · Depend on each other · Good to kick in for others
Focus on impact
· Looking out for the next guy (in terms of doing your work in a way that makes it easier for the next person) forces you to be a team player · Be responsible for your impact—not just your intent · Don't prejudge other people's intent—especially about past events · Avoid assumptions
Address issues
· Remember you *can* work things out · Raise issues in a way that the group can hear the concern and work with it · Listen to each other · Listen → Ask for feedback on your understanding/paraphrase → Revise and correct your view · Speak up

a set of parallel bars; houses of white suburban kids don't typically burn down (the assumption being that fires happen more often in low-income, poorly maintained housing in the inner city); but one might think that a university professor had been a precocious reader. Truth is, I was once a reasonably agile gymnast, and my house did burn down—but I was nowhere close to reading at age four.

By introducing some unexpected information about one another, this exercise not only deepened the participants' knowledge of coworkers; it also illustrated the danger of generalizing about others based on surface knowledge. The opportunity to "work" together in a different way introduced them to new aspects of one another. Joe's singing and sharp wit as well as his creative use of the blocks shifted his public image from lazy to clever and fun. Roy shed some of his reputation as "rigid." Incorporating some playfulness generated considerable laughter and defused some of the tension. The enjoyment of one another further strengthened the team. Debriefing these short exercises helped to make the links: What did you notice/learn about yourself? What assets did you bring to the task? What did you notice about the contributions of others? What did you notice about the team? What helped you to work together? What parallels do you see to daily life as a team?

On the change side of the equation, we concluded each session by asking for action commitments. Each team member identified one or two specific steps that he could commit to take within the following month. To enhance thoughtfulness about implementation, we also asked participants to identify what would help them take those actions and what might get in the way—in essence, to analyze the forces at multiple levels that could influence their follow-through. Then we asked each person to specify a plan for addressing those forces and for monitoring his progress toward fulfilling his action commitments (e.g., checking with a supervisor or coworker or asking for help and support on a regular basis). These plans were written on work sheets that were collected by Tim, the team supervisor, who agreed to follow up. Commitments to actually take action are a useful bridge between the consultation and daily life. The real change happens when new ways of being are actually enacted in the ongoing work relationships.

It did not seem critical to frame the consultation with Security as focused on "diversity" issues explicitly even though it built on the major themes of the Workplace Chemistry Initiative. We spent time helping team members understand how they each experienced their work at ChemPro in an effort to validate the multiple realities among team members. We focused on developing a collective appreciation for their level of interdependence. We also worked on specific behavioral skills for giving constructive feedback and mechanisms for holding each other accountable for their *impact* on one another.

DRYING UNIT: A STIGMATIZED TEAM

The consultation with the Drying Unit was somewhat similar in structure to the work with Maintenance and Security; however, a unique aspect was the need to include broader organizational issues. Drying is the last step in the process of developing ChemPro's specialized chemicals. The substance arrives there wet, and the workers in Drying have to carefully place it on a conveyor belt that goes through ovens where it dries such that it can be ground into uniform crystals. Two groups of workers, one at the "wet end" and one at the "dry end," share twelve-hour shifts. Eight of the people on the unit were women, two of whom were European immigrants with English as a second language; three were women of color (two African Americans and one Latina); and three were U.S.-born white women. The seven male operators included two European immigrants (one with limited English), and the rest were U.S.-born white men. Their manager was a white male, and their team leader was a Caribbean-born black man. Technical advisers included two white men and one white woman. This was clearly the production unit within the plant with the greatest demographic diversity.

This was a colorful group in other ways as well. It was a group of individuals with very different styles and lots of conflict—some within the immediate work group, some between the wet and dry ends on a single shift, and some between shifts. There were complaints of name-calling; a couple of workers were described as "hotheads;" conflicts on one shift had resulted in shouting matches on more than one occasion. Not surprisingly, workers described a lack of trust and a sense of "always being on guard." On the other hand, the majority of the workers had dedicated many years to the company and were considered strong and steady contributors.

Here again, we began with interviews and the collaborative development of a plan with the manager. The team generated a vision that included people talking to each other more, helping one another out, and complaining less. They also hoped to get to a place where they could be more open, trusting, and comfortable with one another. Much of the work with this team proceeded in ways similar to work with the other departments. It was the nature of the barriers to teamwork within this group that was striking and deserves further comment here.

Some barriers were familiar, such as feeling overloaded and stressed, having a hard time giving one another direct feedback, and cynicism about the potential for change. However, unlike the situation on other units, there was also a collective sense that the work of this unit was devalued by the rest of the plant. The Drying workers felt like second-class citizens, and indeed they were treated that way. Members of the male-dominated Processing Unit proclaimed them "wimps" and had been overheard in the lunchroom vowing not to become a "women's unit like Drying." Some described Drying as the "dumping ground for non-performers," since a few people with back injuries had been transferred to the unit because it did not require as much heavy lifting as other production units. In addition, the highest possible pay grade in Drying was lower than that in other production units. This pay grade difference institutionalized the Drying team's lower status—the precision work of producing quality crystals was literally less valued than the more physical labor of boiling and cleaning kettles. The existing hierarchy of tasks within ChemPro could be seen as embodying a set of values that considered "men's labor" more important than "women's labor." Questioning the values embedded in such policies is a critical aspect of diversity work.

The dynamics internal to the Drying team could not be fully addressed without taking into consideration both the informal devaluing of the work by other units and the codification of that lack of value in the pay grade system.

TABLE 4.2 · TEAM ASSESSMENTS OF CHANGE

DIMENSIONS OF TEAM VISION	6 MONTHS AGO	NOW	AMOUNT CHANGE
Maintenance Team (n = 13)			
Respect for personal differences	4.50 (1.00)	5.00 (1.08)	.50
Interpersonal openness and honesty	4.25 (.87)	4.92 (.95)	.67
Good communication	4.33 (.98)	4.85 (1.07)	.52
Acceptance of responsibility	4.17 (.94)	4.77 (1.01)	.60
Shared workload	4.25 (1.22)	4.69 (1.32)	.44
Management support and backup	4.27 (1.35)	4.83 (1.47)	.56
Planned workloads	4.27 (1.19)	4.75 (1.22)	.48
Security Team (n = 6)			
Positive attitude toward work	4.00 (1.26)	5.67 (1.03)	1.67
Personal relationships with one another	3.33 (1.37)	5.50 (1.64)	2.17
Dealing with today	3.20 (1.48)	5.20 (2.05)	2.00
Professional image	5.17 (1.33)	6.33 (.82)	1.16
Neatness	5.00 (.89)	5.83 (.75)	.83
Support for one another	3.20 (1.48)	5.50 (1.05)	2.30
Appreciation and respect	3.50 (1.52)	5.33 (1.63)	1.83
Communication at shift change	3.67 (1.51)	6.00 (.89)	2.33
Acting as team players	3.20 (1.79)	5.75 (.99)	2.55
Drying Team (n = 17)			
Helping each other	4.53 (1.50)	5.65 (1.50)	1.12
Work ethic	4.76 (1.15)	5.24 (1.09)	.48
Sense of equality	5.12 (1.50)	5.59 (1.37)	.47
Two-way communication	4.59 (1.84)	5.53 (1.59)	.94
Respect	4.81 (1.91)	5.29 (1.90)	.48
Positive attitude toward work	4.18 (1.63)	5.06 (1.68)	.88
Stress-free relationships	4.06 (1.60)	4.47 (1.77)	.41
Managing external influences	5.06 (1.75)	5.41 (1.46)	.35

This was essential context for understanding the challenges of team building with this particular group of workers. The reevaluation of the pay grade, however, had to be championed by HR and addressed through formal personnel channels all the way up through Corporate. Even though addressing pay inequities was not the primary goal of our consultation, the team-building workshops did serve the purpose of providing a setting for operators to raise these concerns constructively and thereby rendered the issue a higher priority for their manager and HR. Again, the process of giving a public voice to an issue in a legitimate setting made it harder to ignore.

Within a couple of months, the workers did indeed receive word that their pay grade would be raised. This change, alongside a reorganization that meant that the unit would be getting a new manager, spurred us to devote consultation time to developing a team strategy for communicating a new team image to their new leader and to the plant as a whole. The unit's increased standing became a status to uphold in contrast to their previous reputation, which they had found demoralizing. This shift, probably more than any further delving into the interpersonal conflicts, became the foundation for ongoing improvements in team functioning.

TAKING STOCK

During the last phase of consultation with all the various teams, participants were asked to assess their progress on each dimension of their collaboratively developed team vision. They were asked to rate how they viewed their team when they began the team-building work and how they viewed the team at our final meeting. The ratings indicated some progress over time (see table 4.2). This type of assessment has many methodological limitations (e.g., self-rating, retrospective ratings concurrent with rating of "now") and could not be construed in any way as an "objective" longitudinal measure of progress toward achieving the team goals. However, it did capture the participants' collective *experience* of improvement and, as such, it provided a stimulus for discussion. The teams could celebrate those dimensions that they felt had improved, and they could develop further action plans for those areas they felt had been relatively ignored or stagnant.

alternative approaches to addressing team barriers to diversity

Each team was its own unique concoction of colliding elements, and the approach adopted for some would not work for all. This became quite clear to us in our work, and therefore some of the team consultations did not involve the process described above of collectively generating a team vision, conducting a force field analysis, and defining action steps. On two units in particular, the nature of the barriers to teamwork led us to recommend alternative strategies. One team—Processing—had such an intense culture of "independence" that we recommended more structural interventions. Another team—Prepping—faced challenges related to changing skill expectations and basic competencies that needed to be addressed prior to team visioning. The different approaches to team-building efforts with these units illustrate the importance of "fitting" the intervention to the particularities of the work group in question and avoiding the one-size-fits-all mentality—even *within* the same organization. The formulas for action had to be reevaluated and molded to the unique chemistry of each group.

PROCESSING: A CLASH BETWEEN INDEPENDENCE AND DIVERSITY

Processing was a manufacturing unit in which the twenty-eight workers were predominantly white men (86 percent). I consulted with this team early in my work at ChemPro and then again three years later. During my first consultation, there was one recently hired African American woman and three African American men (11 percent). Michelle, the lone woman, was no longer there three years later. Members of this unit were the highest paid among the plant operators and, by and large, felt they did their jobs well. They were proud that theirs was considered the most physically demanding work in the plant even though it was becoming increasingly computerized and mechanized, thus reducing the requirements for brute strength and theoretically opening up the jobs to more women.

The unit had a reputation for being inhospitable to both women and people of color. When I had given a round of feedback about the initial plantwide survey, this was the unit that responded to the finding that women and people of color experienced harassment at work with comments such as, "Slavery is not my fault so why should we have to worry if 'they' aren't comfortable here?" and "It's *their* problem if they can't take a joke." In Processing, a lack of emphasis on connection had on numerous occasions undermined efforts to diversify the predominantly white male group.

During my first consultation with this unit, I conducted interviews with team members where I probed for shared values about work and work relations. The prevailing attitude was that "you are on your own" (which included the assumption that newcomers should learn their own way around). Informal, but deeply held, values upholding an independent culture were mentioned in one shape or form by most workers. These values can be categorized into four themes: (1) Let others behave however they want as long as it doesn't affect you directly (e.g., "Best off coming in, keeping your mouth shut, do your job and leave"); (2) Don't ask others to adjust to you (e.g., "If you don't like how things are going, you need to figure out a way to cope"); (3) You don't have to be nice or help others (e.g., "We're here to make money, not friends"); and (4) People should not go to management with their concerns (e.g., "My business is nobody else's"). Theirs was a culture of independence even to the extent that there was little sense of a managerial presence or any hub or core group to reinforce accountability. Team members of color described feeling watched and criticized but rarely talked to directly.

Some of the dynamics that emerged for the lone woman on the production unit are a good example of the complicated alchemy. The men were warned by management to "be respectful." At first, the men helped Michelle do her job. Oftentimes they did her work for her instead of teaching her how to do it herself, particularly if it involved heavy lifting. This was likely informed by cultural beliefs about what behavior would be considered respectful of women. Over time, however, some coworkers felt they were "carrying her." The growing resentment was widely discussed among the men, particularly in the lunchroom. Some were quite vocal in their belief that women should not be doing these jobs. However, the concerns were never discussed directly with Michelle. Instead, most of her coworkers simply began avoiding her and ignoring her requests for assistance. She felt unwelcome. She tried to garner support from some of the African American men, and they expressed some empathy, as they had experienced ostracism similar to hers. When she started getting so frustrated that she yelled abusively at her coworkers and walked off the job, her white male coworkers began to more actively close ranks against her. Her African American male coworkers felt somewhat caught in the middle.

When Michelle eventually pressed charges of sexual harassment, she broke such a sacred rule (viz., don't go to management) that the closing of ranks against her was complete. An internal investigation of the charges was conducted between my two interviewing visits. My first interviews were quite wide ranging with discussion focusing on varied sources of concern about team relations. Just before my second visit, unit members had received word that Michelle was going to be moved temporarily to another unit while the investigation proceeded. During this second visit, complaints about her predominated, and I witnessed a most amazing convergence of views over the course of ten interviews across two different shifts. The details of arguments and defenses grew more and more alike from interview to interview to such an extent that I began hearing sentences repeated verbatim. The men gave identical examples about women who had successfully worked on their unit in the past (albeit for a short time). They each began to argue that all they were doing was treating her exactly as they treated the other "guys"—and weren't *they* really the ones being harassed by having to do her job for her and by having to endure her complaints and now a formal investigation.

The swiftness with which this group of extremely independent workers created a unified front was mind-boggling. All issues and concerns *among* the white men disappeared; in fact, several pronounced that "everything was just fine on this unit until she arrived." The only two voices that seemed independent of this tide were two African American men—the only workers of color on those shifts. In contrast to their white coworkers, they did not restrict their interview comments to the sexual harassment situation but also talked about other areas of concern including dynamics of racial exclusion on the unit. While a bit more sympathetic, even they felt they could not come to Michelle's defense at this juncture. In light of the closing of ranks, their risk of personally facing isolation had now become quite high.

The men were eventually deemed "not guilty" of sexual harassment, and the charges were dropped. The investigators decided that Michelle's case did not meet the formal requirements for "unwelcome sexual advances, requests for sexual favors, and other verbal or physical conduct of a sexual nature . . . when this conduct explicitly or implicitly affects an individual's employment, unreasonably interferes with an individual's work perform-ance, or creates an intimidating, hostile, or offensive work environment."[9] Additionally, she was not blameless in regard to the increasing tensions. Not long afterward, she quit.

Despite not meeting the formal criteria for action, the problems that led to Michelle's charge of sexual harassment were clearly shaped by informal team dynamics that marginalized women and then blamed them for their uncomfortable working conditions. The unit had developed a culture that was experienced as hostile by women and people of color (i.e., people outside the white male group were defined as "outsiders"). In this case, being a lone woman and being in a minority as an African American placed Michelle out-side the majority on multiple dimensions. The focus for her coworkers was on her gender far more than her race, most likely because she was the sole representative on that dimension and because the prestige of the job was based on a quality associated with "maleness" (i.e., brawn). By virtue of being different, she was a force that could potentially shake their collective belief about how things ought to be. As a result, even though this group strongly emphasized autonomy and independence from one another, its white male members had an uncanny capacity to come together and coalesce to protect the status quo. A woman's perspective and her experiences of events had vir-tually no visibility and played no role in shaping the dominant culture of the unit. HR felt somewhat discouraged by its limited success in breaking into the male culture of Processing but was willing to renew the effort. Rather than back off, HR continued to press for increased accountability for team-work and pondered whether "next time" two women should be hired at once and put on a shift together.

Another way to understand the diversity challenges that faced Processing is in terms of a dynamic interplay of the organization's articulated value for employee empowerment, the high prestige of the jobs, and the relative demographic homogeneity of the unit. This combination seemed to embolden a strong, monolithic team culture based on independence, a focus on one's own job, scanning the environment for its impact on oneself, and the maintenance of a self-protective stance (e.g., "It's not *my* job"). The unit had also developed practices that helped to maintain this individualized culture. People rarely dealt with each other directly, yet rumors and indirect communication about interpersonal concerns abounded. There were few settings where workers could meet face-to-face to discuss team issues. The emphasis on a very *individualized* form of empowerment pushed potential attention to interdependence underground and constrained both management and co-workers from holding people accountable to one another for working across differences as a team.

The effect on the men of color and the lone woman of color was to pressure them to adapt to the preexisting and often unspoken rules about appropriate behavior. Some rules included expectations that workers should tell each other, and not the supervisor, when they needed to leave early and that being considered a good team member included stopping by the coffeepot at shift change to banter about sports. The irony, of course, is that in groups with such unspoken rules those who are marginal are never told the rules in the first place, and these sorts of informal rules are fully apparent only when someone has broken one. In this case, not only did the minority group members not know that the coffee klatch was expected; they also felt less comfortable confiding in coworkers about scheduling constraints or other daily concerns. Probably both as cause and effect, their behavior was judged differently. For example, the reasons ascribed for African Americans leaving early tended to be person-centric (i.e., lazy), whereas for the white men the attributed reasons were situational (e.g., family concerns or medical appointments).

If my work with this team had begun with the collective development of a shared team vision, it could have unwittingly strengthened rather than challenged these problematic norms. Instead, I opted to work more directly with the unit managers to help them recognize—and confront—the elements of the team culture that created such barriers to diversity. In my work with the managers and team leaders, I contrasted "individualized empowerment" with "collective empowerment" (see table 4.3). Individualized empowerment can set up a culture that is not supportive of diversity and where management is constrained in holding people accountable for teamwork.

TABLE 4.3 · CONTRASTING MODELS OF EMPOWERMENT

INDIVIDUALIZED EMPOWERMENT	COLLECTIVE EMPOWERMENT
Focus on independence	Focus on interdependence
Accountable primarily to oneself	Accountability to the team
Focus on own job and getting it done well	Thinking about the overall team functioning
Scanning the environment for impact on self	Being aware that whatever you do will have an impact on others
Self protective stance ("That's not my job")	Looking out for the team ("How can I help?")

I urged the managers to decide whether they considered the need for change important enough to expend the energy required to shift the unit culture. If they were committed to change, they would need to create a readiness for teamwork by disrupting the status quo (unfreezing the system) on two fronts: first, through changes in basic expectations (e.g., making expectations for teamwork explicit and included in performance evaluations), and second, through an increased managerial presence even if that would feel counter to the individualized empowerment being promoted by the company (including greater supervision and oversight, as well as facilitated team meetings to discuss team functioning). If creating more inclusive and cooperative teams was the goal, the Processing Unit was not ready for the degree of independence it had been granted. This analysis seemed to hit a responsive chord. I worked with mangers to outline strategies for communicating strong expectations for collective empowerment, both by celebrating ways of supporting one another and by holding workers accountable for their impact on team functioning though regular team meetings and incorporating this criterion into performance evaluations. The leadership group opted to move forward with these recommendations on their own, so my work with this unit was temporarily done.

A little over two years later, Keitha asked me to do an assessment of ongoing issues on this unit to help set the stage for a unit manager—Julia, a Latina with strong engineering skills and a recent MBA—due to arrive on the scene in a couple of months. Keitha was concerned about both ongoing tensions among team members and newly emerging complaints from workers in reaction to the management styles of the team leaders. The primary goals were to assess the varied team cultures from shift to shift (with particular attention to management and coaching styles) and the potential climate for supporting women workers. I agreed to do a general assessment and make recommendations to a team consisting of the new unit manager, the previous acting manager, two team leaders (each responsible for half of the unit), Keitha, and Rich.

So again, I headed out into the plant to interview workers from each of the four teams (two day and two night shifts). Some issues were similar to those encountered two years earlier, but there had also been progress on many issues. Overall, workers said there was increased attention to ensuring that people were doing their jobs (accountability) as well as to fostering good relations among team members (cohesion). These themes were important aspects of our previous consultation. However, interestingly, the relative emphasis on these two elements of effective, inclusive teams was not balanced in the same ways by all shifts. Those working on the day shifts were more focused on accountability, and those working on the night shifts were more concerned about cohesion. Problems were emerging because both qualities were not being addressed by both teams.

Accountability without a sense of being connected to a team can lead to fending for oneself and interpersonal negativity (e.g., "backstabbing"). Although most agreed that much more energy was being channeled into holding people accountable for making positive contributions, several people on days still did not see the need for teamwork ("I don't really see anyone else during most of my shift so teamwork doesn't have to happen") and did not feel interpersonal tensions could be addressed ("When the other guy doesn't do his job, you just have to grin and bear it—get used to it"). Generally, operators were offended by any coworker (and, ironically, especially the team leaders) who told others what to do: "Who died and made you boss?" As a result, the lack of coordination was self-perpetuating: "If you feel like nobody is helping you, it's harder to help others." They felt that it was not OK to ask others for help, because it would be experienced as an illegitimate demand. Morning meetings were not being used to address emerging conflicts, and there had not been regular full unit meetings in a while. Once again, there were few places for coworkers to really interact with each other about meaningful team issues. Without such times and spaces, workers were taking their frustrations "to the hill" (i.e., HR) versus dealing more directly with one another.

On the other hand, cohesion within a shift group with a low sense of accountability seemed to contribute to a lack of connection to overall Chem-Pro goals (i.e., the production of a high-quality product). Workers on night shifts felt more connected to one another but described their sense that man-

TABLE 4.4 · ACCOUNTABILITY-COHESION BALANCE

	LOW ACCOUNTABILITY	HIGH ACCOUNTABILITY
Low cohesion	Apathy	Fending for self; interpersonal negativity = > Need intervention to increase sense of connection to the team
High Cohesion	Stick together but adversarial relations with organization = > Need intervention to increase connection to ChemPro goals	Effective, positive working relationships

agement did not know them and did not care. Some described themselves as "the forgottens" and noted, "The main contact of night guys with team leaders is when they have done something wrong." The cohesion was built around sharing their sense of invisibility and their collective sense of being "burnt" (i.e., that mistakes were attended to but their hard work was not getting noticed). A dilemma for management was that increased monitoring of the night shifts might increase compliance but would likely also increase alienation.

One set of challenges I put to the Processing leadership is summarized in table 4.4. They needed to build stronger, respectful relationships with operators and help them see that their work was valued (especially on night shifts). On day shifts, they needed to strengthen positive connections and effective communication among shift members. They also needed to develop additional ways for workers to raise issues with one another on the unit before lodging a formal complaint with HR (including setting aside time in morning meeting explicitly for touching base on team relationships, "having management come down and talk more," and designing other places/settings to deal with conflicts).

In order to address some of the concerns about the supervisory style of the team leaders, I drew a distinction between "checking in" versus "checking on." Staying in touch with people and monitoring people's behavior are both strategies for holding people accountable, but the two approaches have very different impacts. "Checking in" or staying in touch can help people stay connected to the work (i.e., feel cared about and more connected to ChemPro). Some newly initiated early morning visits by one of the team leaders were generally appreciated as a sign of support and backup. "Checking on" or monitoring can generate a backlash, which we were beginning to see in the intensifying and converging complaints about another team leader who showed up for a surprise visit at 3:00 A.M. (which was experienced as an effort to "catch us doing something wrong"). We knew from the situation with Michelle that Processing operators were cohesive enough to rally troops in a significant pushback against change—particularly if it was accompanied by what they sensed as a lack of goodwill: "You don't usually see management, but if you do, it's usually bad news." It can be particularly stressful when an emphasis on mistakes is paired with a need for more coaching: "It's high stakes—you learn rules by breaking them, and then risk losing your job for making the mistake."

My recommendations were for the managers to keep the supervisory emphasis on staying in touch rather than surveillance. I challenged them to work on being visible, available, and interested; making expectations about production explicit on a regular basis; giving clear messages about what *outcomes* were important and about how unit regulations were connected to these outcomes; catching people being good, not just bad; doing regular "rounds" early in the morning to check in with people on both day and night shifts. I also recommended that team leaders hold periodic early evening meetings that could include both day and night shifts to share observations and go over expectations. While we went over these issues during my assessment feedback meeting, I recommended that the team leaders could benefit from additional training and mentoring on supervision skills (with particular emphasis on positive, proactive management styles rather than negative, punitive styles) that would focus on meeting production goals more than on addressing infractions of the rules.

I was also asked to assess the team's readiness to accept women into their ranks. Most of the men in Processing truly believed that a woman would be welcome "if she could do the work" and that the primary barrier was the physical nature of the job, not the team dynamics. I took this as an honest, well-intentioned perception; most of the men were willing to be open-minded. However, any acceptance of women would clearly be based on the premise that *she* must adapt to their way of doing things and that they should not have to adapt to her (including on such issues as topics of conversation, style of joking and teasing, and ways of "bonding"). It was clear that there was not much openness to *mutual* accommodation; rather, she would need to fit in "with us." It was also telling to listen to the message embedded in comments like "I wouldn't want my girlfriend to work here." In other words, any woman team member would need to be unlike the women they knew and loved (i.e., be more like a man).

Given that most of the men believed a woman could make it on the unit, it seemed a distraction to argue about whether the physical nature of the work was the primary barrier. Instead, I suggested that the only way to really assess and address the situation would be to actually hire women onto the unit. I agreed with their sense that if women were going to succeed, ChemPro should hire at least two at the same time, preferably onto the same shift. The unit manager and the team leaders would need to *proactively* monitor the situation by coaching everyone in an ongoing manner. Simultaneously, everyone would benefit from the planned job redesign efforts and the installation of new self-cleaning kettles.

It was clear to me that the managers would have to address the issue of who should be adapting to whom. They could do this by emphasizing how mutual accommodation was something the men were already doing for each other (e.g., I heard stories of workers providing backup for shorter male coworkers, older men, and/or workers who simply needed to get into better physical condition). Managers would have to support both the current men on the unit and any newly hired women, working with each group to anticipate the potential pitfalls. The male workers might be tempted to either overprotect or avoid the women—neither of which would be particularly helpful. Any new women might need help seeing challenges from male coworkers as part of the dynamics of change instead of taking the offensive behavior personally.

The consultation was arranged before Julia was hired as department manager, and I began interviewing for the assessment phase before she started full-time. I met with her and the leadership team to give feedback soon after she arrived. While the issues I summarized and the recommendations I offered resonated for the group, it was clear that the new manager needed to develop her own agenda for tightening things up on the unit. Her independence was particularly important as a woman of color on a unit so historically dominated by white men, and she needed to establish herself as a strong independent leader before she could work with recommendations from an outside consultant. Although rushed to advise a unit that I felt some obligation to guide, I also needed to make space for Julia's chosen approach.

PREPPING: CHANGING SKILL EXPECTATIONS

Prepping is literally "on the other side of the tracks" from Processing, and while also predominantly male, it had historically had the largest percentage of people of color (25 percent black men at the time of our consultation). Out of twenty-four workers, there was one white woman, six black men, and seventeen white men, four of whom were first-generation Portuguese immigrants. I was brought in by a black man who had recently been moved over from another management position to supervise this unit because of recent "racial issues."

The reputation of years past was that anyone who gave management trouble would get "shipped off" to Prepping. The unit was also sometimes referred to as the "little mafia," given its reputation for being very close-mouthed. Issues got "settled" within the unit (e.g., fights could break out and no one would talk about it). As in Processing, a primary challenge facing Prepping was to shift from an independent individual focus to a collaborative team orientation. However, rather than being rooted in a sense of superiority and independence, some of the barriers to teamwork here were more gritty and basic. The assessment interviews revealed a unit under considerable stress.

Most team members were hard workers and committed operators, and they seemed to appreciate this about one another. This was not, as its reputation might lead one to suspect, a unit full of uncooperative employees. There were several individuals who were willing to step up and take leadership roles, and most accepted that changing organizational demands meant they would have to get better at working together. However, their experiences varied widely, and, at times, interviewees seemed to be describing completely different units. Some described a friendly, helpful group, while others felt isolated, alienated, and alone. There were, in addition, significant personal, interpersonal, and structural barriers to enhanced teamwork. Even though many of the workers had been on the unit for a considerable length of time, most expressed little sense of working together as a *team*. In a related way, only a few expressed much sense of personal responsibility for improving teamwork. The group's problems had been around for such a long time that people had accepted the current patterns and climate as just the way things were. As a result, the feeling seemed to be that each person just had to learn to live with it. In other words, since these were chronic problems—not a crisis—there was little faith that much could be done to make things different. In fact, there were subgroups that felt that those who bought into any organizational change goals were "traitors."

The primary "glue" that held the group together was the sharing of complaints (and gossip) about one another. One worker described it as "nonstop baby stuff"—talk about who's doing what, who's getting away with what, and who's doing more than who. Another said, interestingly, "You'd never believe the stuff that goes on here. You could write a book about it." The most common mode of interaction was razzing and dismissive banter. Joking, sarcasm, and talking behind each others' backs were recognized by team members as potentially problematic but also as having the positive effect of allowing workers to connect with one another in at least some manner. One person commented, "We need another way to be friendly . . . we can't just be quiet," but other types of interactions were rare. The banter often had very sexist and racist themes. Two workers who took on team leader roles around this time were derided as "the girls." While workers rarely confronted one another around treatment or jokes they found offensive, the tension would periodically erupt.

There had been a "racial incident" just prior to my work with this team. A white operator posed a question to an African American coworker. "If you were offered a million dollars but they called you a n——, what would you do?" The black man was furious, and the white operator appeared to have no clue why his statement might be offensive (even though it was common knowledge that this particular black man had a long history of feeling isolated and discriminated against on this unit). The white man was written up for his comment and still professed confusion about what he had done wrong, "I have no problem with 'them'—I was only joking." This revealed serious personal blinders, an individual shortcoming compounded by the fact that the common "language" on the unit was the sharing of insults, so he thought he was acting in sync with unit norms. Drawing a line between "harmless" banter and offensive racist and sexist comments can be a particular challenge for those who do not think they are accountable for their *impact* on others. The managers, backed by HR, however, sent a clear message that comments like his would not be tolerated.

The unit's general lack of connection to broader organizational goals further intensified the spotlight on interpersonal dramas. In addition, the structure of the unit's work made any resolution of interpersonal tensions difficult. There were few opportunities for the team to meet as a group, and when they did, the agenda was rarely focused on addressing conflicts or other interpersonal issues. Past "injustices" would often linger indefinitely, since there was no forum for resolving them. The team meetings that did occur were typically more focused on planning the work flow and/or communicating information about organization-wide changes.

In fact, during this period there was a major work redesign effort under way, which was consuming significant organizational energy. A consultant from Corporate was actively working with the unit to redesign job descrip-

tions, the division of job tasks, and the flow of the work as well as how decisions were made on a daily basis. With the redesign, there was going to be a
decreasing emphasis on specialization and an increasing emphasis on cross-
training and the ability to do multiple types of tasks. More of the production
work was becoming computerized, and the company was relying much more
heavily on computer-based programs for both skills training and for ongoing
daily communication. Simultaneously, ChemPro was embracing the notion of
"empowered work teams," relegating increased decision making to workers.

In Prepping, there was considerable stress associated with the work
redesign and other changes. The changing expectations would require skills
many workers did not have (e.g., literacy skills, computer skills). Workers
who probably had the capacity to learn the skills feared they didn't. In addition, the advantages of empowered teams were not clear to workers. In many
minds, the advantages of the increased independence did not clearly out-
weigh the stress of the additional responsibilities (particularly when people
were unsure they had the skills and/or unsure how the increased responsibility would be related to reward structures). One worker summed it up simply:
"All the responsibility is driving people cuckoo." Lack of clarity about what
the redesign changes would really mean added to both a sense of worry and
a sense of cynicism about fairness. The stress added to the already strong "us
versus them" culture (operators vs. management; ChemPro vs. Corporate;
workers vs. CEO) and intensified the low trust among coworkers. There was
a sense that it was unfair to hire people for one set of skills and then later
expect another set (even if the "later" was twenty-five years later). Even though
the consultant from Corporate was trying to involve operators in the decision
making around the redesign, the reorganizing efforts were experienced as a
signal of Corporate's lack of caring about ChemPro workers.

Some of the interpersonal tensions on the unit seemed related to ways
people tried to cover up personal anxieties. As would be expected, those who
had difficulties with basic literacy skills were particularly uneasy, since they
were being expected to become not just print literate but *computer* literate.
One worker refused to "sign off" on any of his online training and was not
reading any of the in-house e-mail notices posted at the beginning of each shift.
Some coworkers attributed his refusal to "resistance" or "hostility toward
change," but it seemed very much an issue of saving face—panic, even—
when confronted with the specter of revealing his lack of basic literacy skills.

As with other consultations, my assessment summary was the result of
intensive interviewing. I then met with the unit manager and the team leaders

to share the feedback. By the time of this consultation, I had a good working relationship with this particular manager, one of the few blacks who had been in any sort of leadership role when I began working with ChemPro. He had given me my first tour of the plant in 1995, and I had met with him during our very first round of interviews. He had been a member of our initial Steering Team and supportive of the Workplace Chemistry Initiative over the years.

In the feedback session, I traced several problematic interpersonal patterns that were getting in the way of more effective team functioning and then put the team issues into the broader context of the reorganization and work redesign. Together, we brainstormed several potential action steps including presenting the interview summaries to the team and brainstorming solutions with workers, providing training in conflict resolution or diversity skills, restructuring team meetings so that interpersonal issues could be addressed, developing a worker-based conflict resolution team, getting a critical mass of operators into the Workplace Chemistry Training, and increasing individualized feedback and coaching from the manager and team leaders.

I shared the schema in figure 4.3 with the manager and his leadership group as a way to summarize the dynamics that had emerged in the interviews and to organize action recommendations. The unit culture was contributing to difficult team issues, but this relationship was intensified by the stress associated with all the work redesign efforts. Critical barriers to managing the stress constructively were the lack of skills that would now be required as a result of the redesign and the lack of settings where team issues could be addressed. We agreed that it was critical for the unit leaders to begin by remedying the issues that were intensifying the stress and thereby contributing to the team tensions (the shaded boxes) before we could embark on any broader efforts to change the unit culture. Until the basic skill issues were addressed, we anticipated that the anxiety over the changes would make it impossible to focus on team building and diversity issues. The unit manager began to immediately assess the technical skills each operator needed in order to meet new job requirements resulting from the workplace redesign and self-empowered team goals. This aspect of the work, very much at the individual level of analysis, was impossible to ignore, and the manager was well equipped to move forward on this front without further consultation.

We also agreed that the unit needed settings where workers could more safely and effectively deal with emerging questions, concerns, and conflicts. So rather than delve into interpersonal conflict resolution skills of individual workers, the manager, team leaders, and I strategized about how to structure

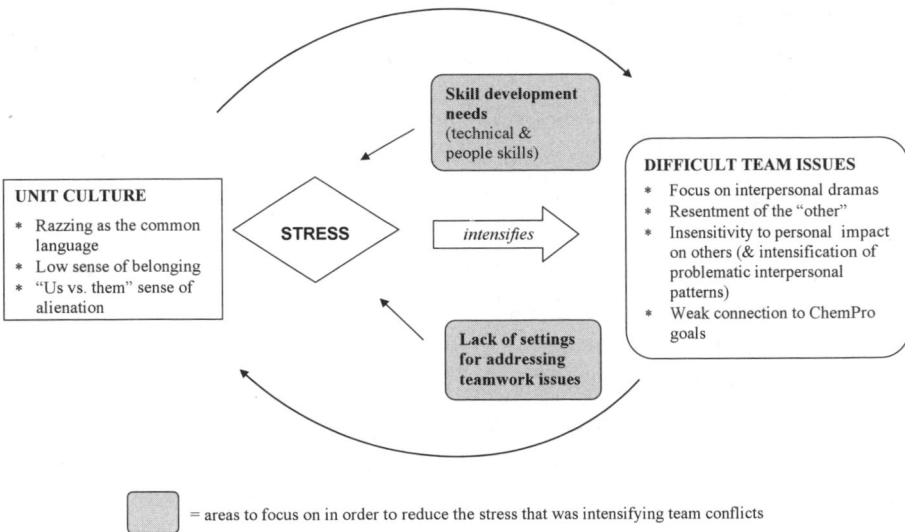

FIGURE 4.3 Prepping Team Issues

settings (like team meetings and shift change meetings) so that concerns could be more comfortably raised. I also consulted with the unit leaders about how they could more effectively facilitate such meetings. In essence, we opted to focus on changing the work environment through these efforts. Moving away from an explicit team-building focus seemed to be a relief to everyone involved (managers *and* workers), and, from all reports, the dual focus on basic skill building and creation of problem-solving settings helped tremendously to relieve the anxiety that was fueling interpersonal tensions.

Clearly, many issues with racial undertones lingered and were left unaddressed by this consultation. We did help reinforce the importance of disciplinary action for "bigoted jokes," but, more than likely, the racist attitudes of some workers were not changed. We did support the new unit manager in the initiatives he had begun, but we did not directly address the concern of at least one black worker that having a black manager limited his protection ("When a black get in charge, he afraid to do anything for black people—afraid of being accused of favorites"), and we did not address whites' feelings of resentment when reprimanded for racist comments (e.g., "You have to watch what you say to 'them,' but they [blacks] don't have to watch what they say to you"). We started where we felt we must. Progress on areas related to inclusion and diversity seemed predicated on—and could build on—taking care of some basic issues first.

ecological reflections: understanding team culture as the essential medium for change

The ecological framework emphasizes the power of context to shape a person's behavior as well as the reciprocal influence that people have on their social settings. In an organization, an individual's work team is the context that shapes life in the most daily of ways. In both formal and informal ways, teams communicate expectations about ways of operating and about what is and what is not considered acceptable. In addition, a work team is the social structure that interprets broader organizational values and conveys expectations about how those values will operate on a day-to-day basis. In our consultations, we observed a wide range of team dynamics that had implications for the genuine inclusion of diverse groups of workers. One powerful influence was the existence of social norms that emphasized sameness. We also saw ways in which the organization-wide priorities for participation had the potential to conflict with diversity values in situations where team autonomy could perpetuate intolerant attitudes. Managers and team leaders are critical in supporting inclusive team processes, but even leadership is best understood as grounded in and shaped by context.

CHALLENGING TEAM CULTURES THAT PRESS FOR SAMENESS

A dilemma plaguing most of our team consultations was the ways in which homogeneity breeds homogeneity. In chemistry, opposites attract—those positive and negative ions seek each other out. This is not necessarily true, however, in human interactions. A preference for homogeneous work groups and an accompanying press for divergent members to conform have been observed in a wide range of groups.[10] Historical forces lay a particular groundwork, which then supports informal processes that continue to hinder effective diversity—in complex and multifaceted ways. At ChemPro, hiring practices yielded a relatively homogeneous workforce, which then reinforced particular informal processes that served to maintain that homogeneity. While the resulting personal connections appeared to increase loyalty to the organization, this "family" culture also intensified a press for people to be alike. For example, a black interviewee noted that the highest-paid man in his group was a white man who "doesn't talk well . . . he talks the way the others want him to talk."

Prevailing societal beliefs about "fairness" also emphasize sameness—so much so as to be a barrier to the meaningful involvement of diverse participants. Common folk wisdom invokes images of "color blindness" as the ideal as we strive to create equitable environments. The reasoning is that we should treat everyone "the same" since, if we are not *really* prejudiced, we should not notice—much less care about—someone's gender, race, ethnicity, sexual orientation, or disability (or other sources of difference for that matter). The implication is that the act of recognizing gender or race is an act of discrimination. However, many have argued that how we make sense of diversity is organized by dominant cultural values, and thus "sameness" embodies a hierarchy of valued ways of being in the world. Discussions of diversity can be haunted by this confusion of sameness and equality, and most settings have not stopped to reflect on the underlying assumptions about sameness and difference that shape their practices.[11] These assumptions, however, become interwoven into an organizational culture and serve as the basic foundation for policies and procedures as well as for informal expectations.[12]

Sameness paradigms suggest that all people should be treated identically. This perspective is at the heart of much of the affirmative action debate: opponents argue that differences in treatment represent inequality. This perspective promotes freedom for people to pursue opportunities but assumes that differential outcomes are a reflection of natural processes. This worldview assumes that if people do not get an equal share, it is due to some *personal* failing. To question such natural outcomes is seen as unjust and unfair. In fact, the acknowledgment that differences exist is mistaken for the creation of differences. This view of sameness stands in contrast to difference paradigms, which incorporate an acknowledgment of variations in access to opportunities, resources, and power based on group membership. Inequality, from this alternative perspective, is seen as resulting from *ignoring* these differences. Difference paradigms are not just concerned with the distribution of resources; they also actively recognize the sociopolitical nature of differences and include historical, cultural, and institutional sources of injustice.[13]

These divergent perspectives have tremendous implications for how a setting will organize to support diverse groups. Sameness paradigms guide the dominant view of equality in our society, undoubtedly because they are so congruent with American values for individualism. Difference paradigms have been a dominant view in much of the literature on the promotion of racial and ethnic diversity and most feminist analyses of gender. Sameness is acontextual; difference frameworks are contextualized and thus more compatible with an ecological perspective. These two types of views do not merely reflect contrasting assumptions; they reflect divergence in very deeply held values about justice and fairness. As Scott and other feminist writers have argued, when difference is posed as the opposite of equality, it presents an impossible choice, since it poses the recognition of historical and current power differences as antithetical to equality. She argues that if we ignore differences in the case of subordinated groups, we "leave in place a faulty neutrality" that begs the question of, sameness relative to what? or according to whose definition of "normative"?[14] This perspective ignores histories that support the assignment of differential values (power) to one group over another. It is essentially an acontextual and ahistorical view.

As we experienced with the team consultations, if unquestioned, this "faulty neutrality" of the sameness paradigm can be further obscured by group dynamics. Research has documented a preference for and attraction to others who are perceived to be more like oneself, which unfolds as a preference for homogeneous work groups, which tend to be more familiar, predictable, and comfortable.[15] Thus, teams tend to select and reinforce members who are most like the dominant group. Without concerted efforts to the contrary, they can emphasize the characteristics that members have in common so much that a monolithic team culture develops, where what is shared by the dominant group becomes considered normative. A strong press for conformity and little tolerance for those who move outside those norms can result.[16]

Without norms to acknowledge that such practices and the accompanying interpretation of behavior exclude some nonmajority members (even if unwittingly), diversity is not supported and people outside the majority group will continue to be defined as "misfits" or, translated into the factory language, "bad workers." The result can be a strong monolithic culture that maintains itself by making anyone who does not fit with the dominant assumptions and norms feel unwelcome, thereby further diminishing their potential to influence the culture of the group. To treat everyone "the same" on these units would be to legitimize the marginalization of those who are not white and who are not male.

CONFRONTING CONTRADICTIONS BETWEEN
PARTICIPATION AND DIVERSITY

A second dilemma that lurked around the edges of all the team consultations was similar to the paradigmatic tensions between sameness and difference. It revolved around contradictions between the organizational values for participation and support for diversity. Research has indicated that participative processes can enhance the satisfaction, commitment, and creativity of organization members. However, the process of promoting broad participation while working to increase sensitivity to the diversity among workers brings with it a delicate balance—particularly when attempted in the context of team and organizational cultures that are built on the preferences of the majority group. In the process of soliciting "participation," minority voices often get lost—sometimes just ignored or considered irrelevant but sometimes more actively defined as an annoyance or distraction or even as "disloyal." In such cases, the goals of worker participation and team empowerment can actually work *against* efforts to promote smooth and productive working relationships across gender and racial differences. The accompanying irony is that while an organization may be adopting initiatives with the hope of enhancing participation and empowerment of people previously excluded from decision making, the group and organizational dynamics can play out such that only those workers who are members of the majority group become fully able and/or comfortable to participate in these new practices.

Employee participation and team empowerment have become popular buzz-words within organization development circles in the United States. Many companies have invested in developing what they refer to as an "empowered workforce" that encourages broad participation in important work-related decisions. As implemented in most U.S. workplaces, the idea has generally been to enable employees to have more control over their work as they are given the responsibility to make more decisions without consulting with others. Such organizationally based empowerment initiatives rarely emphasize accountability for the impact of one's actions on other team members or truly alter the core hierarchy within the organization. Rather, they are interpreted within broader cultural and organizational value systems that embrace autonomy, individualism, and mastery. Employee empowerment initiatives can certainly be interpreted from a more collective value base and emphasize genuine collaboration. But in ChemPro's case, we were not talking about the definitions of empowerment that incorporate collective action or the empowered worker of labor movements,[17] but rather a management approach of dispersing decision making broadly throughout the organization. Thus, while collaborative processes and shared decision making may be promoted in the spirit of broad involvement, they can also unwittingly function to disenfranchise nonmajority members.

ChemPro valued "worker empowerment," and decisions about workplace issues were increasingly being delegated to work teams (from daily problem solving, to work design issues, to scheduling—with some expectation that eventually even performance evaluations and pay raises could be determined by coworkers). The dynamics within both Processing and the Maintenance

Unit, however, illustrate how adopting values that support participation in line with the notion of individual empowerment (e.g., mastery and self-sufficiency) can work against connectedness and, as a result, come into direct conflict with establishing team cultures that support diversity. In such settings, not all members of all groups are necessarily welcome to participate in the same way. Greater inclusion of women and members of marginalized racial/ethnic groups is best supported when attention is paid to the great diversity in terms of how people would prefer to participate and whether the substance of their participation would be syntonic with their team culture. In fact, the ethic of independence and lack of accountability on these units was buoyed by an organizational language of empowerment. If attention is not paid to the *context* of participation—in terms of individual preferences as well as dominant team values—not all voices and perspectives will be represented. When control is conceded to employees without there being some sense of accountability and connectedness to *all* members of the group, it becomes possible for the ethos of the team to be defined in line with the preferences of the dominant group (i.e., white men).

UNDERSTANDING LEADERS IN RELATION TO THEIR TEAMS

I have focused much of this chapter around problematic interpersonal dynamics; however, they are obviously only part of the team story. It seems essential, at this juncture, to return to the role of organizational leaders. Many workplace diversity authors address the critical role of managers in recruiting, retaining, and promoting a diverse workforce, and advice abounds about the requirements for organizational leaders who strive to support a diversified workforce: They should serve as role models. They should be able to span various groups, be proactive in their support, and be prepared to engage in a multileveled approach to facilitating diversity. They need to be keenly aware of their own biases and also be ready to confront the types of team dynamics that lead to ethnocentrism and resistance to change. They need finely tuned facilitation skills, an understanding of how to ensure that minority members are heard, and an ability to mediate conflict situations.[18] No small set of demands!

Ultimately, however, effective leadership of diverse teams cannot be reduced to a checklist of predefined skills. Effective support for diversity is also an issue of how a manager's style "fits" with the dynamics of her/his particular team. A team has a set of dynamic patterns that shape the ways in which diverse workers are included (and/or excluded) in daily work. As is clear from the sample consultations summarized here, these patterns are shaped by such issues as the history and evolved traditions of the team, its demographic makeup, the changing organizational demands, and the current diversity dynamics of the group. Leaders stand in *relationship to these patterns*—not just in relationship to individual team members. That is, leaders help to shape the interactional patterns among team members, at the same time that their behavior is shaped by those very same patterns. The issue is not just how well a leader manages a diverse group but, more importantly, how her/his managerial approach might contribute to, intensify, moderate, and/or in other ways shape the team dynamics—and ultimately the impact of those team dynamics on promoting equity and inclusion among diverse workers. A manager's particular leadership style has an impact on team members' experiences of themselves, of others, of the relationships among team members, and of the possibilities for alternative futures. Simultaneously, the evolving team dynamics shape what ways of being are open to the manager—leaders both alter team patterns and are altered by them. All this works together to construct a team culture, which then becomes an entity or force unto itself. The principles of person-environment adaptation, phenomenology, and interdependence are all at play.

An ecological analysis compels us to consider the requirements for leadership as a function of the particular team context s/he is trying to manage and of the leader's relationship to the patterns that make up that context. For example, in the Maintenance Unit, Jack's reliance on informal networks became a barrier to increasing the diversity within the team. His discomfort with directly confronting conflict further marginalized people outside his informal (all white male) inner circle. The tension that such a style generated could then easily become a rationale for surrounding himself with people who would not confront him and pressure him to change. Although along many dimensions he was a very competent manager, his leadership style was a distinct barrier to increasing diversity. I do not believe for a minute that he intended to exclude anyone, but intentions are largely irrelevant here. It is not the intention but the impact that shapes the ongoing patterns. In the case of Maintenance, these patterns also sat within a broader context—i.e., the culture of the skilled trades, which has been described as reinforcing homogeneity through the system of apprenticeships and mentoring structures.[19] To better support diversity, Jack would have needed to push himself to go further outside his comfort zone and reach out to the members of this team with whom there would be less interpersonal predictability.

In contrast, in Security, the manager's primary task for supporting diversity was to ensure that there were regular meetings structured to promote problem solving about emerging concerns. He also needed to hold team members to the personal commitments made during the consultation and periodically set aside time to facilitate sessions where they could be reminded about what they valued and appreciated about one another. In Drying, essential "diversity skills" for the manager were to advocate effectively to have the pay grade reevaluated and to get out from under the devalued mantle of being the "women's unit."

During both of my consultations with Processing, the unit was in transition from one manager to another, and, each time, some workers complained that part of the problem with the unit was a "lack of a management presence." Over time, the unit managers had included a black man, a white woman, a white man, a different white woman, a different white man, and a Latina—and all faced similar challenges in trying to break into the fiercely independent culture of the unit. The challenge for leadership was to earn the respect of the workers while also challenging their operational style—a heavy hand with a soft glove. Managers needed to set clear expectations for respectful behavior, and promote change both from top down and from bottom up.

In Prepping, the simple fact that the manager was black set up a distinctive set of challenges. He had to navigate a tricky terrain, with some of the whites on the unit accusing him of being "overly" responsive to racial issues while some blacks worried that he was avoiding support for black workers out of a fear that he would seen as living up to the whites' worries about him. That type of bind is very demanding of a leader. S/he has to step up to the challenge of moving forward without taking the inevitable accusations personally. In this case, the Prepping manager was amazingly able to hear the conflicting allegations as reflecting the anxiety that *all* his team members (black and white) were feeling about the rush of impending changes.

The essential diversity requirement for leaders that may emerge from this analysis is that they must develop an ability to assess the unique patterns on their team, understand their role in those patterns, and be able to challenge exclusionary team dynamics generated by those patterns.

SYNTHESIS

In discussing the importance of local knowledge, Phil Mann wisely noted, "Scientifically rational plans to reform or manage society have foundered from a failure to take the nature of the local situation into account [particularly in] addressing questions about program implementation."[20] The ecological perspective requires us to locate our change efforts in the specifics of the local situation—in ChemPro's case addressing the team pressures for conformity, pointing out the value contradictions that reduced accountability, and supporting leadership in challenging exclusionary norms.

A consultation, however, is time limited—an intervention at one moment or during one period in time at best. I was just a visitor at ChemPro who stopped in for a while, messed with the family dynamics, and left. I was not even a very important player in the full family drama. As consultants, we can provoke some shifts, but the real work of organizational change is in the hands of the people who populate the organization on a daily basis over time. To support their work beyond specific training workshops and consultations, we can work with them to establish some practices that institutionalize a value for and commitment to diversity that becomes part of the regular fabric of organizational life.

synthesis

ASSESSING AND INSTITUTIONALIZING CHANGE

IN CHEMISTRY, "SYNTHESIS" is the formation of a more complex compound by combining simpler compounds or elements. In organizational work, we are also interested in understanding how separate elements of a change initiative combine to affect the organization as a whole. Harking back to where we started, the overall goal of the Workplace Chemistry Initiative was to develop an organization in which the contributions of diverse people would be valued and fully tapped toward accomplishing the goals of the organization. The vision, as stated by the initial Workplace Chemistry Steering Team, was:

> To create a work environment at ChemPro where every individual regardless of race, gender, and/or disability can work at their best by creating a culture of flexibility and sense of inclusion where all people feel wanted and appreciated.

To address this vision, there were three threads of activities that made up the Workplace Chemistry Initiative: diversity-specific skill development activities (primarily through the survey feedback and the training as described in chapter 3), interpersonal skill and team capacity building (primarily through team consultations as described in chapter 4), and the institutionalization of organizational values for diversity. This last thread (i.e., efforts to incorporate the value for diversity throughout organizational practices) is the focus of the current chapter.

In addition, this chapter will look at the *impact* of the combined efforts on the organization as a whole. Beyond the stories and warm greetings from workers you have grown fond of, how do you really know if years of work on diversity concerns have had an enduring impact? This is no simple task, yet at ChemPro we wanted to document changes both for rationalizing all the effort that had gone into the initiative and for clarifying what next steps were needed.

efforts toward institutionalization

Some work to activate organizational-level structural and cultural change was integrated into the training and the consultation activities. I have already described the development of internal change agents (the initial Steering Team and the cotrainers) and the identification of an internal group to advocate for diversity goals (the People Team)—both important institutionalization strategies. There were additional simultaneous efforts aimed at weaving values for diversity into the fabric of daily life—some independently implemented by HR and some developed in collaboration with our group. Attention was devoted to addressing diversity goals in hiring practices and priorities, criteria for performance appraisals, policies for disciplinary actions, leadership development, succession planning, and work-life policies. Incorporating the value for diversity into ongoing organizational policies and procedures is oft touted as the missing piece in workplace diversity initiatives.[1]

HIRING AND RETENTION

Under the HR leadership of both Keitha and Rich, there was a concerted effort to recruit and hire a more diverse workforce. Given the combination of fairly low turnover and downsizing, there was not much opportunity to dramatically change the complexion of the workforce, but the desire was there.

To assess employment patterns over time, we chose to look at three-year intervals. That is, we summarized personnel data for the year just before we began working with ChemPro (Year 0) and for Years 3 and 6.[2] Information was gathered though affirmative action reports and personnel turnover summaries. While none of the demographic changes reached statistical significance, the patterns are interesting. Over the years, the overall size of the plant workforce decreased slightly. With the reduction in force, the overall percentage of females within the plant declined slightly. Before we began, out of 211 employees, 17.1 percent were female. By Year 3, the size of the plant had decreased by 11, bringing the total number of employees to 200, with 16 percent female. By Year 6, the plant had decreased again by another 5 employees, bringing the total to 195, 15.9 percent of whom were female. Eight of the 43 (18.6 percent) employees hired into permanent positions since the beginning of the Workplace Chemistry Initiative were women; however, approximately the same percentage (18.0 percent) of the 59 full-time people who left during that time were also women (and 18.9 percent of the 37 who left since Year 3 were women). What all this boils down to with respect to the employ-

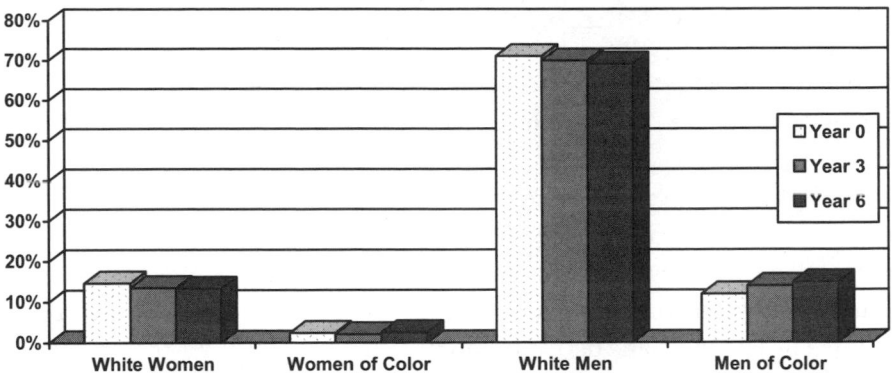

FIGURE 5.1 Plant Demographics over Time

ment of women is that the plant maintained the status quo. The change of note is that the percentages of women who were black, Asian, and Latina gradually increased over time (13.9 percent in Year 0, 15.6 percent in Year 3, 16.1 percent in Year 6) (see figure 5.1).

The company made more progress in hiring and retaining people of color than women. The percentage of workers of color by Year 6 was 17.4 percent (primarily African American, Caribbean black, Latino/a, and Asian workers)—up 3 percent since the start of our work. However, the gender ratios among people of color paralleled the ratios plantwide, (i.e., still skewed by sex). Over a third (37.2 percent) of the 43 employees who were hired over the six years were people of color. Similarly about 34 percent of the 32 employees hired since Year 3 were people of color. In terms of attrition, about 20 percent of those who had left over the six years were people of color. Unlike the trends for white women, the hiring of people of color—mostly men—outpaced attrition.

These gender and race patterns may be related to the fact that most hiring was occurring for operators on the plant floor. Simply put, there were more opportunities to diversify where there were more job openings. However, these were jobs heavily dominated by men, and the new hires did little to change that. The whole plant remained highly segregated along gender-stereotypical lines. Males continued to dominate the Production and Facilities departments, while women were better represented in administrative and laboratory positions (see figure 5.2).

The plant also remained fairly segregated by race. People of color were never the majority in any department, but by Year 6 there was higher representation in Production (22.7 percent) *and* Labs (25 percent) (up from 15.7

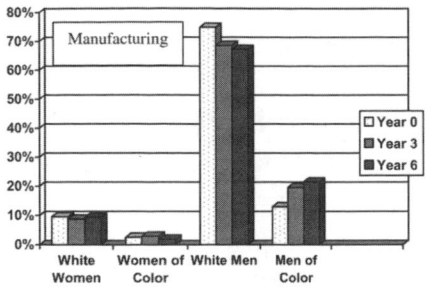

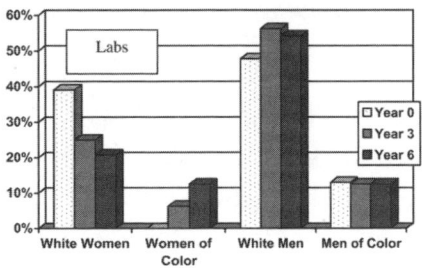

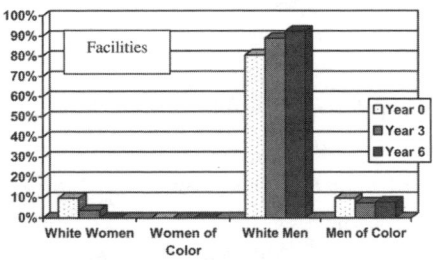

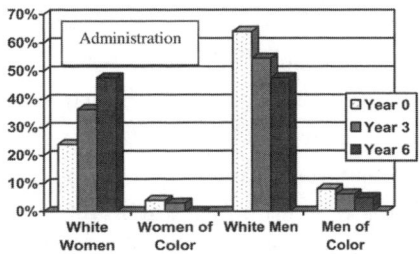

FIGURE 5.2 Demographics for ChemPro Departments

percent and 13 percent respectively) than in other areas. The pattern whereby most people of color in Production were clustered within Prepping remained fairly stable.

In sum, there was an increased presence of diverse employees in some quarters of the plant but not in others. While the overall representation of white women declined slightly, the percentage of workers of color increased. It is also worth noting that the increases in diversity occurred in the department in which there was the most turnover and thus the most opportunity for hiring from the outside (i.e., in Production). Simultaneously, women and people of color were becoming a significant proportion of the workers in Labs.

PROMOTION

In addition to hiring efforts, ChemPro was proactive in the identification and promotion of a diverse group of leaders. It instituted a process of providing additional training and development for workers who were considered to have management potential. Some organizations have developed programs specifically for leaders from underrepresented groups. ChemPro opted not to adopt a separate process. So the people identified for leadership development still included many white men (as that was still the majority in the larger pool of potential nominees); however, increasing numbers of people of color and women were also identified. Particularly within a relatively small plant, the development of leaders cannot easily become singularly focused on members of minority groups without being dismissed and resisted as reverse discrimination.

The supervisory structure of the Production Department shifted over time, but the basic hierarchy involved a Production Department manager, unit supervisors for each of the five manufacturing units, and team leaders under each unit supervisor. The team leaders were responsible for decision making and supervision of much of the daily work on the plant floor. In the early stages of the Workplace Chemistry Initiative, one aspect of leadership development involved capacity building for these team leaders. They all met together with Keitha on a regular basis in what she described as "case study meetings." These groups were an important strategic intervention, since the team leaders were the people most directly responsible for putting the diversity values into action. As Keitha reflected:

> We [upper level managers] didn't have to live with it like they did. The
> team leaders had to live with it in a very day-to-day, nitty-gritty way. So

for them, they had to change their whole decision making style—because that was really what we were asking them to do . . . Management can say all these nice things about "We want diversity. We want to do this," but the people who actually have to make the change are those first level supervisors.

Keitha organized these groups to help build supervisory competencies and provide support because she recognized the enormity of the shift in expectations:

It was a struggle. I think they were our weakest point in the organization, to be honest with you, because they were part of that old boy network . . . When you think about it, we were trying to change their whole mind set. Most of them had been operators for years, so it really was a change for them to not work from a favoritism perspective but instead base decisions on what was fair for all the individuals on their teams. So we worked with them on their everyday problems . . . they would raise an issue, we would discuss it and talk about ways they could solve it . . . I think it was helpful.

One of the most visible markers of the diversification in leadership was the eventual hiring of men of color into these team leader positions. When we began at ChemPro, the Production Department manager was a white woman, and there was one white woman and one black man among the five unit supervisors, but there was an entirely white male slate of team leaders. Between Years 3 and 6, a reorganization of the supervisory structure divided the production units into two sections called Manufacturing-1 (Prepping and Mixing) and Manufacturing-2 (Washing, Processing, and Drying). Each had its own supervisor, with team leaders under that person. Right after this reorganization, the supervisors for both sections were white men, but two of the four new team leaders in Manufacturing-1 were black men; two were white men. In Manufacturing-2, there were two white male and one black male team leaders. In Year 7, the presence of leaders of color increased further. Two black men were transferred to take over as supervisors of both sides of manufacturing, and half of the team leaders were black men.

What was notable here, however, was not only the numbers. Change was evident in the seemly simple fact that these black men accepted the positions. One of these new team leaders had been offered the position multiple times and had turned it down. Not only was he reluctant to be a "token black," but his wife had apparently encouraged him not to "be an Uncle Tom" or "go over to the other side." These new team leaders of color were also faced with rumblings at work about "being unqualified" and "only got the job because s/he's black." Behind any increasing numbers are complicated interpersonal dynamics—both inside the workplace and in people's lives outside. Stepping from "worker" to "management" is a shift in identity for any line worker but fraught with even more potential dangers for members of minority groups. Rich described the challenge as follows:

> I was highly impressed with Byron. I talked to him several times about becoming a team leader. He didn't want anything to do with it because he didn't want to be segregated from his crew, and he thought he'd be looked upon as management and so forth. And then finally one day I think the light went on and he said "look I gotta take care of myself and my family. What's this about?" And he asked me, and I said "okay" . . . We actually talked about this in the meeting when we knew we were gonna put Byron in the team leader position. "They are gonna assume that we are putting him in this position because he his black. And, so what are we gonna do about it?" And I said "well, we're not going stop that perception no matter what we do" . . . We put him in there and he went through hell. He was going to quit several times. I talked him out of it. They keyed his car. They just did nasty things to him and he wanted to quit but I said, "Why let them win? In case the next person happens to be a person of color, you don't want them to win" . . . That's how we've gotta keep doing it, you can't let them win. So I think Byron felt supported by Warren and me.

It had gotten a little better to be a black employee but not necessarily a black supervisor. There was still work to be done.

The top leadership team had also become somewhat more diverse over time. When we began, it consisted of five white men, one white woman, and one Asian man. Three years later, the leadership group had grown to nine people and had shifted from about 71 percent white men to over 55.5 percent women and people of color (44.4 percent women and 22.2 percent people of color, including Keitha, a black women, as well as three white women and a black man). By Year 6, the percentages had dipped to 36 percent women and/or people of color among the top eleven leaders (two white women, one woman of color, and one black man) but still remained higher than when we began. When we went back out to the plant about three years later, the leadership group was all white but half women. We learned that they were openly talking about gender and work/communication styles by all reading *Talking from 9 to 5* by Deborah Tannen and discussing it chapter by chapter.

PERFORMANCE APPRAISAL CRITERIA

Numbers of people are part of the story. Perhaps most noteworthy was the increased visibility of women in the ranks of leadership and the willingness of people of color, with some support from management, to begin to challenge the strong informal sanctions that had kept them out of management jobs. However, while representation is an essential component—clearly, there is no diversity to manage if you don't bring diverse people into the organization—there also needs to be some institutionalization of the expectation to *value* the diversity. Along these lines, I worked closely with Keitha, then Rich, on integrating diversity competencies into performance evaluation criteria. ChemPro already had effective performance appraisal (PA) mechanisms in place; my task was to advise HR about ways to incorporate new dimensions relevant to the inclusion of diverse groups.

We worked together to add diversity-related performance criteria for people at all levels of the organization; however, we considered leadership expectations particularly important leverage points. In the late 1990s, HR started conducting a "360-degree evaluation" of all people in any sort of leadership role. A "leader" included anyone who had the responsibility to do performance evaluations of others and/or was responsible for leading or directing the work of others. This group included upper-level managers, department managers, unit supervisors, and team leaders. The "360" involved soliciting input from the people who surround the manager, including his/her direct supervisor, peers, supervisees, *and* the president.

The 360 performance criteria were organized into categories based on the company's five core values of respect for employee dignity, integrity, trust, credibility, and continuous improvement and also included two leadership dimensions, which were *creating an exciting and rewarding workplace* and *building a performance-based culture*. The evaluation templates already included thirty-one specific criteria organized into these seven categories. I worked with HR to articulate nine additional diversity-specific criteria plus two other, more general criteria related to effective leadership of diverse groups. For example, under the "dignity" dimension, ChemPro already included *values and champions human differences*. We suggested adding more detail: *treats both men and women employees fairly, treats employees from all racial backgrounds fairly, treats employees of different ages fairly,* and *treats employees with disabilities fairly.* Under "integrity," we added a dimension important to diversity even though not directly signaling diversity content: *shows a high degree of personal integrity in dealing with others.* Under "creating an exciting and rewarding workplace," we added: *appreciates and encourages differences in people* and *effectively interacts with others.* For several years, our university-based group took on the task of summarizing the evaluations from all sources and providing individualized feedback for each leader.

Given that about a third of the final dimensions were relevant to the full inclusion of diverse groups and the effective management of differences, the performance evaluation process sent a clear message that fairness and equitable treatment were important values for the company. In addition, there was symbolic reinforcement of these values in the fact I coordinated the feedback summaries and our university group had become, in many people's minds, synonymous with the Workplace Chemistry Initiative.

PAs come along only once a year, so ongoing expectations for behavior in the plant were also critical. Warren established what he referred to as a "zero tolerance" policy for any behavior that was intimidating, harassing, or conveyed intolerance or bias toward any group. He made it clear that he expected HR and all managers to hold to the same standard. He not only threatened but he also followed through with disciplinary action against workers who engaged in inappropriate behavior. He was steady in his commitment to this policy over the years. As Rich reflected, "If I had gone in any other direction than severe repercussions for an offense, he would have been upset with me."

We had hoped that we might be able to track performance ratings and salaries over time and even do some comparison by race and sex. This would have provided a glimpse of changes in key indicators of performance and equity in reward structures. However, these data are highly confidential and very difficult to access. We had partial access but finally decided it would not be professionally responsible to work with incomplete data. It would not do justice to the story, and it would be unethical to draw any conclusions about such important dimensions if we could not more confidently stand by our data.

changes in organizational values

It is a cliché to say that oil and water don't mix. However, if you change the initial context—for example, add an emulsifier to the water—you can indeed create an "openness" to oil such that the two substance can mix. At ChemPro,

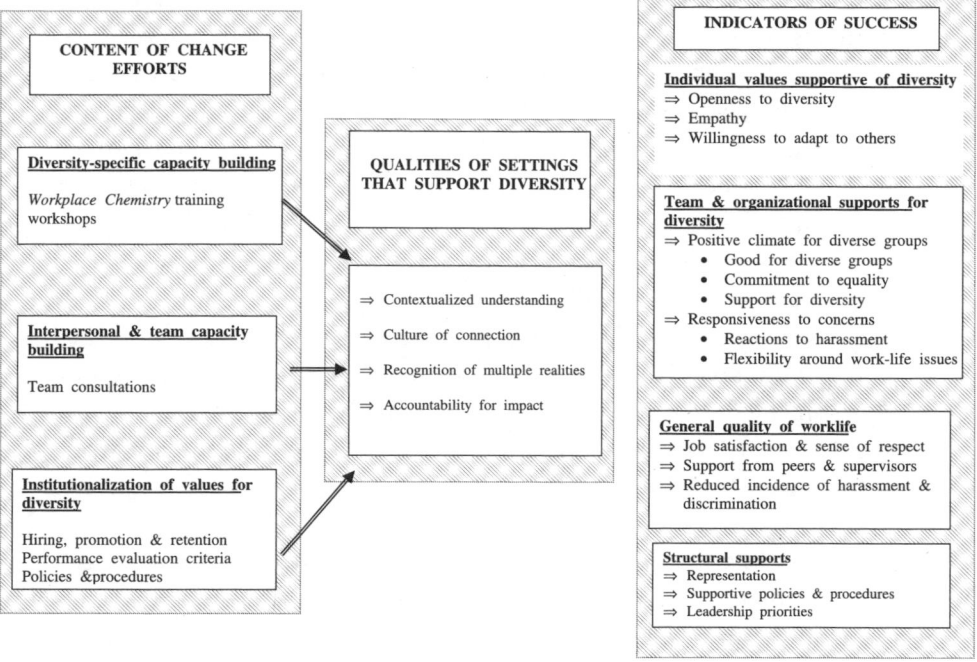

FIGURE 5.3 Indicators of Success

we were striving to create an *organizational context* that was open to diversity and would enable a diversified workforce to thrive. Thus, in addition to looking at changes in numbers and in evaluation structures, we wanted to assess changes in the organizational qualities consistent with the guiding model (i.e., changes in the organizational capacity for contextualized understanding, culture of connection, recognition of multiple realities, and accountability for impact). See figure 5.3 for an overview of what we defined as the indicators of success.

Capturing this type of information is anything but an exact science. It is reasonably straightforward to ask for feedback on specific training activities. As described in chapter 3, we were able to gather participants' reflections about the training workshop components, assessments of what made the training useful, and personal observations about behavioral outcomes of the training. However, it was critical to go beyond this—not only because the training was only one aspect of the full initiative, but also because, ideally, even training will have an impact beyond the workshop setting and beyond the attitudes and behavior of individual participants. In chapter 4, I described how we evaluated the consultation activities by asking participants for their self-assessments of team progress toward their collaboratively developed team vision. While limited in objectivity by design, this allowed at least a window into changes in team values and cultures. We also talked with managers and the leadership team regarding their impressions of changed team dynamics. Even after the reviews of the training and consultation components, there remained further evaluation challenges. Most importantly, we wanted to know more about how the Workplace Chemistry activities might have affected broader organizational sensibilities.

Since our work with ChemPro began with a plantwide survey, we had some important quantitative benchmarks against which to compare the situation over half a decade later. In Year 7, we proposed a follow-up survey. The company's desire to return to the issues assessed at the beginning of Workplace Chemistry Initiative provided a unique opportunity to look at changes over time.

At both points in time, the surveys were distributed to all employees. People were then given the option to either send their responses directly to us at the university or meet with us off-site at a nearby recreation hall during paid work hours. In Year 1, we received 141 responses from the 210 employees (67 percent response rate). Six years later, we received 162 responses from the 188 full-time employees (a response rate of approximately 86 percent). In Year 1, 18.6 percent of the responses came from women, and 15.6 percent came from people of color. In Year 7, 17.6 percent of the respondents were women, and 22.3 percent were people of color. While still in a minority, women and people of color responded to each survey at a slightly higher rate than did their white male coworkers. On both surveys, we heard from people on every unit and at every level of the organization. Employees were assured that their participation was entirely voluntary, that their responses would be completely confidential, and that their decision about whether or not to participate would not affect their job in any way. All results were shared in summary form so individual responses could not be recognized.[3]

Both the original survey and the follow-up were designed by our university group in consultation with HR and the People Team. On the initial survey, we had asked employees across the plant about a wide range of issues. As described in chapter 3, the diversity focus was folded into a survey that also covered such issues as overtime preferences and leisure-time activities. Six years later, we repeated the questions from the original survey that were most directly related to diversity dynamics. We augmented the follow-up survey with some additional questions about supervisor supports, since this was a top concern within HR at that time. We asked about individual values and about team and organizational supports for diversity as expressions of the setting qualities that we had worked to foster. We also wanted to probe broader indicators of the quality of work life (including satisfaction, experience of respect, support from supervisors and peers, sense of fairness, and incidence of harassment and discrimination) and compare responses from the various subgroups within the plant. To develop the survey, we adapted some preexisting scales and also developed some measures specifically for use with Chem-Pro. Almost all the sections of both surveys asked participants to rate their experiences on 5-point scales.[4] The comparison of the two surveys revealed areas of progress as well as areas for continued attention.[5] I have included some key tables and charts in the text; additional figures and tables of results can be found in appendix C.

INDIVIDUAL VALUES SUPPORTIVE OF DIVERSITY

Three personal perspectives central to diversity were assessed on the surveys. We labeled these variables *conservatism about diversity, empathy,* and *concerns about adapting to differences.* Scores on *conservatism about diversity* indicate the extent of agreement with a particular set of beliefs about efforts to promote equity among diverse groups. A high score on the scale indicates a lack of support for organizational efforts to address diversity and reflects the view that concerns related to bias or discrimination are up to the individuals involved (versus the organization) to solve. This is an acontextual perspective in that it ignores the influence of differential access to resources among various demographically defined groups and downplays the impact that such issues as societal expectations and discrimination can have on people's lives. Our hope was that the Workplace Chemistry Initiative would result in greater openness to collective, context-sensitive approaches to diversity.

Empathy is the ability to put oneself in another's position and/or to listen and understand another person's perspective even when one disagrees. Empathy was one of the skills we considered essential both for creating a culture of support and for enabling workers to learn about and appreciate the uniqueness of their coworkers. Without empathy, it would be very difficult to recognize the wide range of experiences—or "realities"—and the forces that render one person's experience of an event different from that of another. The training and consultation components that promoted "both/and" perspectives as well as those that provided opportunities to learn about coworkers' lives were geared toward enhancing empathy. A person who felt s/he had strong empathy skills would score high on this survey scale.

The measure of *concerns about adapting to differences* included items that assessed attitudes about whether one should be asked to adapt to the needs of others (e.g., as opposed to feeling resentful if asked to consider changing one's way of operating because of a coworker's unique abilities, situation, and/or culture). The Workplace Chemistry Initiative emphasized the importance of thinking about oneself in the context of a group and understanding how team members each shape and influence the work demands and opportunities faced by their coworkers. The willingness of individual workers to adapt as necessary to enhance the positive functioning of the collective was an important aspect of both the training and the consultation work. The discussion of "accountability for impact" emphasized the requirement to be cognizant of and responsible for how your behavior affects others. A high score on this scale indicates high resentment if asked to change to adapt to others.

The results revealed that beliefs about the value of addressing diversity issues were less conservative on the follow-up than they had been six years earlier (see figure 5.4). On the Year 1 survey, the ratings of whites had been significantly more conservative than those of people of color; men had been significantly more conservative than women. In particular, white employees

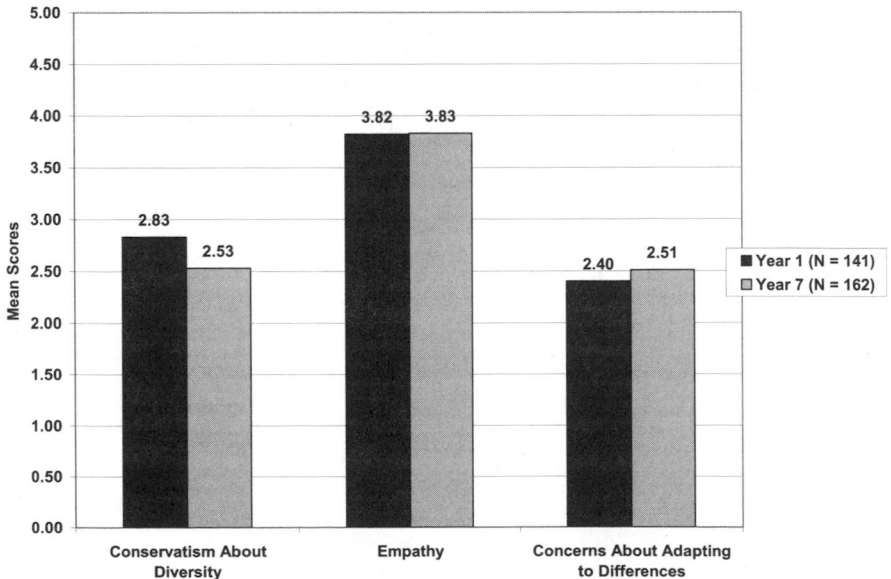

FIGURE 5.4 Individual Values Supportive of Diversity: Year 1 vs. Year 7

TABLE 5.1 · INDIVIDUAL VALUES SUPPORTIVE OF DIVERSITY: COMPARISONS BY RACE AND SEX

	OVERALL	POC	WHITE	SIG	WOMEN	MEN	SIG
Year 1	$n = 141$	$n = 21$	$n = 114$		$n = 26$	$n = 114$	
Year 7	$n = 162$	$n = 28$	$n = 122$		$n = 28$	$n = 131$	
Conservatism about diversity							
Year 1	2.83 (0.80)	2.27 (0.80)	2.94 (0.75)	$<$ .001	2.45 (0.74)	2.91 (0.78)	$<$ .01
Year 7	2.53** (0.96)	2.05 (0.89)	2.61** (0.93)	$<$ .01	2.31 (1.07)	2.56** (0.94)	
Empathy							
Year 1	3.82 (0.87)	3.95 (0.95)	3.79 (0.88)		3.77 (0.91)	3.84 (0.87)	
Year 7	3.83 (1.07)	3.89 (1.13)	3.84 (1.08)		3.82 (1.06)	3.82 (1.08)	
Concerns about adapting to differences							
Year 1	2.40 (0.52)	2.39 (0.67)	2.41 (0.50)		2.22 (0.53)	2.45 (0.52)	$<$ .05
Year 7	2.51 (0.72)	2.41 (0.71)	2.50 (0.74)		2.46 (0.60)	2.51 (0.75)	

**$p < .01$ for comparison of Year 1 vs. Year 7
NOTE: The table numbers are the mean rating of participants on scales that ranged from 1 to 5. The numbers in parentheses are the standard deviations.

had more strongly endorsed the views that affirmative action promotes discrimination against whites and that we have gone too far pushing for equal rights in this country. Whites and men reported significantly less conservative views at the time of the follow-up, and the gap between women and men was no longer statistically significant in Year 7. However, whites' views remained significantly more conservative than those of workers of color (see table 5.1 for differences by race and sex.)

People throughout the plant described themselves as moderately empathetic—with little change over time. Similarly, people reported that they were generally not terribly concerned about having to adjust to varied coworker needs, although ratings on this dimension crept up a bit over time for all groups. Initially, men were more negative about being asked to adapt than were women, but by Year 7 ratings did not seem to vary significantly by race or sex mainly because women's ratings of concern went up more than men's did.

From these results, it appears that beliefs about the value of attending to diversity may have been the most accessible to change (i.e., the reduction in conservatism). The Workplace Chemistry Initiative, the emphasis placed on diversity by management and Corporate, as well as the attention of mass media during the 1990s may all have played a role in this increased openness. In contrast, average empathy ratings did not change much over time. It may be that this particular organizational change effort simply failed to increase individual skills for empathy and/or that this particular quality is not as susceptible to change. Additionally, self-reporting is inherently limited, and self-assessments of empathy may be independent of actual skill levels, such that the lack of evidence of change in empathy might be at least partly an artifact of the measures and measurement strategies used. Moreover, given our inability to match surveys (i.e., to compare pre and post for specific individuals), we could only analyze mean ratings for groups that consisted of slightly different people at time 1 versus time 2. This more severely limited our ability to interpret findings for a very personal skill such as empathy than for other attitudes or dynamics where we could argue that change in collective beliefs—regardless of the specific individuals who populate that collective—signaled positive change and progress for the organization as a whole.

Changes in people's willingness to be flexible and adapt to the diverse styles and situations of coworkers were not as expected. Although the changes were not statistically significant, the trend was toward increasing rather then decreasing levels of concern. On reflection, this dimension may be tougher to influence than other factors, since it is not just a philosophical issue. Being expected to bend to others' needs and priorities has very real implications for the manageability of workers' daily lives. From informal conversations, we learned that being asked to alter a schedule for a coworker with a sick child was annoying to some; seeing that bereavement leave might be set up differently for people with different religious traditions seemed deeply unfair to others; understanding cultural differences in how to approach conflicts was not easy for others. As one white man expressed it,

> We know they have to hire people of color, but they hire minorities that hardly speak English and don't understand your directions and keep doing the job wrong. Then the Safety Department wants you to sign them off as being a safe worker . . . You complain to HR, and they say "Get use to it. We have to hire them." I don't want to get use to it. I want to work with people who speak English.

Along these lines, it is interesting to note that the corners of the plant where there was the most concern after six years of the Workplace Chemistry Initiative were the departments that indeed had the most diversity—the Labs and the manufacturing units. This finding could reflect some settling in of the reality that the rules of the game were indeed changing, and workers were finding this came with some costs or, at least, inconvenience. It is possible that Year 7 ratings in the more diverse departments were a more realistic measure of feelings about having to adapt to differences among team members. It would indeed be odd to think that the relatively homogeneous departments were actually the departments *most* willing to work with diverse groups— even though they rated themselves as more accepting. An additional caution is needed to avoid overinterpreting any rise in ratings. Even though concerns went up slightly from Year 1, the good news is that scores were all still below midrange on the scale (i.e., below 3 on the 5-point scale). People may have been grappling with what adapting to diversity meant to them, but they were still, for the most part, neither reactionary nor totally rejecting.[6]

We also did some comparisons between the ratings of managers and those of hourly workers. Managers were particularly committed to the expectation that workers should adapt to differences in the workplace; they were also more enthusiastic about the value of attending to diversity (i.e., less conservative). It should perhaps not be surprising that those with greatest control over their work were the most open to altering their patterns to adjust to others. The personal accommodations required of managers and organizational leaders were undoubtedly less disruptive and involved more choices about alternatives than those required of workers at the other end of the hierarchy. For example, shifting a meeting time to accommodate a colleague's child care crisis is very different than having to work overtime on the plant floor to make the same sort of accommodation. In addition, it may be that the enhanced attention to diversity expectations—particularly in the evaluations of leaders—was paying off. Not only were people in management roles significantly less conservative and more willing to adapt; they also changed over time to become even more open to diversity, while hourly workers became more concerned about adapting to differences (see table 5.2).

TEAM AND ORGANIZATIONAL SUPPORTS FOR DIVERSITY

In addition to changing individual attitudes, we hoped that the years of work with ChemPro would also increase the team and organizational supports for diverse workers. We looked at several related dimensions. We asked about the diversity climate of the organization including the extent to which ChemPro was seen as a good place for various groups of people to work (*good for diverse groups*), management was seen as serious about treating people equally (*commitment to equality*), and supervisors demonstrated a value for and understanding of diverse workers (*support for diversity*). In addition, we asked about

TABLE 5.2 · INDIVIDUAL VALUES SUPPORTIVE OF DIVERSITY:
COMPARISONS BETWEEN MANAGERS AND WORKERS

	MANAGERS	HOURLY WORKERS	SIG
Conservatism about diversity			
Year 1	2.46 (0.91)	2.86 (0.73)	< .05
Year 7	1.84* (0.78)	2.64+ (0.99)	< .01
Empathy			
Year 1	3.83 (1.07)	3.83 (0.85)	n.s.
Year 7	3.81 (1.21)	3.86 (1.06)	n.s.
Concerns about adapting to differences			
Year 1	2.02 (0.49)	2.46 (0.50)	< .001
Year 7	1.86 (0.58)	2.63+ (0.74)	< .001

$^+p < .10$ for comparison of Year 1 vs. Year 7
$^*p < .05$ for comparison of Year 1 vs. Year 7
NOTE: The table numbers are the mean rating of participants on scales that
ranged from 1 to 5. The numbers in parentheses are the standard deviations.

responsiveness to concerns including the likelihood that someone at Chem-Pro would challenge degrading comments and jokes (*reactions to harassment*) and the extent to which workers felt they could ask for flexibility in order to deal with demands outside work (*inflexibility around work-life integration*[7]). Note that higher scores on all but *inflexibility around work-life integration* were what we were aiming for; we hoped, of course, that *inflexibility* would be reduced (see figure 5.5).

People reported positive diversity climates. They felt that ChemPro was generally a good place for diverse groups to work, and there was an overall positive sense that the organization was committed to equality and that supervisors provided support for diversity. However, for the plant as a whole, ratings of *commitment to equality* fell over time. To unravel these results, it is useful to look at how the patterns differed for different demographic groups (see table 5.3). In Year 1, women had been significantly more negative than men both about whether ChemPro was a positive environment for diverse groups and about the extent to which there was an organizational commitment to equity. By the follow-up, women's ratings on both diversity climate dimensions rose significantly, and men's dropped (particularly on ratings of *commitment to equality*). These patterns combined to eliminate the *statistical* differences based on sex by Year 7. Looking at the results by racial groupings,

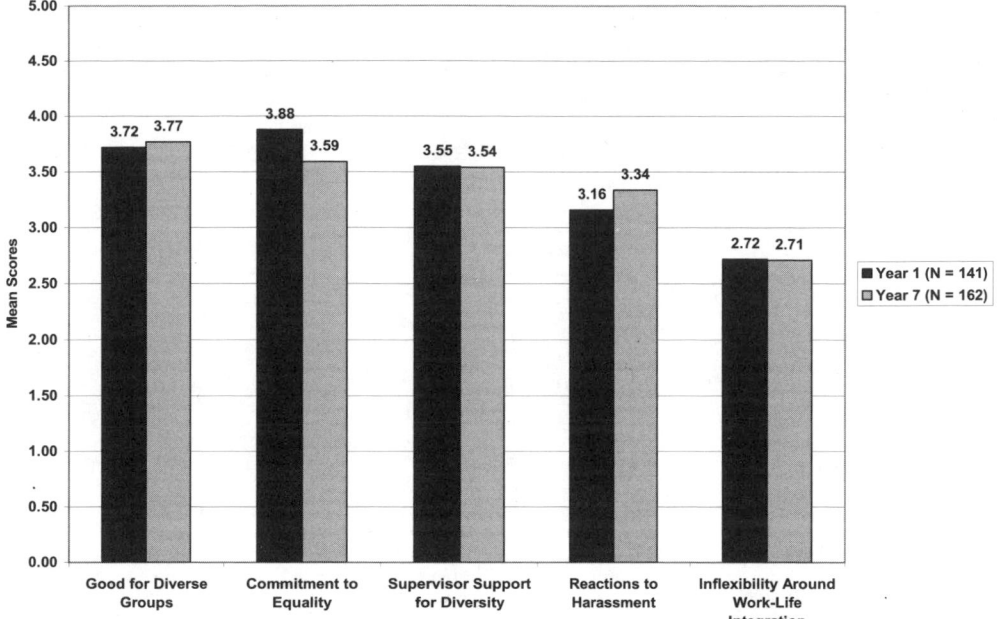

FIGURE 5.5 Team and Organizational Supports for Diversity: Year 1 vs. Year 7

the drop in perceptions of commitment to equity was also significant for whites. Thus, what looked like a simple change plantwide, actually included different patterns for different groups.

Supervisors got generally positive marks from everyone for their *support for diversity* (means of a little over 3.5 for both Year 1 and Year 7). There were no statistically significant differences based on race or sex for either year. There was an overall sense that the organization would take action to halt harassment and that this responsiveness had improved slightly over the years. People generally experienced some *flexibility around work-life integration,* and women as a group noted some improvement on this dimension from Year 1 to Year 7.

Interestingly, there were not many differences between managers and hourly workers in their assessments of team and organizational supports at the start of the project. By the follow-up, however, people at the top of the hierarchy rated the diversity climate significantly more positively than did workers at other levels of the organization. Some of the divergence was that managers saw improvement over time on the climate being *good for diverse groups,* on *support for diversity,* and on *reactions to harassment.* Hourly workers, on the other hand, gave the organization lower marks on *commitment to equal-*

TABLE 5.3 · TEAM AND ORGANIZATIONAL SUPPORTS FOR DIVERSITY: COMPARISONS BY RACE AND SEX

	OVERALL	POC	WHITE	SIG	WOMEN	MEN	SIG
Year 1	$n = 141$	$n = 21$	$n = 114$		$n = 26$	$n = 114$	
Year 7	$n = 162$	$n = 28$	$n = 122$		$n = 28$	$n = 131$	
Good for diverse groups							
Year 1	3.72 (0.64)	3.88 (0.63)	3.71 (0.64)		3.15 (0.63)	3.85 (0.58)	< .001
Year 7	3.77 (0.83)	3.52 (0.92)	3.83 (0.76)		3.71* (0.90)	3.80 (0.81)	
Commitment to equality							
Year 1	3.88 (0.86)	3.79 (0.73)	3.94 (0.85)		3.29 (0.94)	4.04 (0.74)	< .001
Year 7	3.59** (1.06)	3.63 (1.09)	3.62** (1.04)		3.82* (1.00)	3.55** (1.08)	
Support for diversity							
Year 1	3.55 (0.93)	3.81 (1.02)	3.53 (0.90)		3.48 (0.86)	3.58 (0.93)	
Year 7	3.54 (1.02)	3.32 (1.08)	3.59 (1.02)		3.52 (1.03)	3.57 (1.02)	
Reactions to harassment							
Year 1	3.16 (0.98)	3.33 (0.75)	3.13 (1.02)		2.94 (1.11)	3.21 (0.96)	
Year 7	3.34 (1.03)	3.50 (0.93)	3.35 (1.05)		3.39 (0.99)	3.32 (1.05)	
Inflexibility around work-life integration							
Year 1	2.72 (1.05)	2.79 (0.93)	2.71 (1.09)		3.00 (0.99)	2.67 (1.06)	
Year 7	2.71 (0.97)	2.79 (1.06)	2.66 (0.94)		2.46+ (1.15)	2.74 (0.92)	

$^+p < .10$ for comparison of Year 1 vs. Year 7
$^*p < .05$ for comparison of Year 1 vs. Year 7
$^{**}p < .01$ for comparison of Year 1 vs. Year 7
NOTE: The table numbers are the mean rating of participants on scales that ranged from 1 to 5. The numbers in parentheses are the standard deviations.

ity and *support for diversity* (see table 5.4.). These findings overlap with the observation that, in Year 7, workers in the Production Department had lower ratings on most dimensions of diversity climate than did people in other departments—in contrast to Year 1, when they had had higher ratings than others on *commitment to equality* and *support for diversity*.[8]

There is both good news and some challenging feedback in these results about team and organizational supports. On all the dimensions measured, ChemPro received fairly positive ratings. Women were experiencing Chem-Pro as a more positive, flexible, and inclusive place to work than they had been when we began. Men, on the other hand, with their slipping rating for the organization's commitment to equality, may have been expressing con-

TABLE 5.4 · TEAM AND ORGANIZATIONAL SUPPORTS FOR
DIVERSITY: COMPARISONS BETWEEN MANAGERS AND WORKERS

	MANAGERS	HOURLY WORKERS	SIG
Good for diverse groups			
Year 1	3.89 (0.66)	3.70 (0.64)	n.s.
Year 7	4.30* (0.59)	3.69 (0.88)	< .01
Commitment to equality			
Year 1	4.17 (0.61)	3.85 (0.87)	< .10
Year 7	4.38 (0.88)	3.36** (1.08)	< .001
Support for diversity			
Year 1	3.72 (1.02)	3.54 (0.91)	n.s.
Year 7	4.40** (0.56)	3.32+ (1.05)	< .001
Reactions to harassment			
Year 1	3.12 (1.04)	3.19 (0.99)	n.s.
Year 7	3.88* (0.91)	3.28 (1.07)	< .001
Inflexibility around work-life integration			
Year 1	2.45 (0.82)	2.80 (1.07)	n.s.
Year 7	2.22 (0.73)	2.81 (0.97)	< .05

$^+p < .10$ for comparison of Year 1 vs. Year 7
$^*p < .05$ for comparison of Year 1 vs. Year 7
$^{**}p < .01$ for comparison of Year 1 vs. Year 7
NOTE: The table numbers are the mean rating of participants on scales that ranged
from 1 to 5. The numbers in parentheses are the standard deviations.

sternation about the new landscape that was now more explicitly attending to
race and gender. The areas of the plant where ratings of team and organizational supports went up fairly consistently over time were the Labs and the
administrative positions. These are groups with proportionally more women,
so this undoubtedly reflects a dynamic that interacts with the findings related
to sex differences.

QUALITY OF WORK LIFE

While fostering supports specific to diversity (at the individual, team, and
organizational levels) was a primary focus of the work with ChemPro, we certainly hoped that our work would also translate into improvements in the
general quality of work life for everyone. To assess this, we looked both at
indicators of positive feelings about work (*sense of satisfaction, respect,* and *sup-*

port from peers and supervisors) and at the incidence of specific problems related to discrimination and harassment (both observed and directly experienced). These are broad dimensions undoubtedly influenced by factors well beyond the Workplace Chemistry Initiative. However, since a major goal of the initiative was to foster a more supportive and inclusive work climate, we wanted to know how workers' general experiences on the job had changed over the years of our involvement and how the experiences of members of different identity groups might compare.

Satisfaction, Respect, and Support. When the Workplace Chemistry Initiative began, employees of ChemPro reported feeling moderately satisfied and respected in their jobs, but *job satisfaction* was significantly higher among men than among women. Six years later, women's ratings were beginning to catch up with men's such that there was no longer a statistically significant sex difference. While *satisfaction* and *respect* scores went down somewhat for people of color, they had started out higher than those for whites and remained slightly higher on the Year 7 survey. There were no significant differences based on race for ratings during either time period. In short, the patterns for ratings of *satisfaction* and *respect* were much like the results for team and organizational supports, with the most evident change being some increasingly positive experiences for women (See figure 5.6 and table 5.5.)

Over the six years, ratings of *satisfaction* improved for most job groups but decreased for workers on the plant floor. In Year 7, workers in Manufacturing-2 reported the lowest satisfaction and lowest sense of respect of all departments, whereas in Year 1 the highest ratings of satisfaction had been in the production units. In Year 7, employees in the Facilities Department reported by far the greatest satisfaction. The most noteworthy improvements in job satisfaction over time were in the Labs and in office positions; however, the Labs remained lower than the other non-production units. From participants' comments, it was apparent that the decreased satisfaction among the production operators was due in large part to the much leaner staffing patterns. Interestingly, when comparing managers and hourly workers, there were no significant differences in *job satisfaction* or *respect* on either survey. It is again interesting to note, however, that both Production and the Labs were relatively more diverse than the more satisfied departments—providing some incentive to give this aspect of the pattern further attention.

At the onset of our work, people had reported moderate levels of support from supervisors and cohesion among coworkers. There were no significant

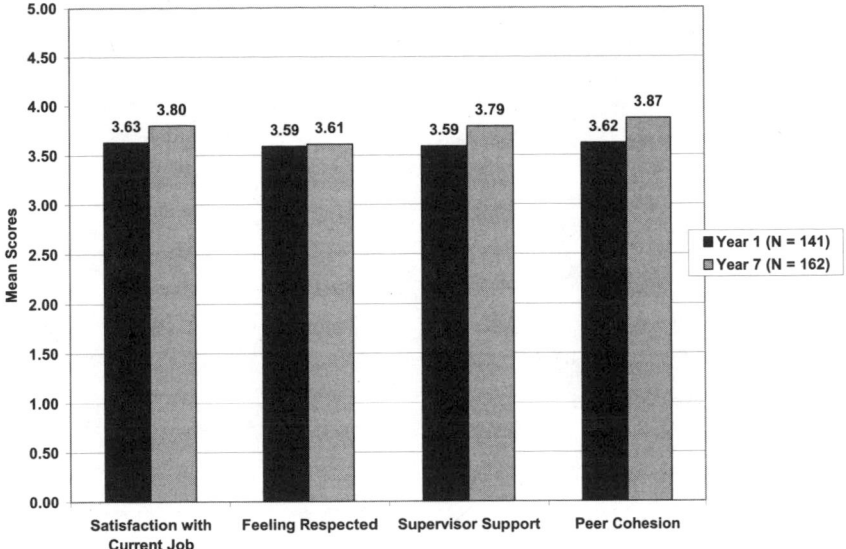

FIGURE 5.6 General Quality of Work Life: Year 1 vs. Year 7

differences between demographic groups in terms of *support from super-visors,* but women were significantly less pleased with their *relationships with coworkers* than were the men. By follow-up, *supervisor support* and *peer cohesion* had improved for most groups,[9] and because improvement in women's scores outpaced increases for men, the gender differences disappeared. While there were no significant differences in ratings of these types of organizational supports for people of different races, there was, however, a significant difference on one question in Year 7, with people of color being far more likely than whites to say they were exposed to some hostility from their supervisor (white $X = 3.85$; people of color $X = 4.32$, $p < .05$).

Managers reported significantly more positive experiences of *supervisor support* and *peer cohesion* than did hourly workers. Over time, managers logged significant improvement in *supervisor support,* while hourly workers noted improvement in *peer cohesion* (see table 5.6). As was true for *job satisfaction* and *respect,* the Year 7 ratings of *supervisor support* and *peer cohesion* were highest in Facilities and lowest in Production. While ratings of *supervisor support* and *peer cohesion* in the Labs increased over the six years, their ratings of *peer cohesion* remained low relative to other units.[10]

Harassment, Discrimination, and Unfair Treatment. We hoped, of course, that changes in the climate of support for diverse groups would also translate into

TABLE 5.5 · GENERAL QUALITY OF WORK LIFE: COMPARISONS BY RACE AND SEX

	OVERALL	POC	WHITE	SIG	WOMEN	MEN	SIG
Year 1	$n = 141$	$n = 21$	$n = 114$		$n = 26$	$n = 114$	
Year 7	$n = 162$	$n = 28$	$n = 122$		$n = 28$	$n = 131$	
Job satisfaction							
Year 1	3.63 (1.39)	4.05 (1.23)	3.56 (1.41)		3.04 (1.49)	3.77 (1.34)	< .05
Year 7	3.80 (0.98)	3.89 (0.96)	3.78 (0.96)		3.61^+ (0.96)	3.86 (0.97)	
Feeling respected							
Year 1	3.59 (0.98)	3.75 (1.12)	3.55 (0.96)		3.31 (1.16)	3.67 (0.92)	
Year 7	3.61 (0.98)	3.61 (1.10)	3.62 (0.95)		3.54 (1.17)	3.64 (0.94)	
Supervisor support							
Year 1	3.59 (1.02)	3.88 (1.04)	3.56 (1.02)		3.24 (0.99)	3.67 (1.02)	
Year 7	3.79 (1.01)	3.75 (0.98)	3.83* (1.02)		3.56 (0.96)	3.87 (1.00)	
Peer cohesion							
Year 1	3.62 (0.83)	3.83 (0.84)	3.59 (0.82)		3.28 (0.81)	3.69 (0.82)	< .05
Year 7	3.87* (0.88)	3.95 (0.77)	3.88* (0.91)		3.96* (0.72)	3.85 (0.92)	

^+p < .10 for comparison of Year 1 vs. Year 7
$^{**}p$ < .05 for comparison of Year 1 vs. Year 7
NOTE: The table numbers are the mean rating of participants on scales that ranged from 1 to 5. The numbers in parentheses are the standard deviations.

reduced instances of harassment, discrimination, and unfair treatment. To look at these issues, we asked people both about their observations of the treatment of others and about their own personal experiences with harassment and discrimination (see figure 5.7).

In Year 7, people reported few observations of *harassment of or discrimination against others* based on race or gender, which reflected a significant decrease over time. All demographic groups reported significant decreases, and gender differences that were significant in Year 1 disappeared. On the other hand, observations of *generally offensive behavior* (e.g., generally offensive, racist, and sexist comments or jokes) rose significantly in Year 7, with over 70 percent of respondents—both men and women, both whites and people of color—witnessing at least some offensive, sexist, or racist jokes or comments. The greatest increases were in the reports by whites (up 27.3 percent) and men (up 29.3 percent). (See table 5.7 and supporting tables in appendix C.)

TABLE 5.6 · GENERAL QUALITY OF WORK LIFE: COMPARISONS
BETWEEN MANAGERS AND HOURLY WORKERS

	MANAGERS	HOURLY WORKERS	SIG
Job satisfaction			
Year 1	3.75 (1.41)	3.61 (1.39)	n.s.
Year 7	4.00 (0.71)	3.75 (1.06)	n.s.
Feeling respected			
Year 1	3.74 (0.81)	3.58 (1.02)	n.s.
Year 7	3.90 (0.64)	3.58 (1.04)	n.s.
Supervisor support			
Year 1	3.62 (0.94)	3.59 (1.06)	n.s.
Year 7	4.51** (0.51)	3.60 (1.04)	< .001
Peer cohesion			
Year 1	4.07 (0.63)	3.52 (0.85)	< .01
Year 7	4.40 (0.75)	3.74[+] (0.89)	< .01

[+]$p < .10$ for comparison of Year 1 vs. Year 7
**$p < .01$ for comparison of Year 1 vs. Year 7
NOTE: The table numbers are the mean rating of participants on scales that ranged
from 1 to 5. The numbers in parentheses are the standard deviations.

We also looked at perceptions regarding whether some groups were treated more harshly than others (*unfairness*). All ratings on this dimension were fairly low (and all subgroup means were below 2.55 on the 5-point scale), indicating only modest endorsement of the notion that some groups were treated unfairly—although men were significantly more positive than women about the level of fairness at ChemPro (in both Year 1 and Year 7). Again, looking at responses to various individual items was revealing. An interesting finding in Year 7 was that whites, people of color, and women each described more inequities directed toward their *own* group than others did. That is, whites were significantly more likely to say that whites were penalized more than people of color for mistakes, while women perceived that females were penalized more than men. People of color rated the organization significantly higher than whites did on whether it was a good place for white males to work. Whites rated the organization significantly higher than people of color did on whether it was a good place for people of color to work.[11]

We then asked about people's *own personal* experiences of sexual harassment, gender harassment, and racial harassment. Reports of *sexual harass-*

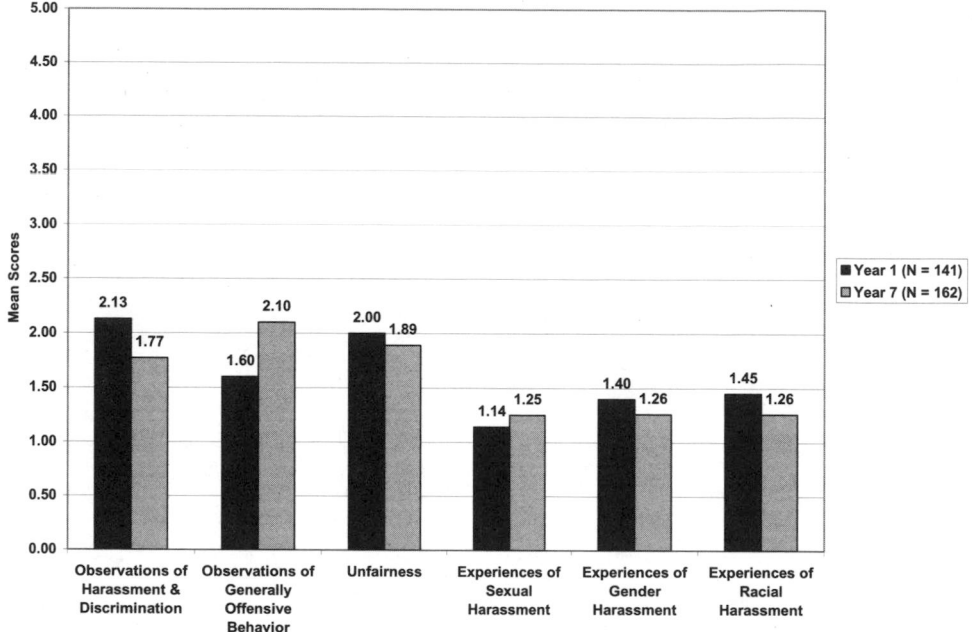

FIGURE 5.7 Harassment, Discrimination, and Unfair Treatment: Year 1 vs. Year 7

ment (i.e., unwelcome sexualized attention, touching, or pressure for dates) were infrequent on both surveys—even though participants were asked to rate experiences over a five-year span. However, noting that overall scores on the sexual harassment scale went up slightly on the second survey, I felt compelled to look more closely at the individual survey items and at subgroup means.[12] There were negligible changes in amount of unwanted touching experienced by women, and their reports of unwelcome pressure for dates went down from 3.8 percent to zero by the seventh year. Women's reports of unwelcome suggestive looks and/or flirtation stayed about the same (with roughly a quarter reporting these in both years). The increases over time were mainly in the ratings by *men* on items asking about "unwelcome suggestive looks or gestures" and "unwelcome flirtation/sexual attention." It is altogether possible that the looks and gestures were not even related to sex or gender, and it is likely that the unwanted sexual attention for the men would not meet the "hostile climate" standard used to define sexual harassment.

Almost 62 percent of the people of color and 62 percent of the women had reported at least some experiences of *racial or gender-based harassment* or discrimination on the original survey (compared with 13.4 percent of whites

TABLE 5.7 · OBSERVATIONS OF GENERALLY OFFENSIVE BEHAVIOR

HOW OFTEN HAVE YOU OBSERVED ANY OF THE FOLLOWING BEHAVIORS WHEN AT CHEMPRO OVER THE LAST FIVE YEARS?	TOTAL N	FREQUENCY			% OF EACH POPULATION WHO HAVE EXPERIENCED THE PROBLEM			
		Never	1–2 times	Some to very frequently	% POC	% White	% Women	% Men
Year 1					n = 21	n = 113	n = 26	n = 113
Overall	139	70	30	39	61.9	47.3	65.4	45.5
Teasing, jokes, or remarks you find generally offensive	139	88	22	29	38.1	35.7	50.0	33.0
Jokes or comments you consider sexist	139	101	16	22	19.0	27.7	57.7**	19.6**
Jokes or comments you consider racist	139	90	28	21	61.9**	30.4**	50.0	31.3
Year 7					n = 28	n = 122	n = 28	n = 131
Overall	162	42	56	64	75.0	74.6	71.4	74.8
Teasing, jokes, or remarks you find generally offensive	162	49	63	50	71.4	69.7	67.9	70.2
Jokes or comments you consider sexist	162	54	59	49	60.7	68.9	67.9	66.4
Jokes or comments you consider racist	162	66	56	40	53.6	61.5	57.1	59.5

$**p < .01$

and 9.8 percent of men). Six years later, 25 percent of the people of color reported some problems based on their race, and 25 percent of the women reported issues based on gender (compared with 13.9 percent of whites and 14.5 percent of men) (see table 5.8). This is fairly dramatic improvement; however, it is important to remember that *any* continuing incidents were still concerning.

Interestingly, there were few differences between managers and hourly workers in either their *observations of discrimination against others* or their *personal experiences* of harassment and discrimination. The one place where they differed was in terms of their perceptions of *unfairness* in Year 7, when hourly workers were significantly more negative than managers.[13]

So there is mixed news in the data about harassment and discrimination. Frequencies of all types of problems were fairly low, and there were significant reductions in harassment and discrimination—both in terms of parti-

TABLE 5.8 · PERSONAL EXPERIENCES OF HARASSMENT AND DISCRIMINATION

HARASSED OR DISCRIMINATED AGAINST AT CHEMPRO OVER THE LAST YEAR BECAUSE OF:	TOTAL N	FREQUENCY			% OF EACH POPULATION WHO HAVE EXPERIENCED THE PROBLEM			
		Never	1–2 times	Some to very frequently	% POC	% White	% Women	% Men
Year 1					n = 21	n = 113	n = 26	n = 113
Race/ethnicity	139	107	10	22	61.9***	13.4***	26.9	21.4
Gender	139	111	10	18	20.0	18.6	61.5***	9.8***
Family responsibilities	140	116	10	14	14.3	15.9	30.8*	13.3*
Sexual orientation	140	133	4	3	9.5	2.7	15.4**	2.7**
Health/disability	140	123	7	10	19.0	9.7	19.2	10.6
Year 7					n = 28	n = 122	n = 28	n = 131
Race/ethnicity	162	136	16	10	25.0	13.9	10.7	17.6
Gender	162	136	14	12	3.6*	18.9*	25.0	14.5
Family responsibilities	161	137	15	9	14.3	14.0	17.9	14.6
Sexual orientation	162	153	4	5	3.6	5.7	3.6	6.1
Health/disability	162	143	11	8	7.1	10.7	14.3	10.7

*p < .05; **p < .01; ***p < .001

cipants' own experiences and in their observations about the treatment of others. The incidence had not, however, been reduced to the hoped-for zero level, and there were increases in observations of some problematic behaviors. The increases in *generally offensive behavior* as well as in overall reports of *sexual harassment* were complicated to interpret. The most dramatic changes in observations of offensive treatment were reported by the groups least directly affected. In fact, the number of people of color who noted racist jokes or comments actually went down, while every other group reported increases. The numbers of women noting sexist jokes or comments remained relatively steady, while all other groups reported an increase. These patterns would seem to indicate an increased awareness among whites and men to the experiences of women and people of color. That is, rather than capturing a new phenomenon, they may well have tapped an increased sensitivity to sexist and racist interactions that had long permeated the plant but were only now being noticed as such.

from evaluation to next steps

The picture that all these data drew was a complex one—some significant progress combined with some lingering concerns. However, there is so much information that it is easy to get lost in the details. So what does it all mean?

We learned that there was an increased awareness of the importance of diversity. There were lower reports of discrimination and harassment, and a greater confidence that others would challenge sexist and racist comments. The general consensus was that the company would proactively address harassment. These are all important indicators of improved organizational supports for diversity. Also significant was the increased presence of women and people of color in the plant. While the actual numbers of women did not increase, they became more visible among the plantwide leadership. There was somewhat increased hiring of people of color—particularly within Production—but perhaps more important was the increased representation of people of color in team leadership roles.

It was also noteworthy that women reported increased satisfaction and an increased sense that ChemPro was a good place for diverse groups to work. These findings were particularly reassuring since the pre-post training assessments had made me worried that women might not have felt fully validated by the workshops. After our years of work, a stronger consensus had emerged that ChemPro, as a whole, provided a work environment that would not tolerate gender and racial bias and discrimination. In sum, the commitment this organization made to fostering diversity among workers lasted over time, and the impact was felt at many personal and interpersonal levels. This was particularly impressive given the steady downsizing that was ongoing throughout these years.

Rarely is any change initiative a magic solution when it comes to addressing entrenched interpersonal and cultural patterns. If I were to tell a completely "happily ever after" story, the reader would be right to be skeptical. Women and people of color still faced barriers, particularly in the more intangible forms of offensive jokes and comments and the reluctance of some coworkers to make accommodations for differences in style, approach, and needs. Although improved, women's satisfaction continued to be a bit below men's. Women were still in the minority throughout the plant, particularly in Production. Women had not cracked the ranks of the male (and more highly paid) enclaves of Processing or Facilities. People of color indicated that they were exposed to more hostility from their supervisors than whites were.

People were more concerned about the treatment of their own group than others were (true for whites, people of color, women, *and* men!). Hourly workers seemed to be feeling increasingly stressed and disempowered. Some departments were clearly happier than others.

Through honestly considering the feedback and assessment results, the organization could celebrate the positive changes and, at the same time, develop action plans for the issues that still needed to be addressed. The next steps were entirely up to the leadership at ChemPro, so at this juncture it was essential to renew the sense of partnership with the top leadership team.

MAKING SENSE FOR THE ORGANIZATION

Rich and I designed a workshop for the managers where we asked the group to collaborate in the interpretation of the findings and in outlining how the results might be useful for defining future steps. By this time, Warren had retired. Brian, who had been working at Corporate after a stint as the manager of the ChemPro Facilities Department (Maintenance and Security), came back from Corporate to serve as the new ChemPro president. His style was quite different from Warren's, but he remained committed to the Workplace Chemistry goals. With his blessing, Rich and I convened a group of twelve top managers (six white men including the president, three white women, and three black men). We laid out the following goals:

- · To celebrate the positive changes over time
- · To foster awareness among managers about current diversity-related challenges throughout the plant
- · To affirm the commitment of mangers to creating an organizational culture supportive of diverse employees
- · To brainstorm ways for the leadership to celebrate strengths and address ongoing challenges related to diversity

We created a structure for the workshop that involved asking the managers to first discuss some of their own experiences and values around diversity. We asked them to engage in adapted versions of some exercises we had used during the plantwide trainings. Our thinking was that this experiential component would help create a context for the discussion of survey results that would humanize the challenges and would be anchored in a spirit of understanding. We wanted to begin by reminding the managers of the perspectives and values that had been guiding the Workplace Chemistry Initiative. We asked them to problem-solve in a spirit compatible with an ecological analysis—without casting blame, looking for strategies at multiple levels of analysis, infused with empathy for the experiences of diverse groups, but ultimately committed to holding people accountable for their impact on the inclusive nature of their teams and the diversity climate of the company. These initial discussions did indeed seem to affirm their shared commitment to the issue of diversity and to creating energy for the task ahead. Brian made an impassioned plea for everyone to recognize that "the success of efforts to promote and sustain diversity has been and will continue to be achieved through a team effort."

The first half of the workshop was devoted to interpreting the survey results. I provided an overview of the survey process and initial findings. Rich provided a summary of the current status of diversity issues within the plant. We provided a booklet with about fifty pages of tables to each participant. Then we divided the managers into five subgroups and assigned each one a topic area. Their group task was to review their set of tables, identify three issues that they found particularly "striking," and be prepared to talk about what they found so intriguing about those particular patterns.

At first blush, it might seem crazy to unload so many tables on this unsuspecting group. Remember, however, that this was a data-driven company with a "statistical culture" (as Keitha had explained when introducing me to the organization); these managers were no strangers to numerical outputs and tracking quantitative measures of product quality. In another setting, with participants who did not confront table upon table of numbers on a daily basis, this might not have been an appropriate strategy. A facilitator might have more wisely pruned the tables into a more manageable pile. These ChemPro managers, however, seemed perfectly within their element.

As the subgroups discussed their observations based on the data, we asked participants to reflect on two other issues: What else is going on in the plant that we might not be seeing in the survey data? And what else is ChemPro doing right (i.e., additional ways in which the organization has been successfully moving toward the original vision of the Workplace Chemistry Initiative)? As the groups reported on their discussions, I was excited about their ability to see the subtleties in the data and to relate the numerical findings to specific current circumstances within the plant.

There was general consensus that people throughout the plant had grown increasingly disapproving of racist and sexist jokes and comments. The top managers' sense was that when the Workplace Chemistry Initiative began, many people at ChemPro were oblivious to harassment and discrimination.

The managers took the increased ratings of harassment as a signal of increased awareness, and the increased acknowledgment of generally offensive behaviors as reflecting increased sensitivity. One person observed that, unlike in the past, offensive remarks were no longer dismissed as, "It's a joke" or "That's just Mike." He said, "Today, a more typical response might be, 'That's how Mike used to be.'" They also felt that the message of "zero tolerance" had gotten out and that fears that reporting harassment might make one a target had lessened.

However, they also discussed a very recent distressing situation where offensive pictures on the women's bathroom walls were ignored for months until a female student intern reported them. Once they were reported, the managers had taken swift action. In the workshop discussion, the leaders challenged themselves to grapple with how and why the long-term female employees had tolerated offensive graffiti rather than report it. It seemed inconsistent with their sense of how things had changed. They worried that people had become "desensitized" to some racist and sexist behavior, and that it was perhaps more common than they had thought. They recognized that this situation was evidence that they needed to do more work to assure workers that management was committed to supporting a work environment free from such offensive behavior.

They were not surprised by the findings about greater conservatism among operators and the greater reluctance to adapt to differences. The group felt the greater interest in diversity among the leadership probably reflected a multitude of factors, including that supervisors were more "indoctrinated" toward promoting and sustaining diversity while many operators were feeling that they had little control over the ongoing changes. They also recognized that the "threat" to manufacturing in the United States was a factor casting a shadow on many of the survey results. They knew from their daily interactions within the plant that operators were stressed by the increased job insecurity within the whole industry, and many were worried about a lack of transferability of the job skills learned at ChemPro.

The second half of the day was devoted more intensively to action planning. With the survey-based observations posted all over the walls, we asked each of the leaders to generate at least ten action steps that would address the current situation—either remedy problem situations or accentuate successes. I facilitated a process of gathering up the individual ideas and clustering them into themes, which was much like the process used in the team consultations to generate summaries of team visions, barriers, and resources.

The leadership group agreed that while continuing to work on team building, they needed to recognize that many employees, particularly white male operators, came to the job with more conservative views about diversity and less belief in the value of adapting to diversity. They agreed that they should actively support, and not become complacent about, the finding that women seemed to be feeling more a part of their work teams. They wanted to celebrate the increased sense that sexist and racial comments and sexual harassment should not be tolerated, while also recognizing that women's job satisfaction continued to lag a bit behind men's. They could acknowledge the improvements and the fairly low rates of harassment and discrimination but saw the need to continue to address the issues, since the problems had not totally disappeared. They wanted to follow up on the finding that people of color indicated that they were exposed to more hostility from their supervisors than were whites, and also follow up on the lowered sense of supervisor support and cohesion among operators.

The group agreed that two areas of the organization warranted particular further attention: Production (because of decreased satisfaction, support, and tolerance) and the Labs (because the experiences of individual members seemed to vary so widely). So we set aside time to address issues relevant to these departments. I asked the Production and Lab managers to each serve as facilitator for the discussion about their own department, while I stepped into the role of recorder. This was time for these particular managers to get help and support from their colleagues for addressing the emerging issues on their own units—and thus it made sense to place them in charge of the process and to avoid a scenario where they felt put on the spot and "talked about" rather than "partnered with."

The discussion for Production focused on workers' sense of job insecurity, the lack of reward structures tied to *team* accomplishments, and some growing cynicism that "everything is political anyway." The solutions proposed focused on enhancing worker involvement in decision making and keeping operators better informed about the changing economic pressures and demands faced by the plant. There was recognition that any initiative would need to directly address the worry that attention to diversity was promoting discrimination against whites. The manager and team leaders within Production agreed that they needed to talk more about the difficulties of—and strategies for—adapting to working with diversified teams.

While the Labs were also identified as "hot spots," the concerns were quite different. The emphasis for the Labs was on fostering greater cohesion. Rather than generalized discontent, the problem seemed to be increasing fragmentation. From the informal comments that accompanied the survey administrations, it had become clear that some lab workers felt they belonged to a tight-knit, well-functioning team while others felt alienated—and the differences seemed to be largely shaped by race and gender. A small group of white men described the Labs as close, "almost like a family." They described a very comfortable working environment. At the same time, several other workers were upset that "there are favorites." In particular, two women of color talked about how they felt they were neither listened to nor extended much flexibility around their work arrangements. Additionally, these women felt very uncomfortable raising their concerns with their coworkers and supervisors.

The managers of these two departments gathered up the suggestions of their peers and agreed to formulate plans for working on the identified issues. The discussion then turned to the ongoing role of all organizational leaders in promoting a more inclusive workplace. Again, we asked the leadership group to do some personal reflecting—this time about times when they had observed inequities and wished they had spoken up but had not, and times when they had spoken up and taken action about something they felt was unfair. The vignettes they shared became the backdrop for a discussion of what conditions help people to be proactive about injustice and what sorts of barriers get in the way.

Each manager made a pact with the leadership group to take specific actions toward addressing the issues that had emerged in the workshop discussions. The agreements included general vows to be more conscious of differences, to hold meetings with team members about emerging diversity-related concerns, and to integrate additional criteria about adapting to team differences into the PA framework. Each leader made a public commitment to support the others. Brian concluded the workshop by commending the group for being "open, committed, mutually respectful" and challenged each and every manager to continue to "work to their fullest" to make ChemPro an inclusive and welcoming workplace. This was not an initiative that would "end" but rather a process that would be ongoing.

ecological reflections: appreciating the motion of organizational life

This review of organizational life brings home the lesson that efforts to promote inclusive workplaces cannot be short-term or one-dimensional. The work to create organizational supports for diverse members of our society needs to be sustained and multilayered. As Holvino, Ferdman, and Merrill-Sands put it, "One of the key challenges of a diversity initiative is to have the right mix of synergistic interventions that will maximize change."[14] Additionally, diversity initiatives must take into consideration the unique characteristics and dynamics (i.e., chemistry) of each organization.

While a synergistic mix of strategies may be essential to the success of an organizational change process, this complexity is also what makes it difficult to get a handle on how deeply the initiative has affected the organization as a whole over time. Several dilemmas emerged in our review of indicators of change at ChemPro. The assessment process made apparent how difficult it is to describe a system that is in constant motion. In fact, the results left us all wondering whether even the meanings of the measures we used to assess progress had, themselves, changed over time. The portrait that emerged from our review of organization-wide themes also served as a reminder that not all people or all groups are affected in the same way by an organizational initiative.

RECOGNIZING THAT SYSTEMS ARE IN PERPETUAL MOTION

Using static measures to document changes in an organizational system is like trying to capture the drama of your daughter's championship soccer game with a still camera. Knowing the final score does not really tell you what happened or even how well the team played. You might catch an important moment on film but perhaps not. You don't know which passes connected or how well each player covered her mark. When the dynamics you want to describe are in motion, it is near impossible to record them all in that single photo, because the game is not about the individual players but rather about how the group worked together. A video camera might help, but even that does not tell you all you really want to know about the "spirit" of the game.

Organizational change is ongoing and does not stop while we try to capture it on film. As change agents, we have very few tools with which to record the flow and the "feel" of organizational processes. There is a lot going on at once, and what you do manage to "see" is continuously evolving. With this perpetual motion in mind, it is important to remember that a definable intervention is only one of many influences within an organization. During my tenure at ChemPro, the organization was implementing new approaches to employee empowerment, engaging in multiple reorganizations, shifting reporting structures, revising PA procedures, and implementing cross-training requirements—all technically separate from the Workplace Chemistry Initiative itself.

It is additionally challenging to assess changes occurring within an organization when there are significant simultaneous changes in the social and economic context of the organization. In other words, not only is a system in motion *internally,* but the context within which that system sits is also constantly changing. ChemPro faced a shifting economic landscape, which, particularly in the later years of our work, brought considerable economic pressures and downsizing. This is all obviously important to consider when working to alter individual attitudes, team and organizational supports, and the general quality of work life. Clearly, many influences fed into any changes we might have observed.

Understanding systems as dynamic also highlights the importance of assessing changes in *patterns.* This point became particularly apparent when we were looking at the survey data. Broad summary statistics rarely yielded a useful picture. For many of the key indicators, it was enlightening to consider how *patterns* of change differed by race and/or sex and by organizational position. The relationships between various indicators told a richer story than any single indicator by itself. For example, the departments that were most diverse also expressed the most reluctance to adapt to diverse others. This combination of factors drew a more complex picture of the challenges in the process of learning how to work with a diversified team. The adaptation to diversity was an ongoing process that involved negotiating new ways to work, and with that adaptation came some bumps in the road.

Assessments that take a snapshot of an organization are more appropriately used for hypothesis generation than hypothesis testing. Survey data such as ours technically only *describe* participants' responses to a particular set of stimulus questions at a particular point in time rather than proving any specific connections. Additionally, not all change can be easily quantified. "Humanizing coworkers" is very difficult to operationally define. Organizational "culture" is a notoriously difficult construct to measure. Further, there is the impossibility of separating out which initiatives, influences, or broader trends have been the key catalysts for any specific shifts. Nonetheless, survey results can raise useful questions about possible links and point to issues for organizational leaders to explore more fully. They provide a window into possible connections and areas to explore.

Qualitative information to complement the quantitative is extremely useful.[15] The written comments on the surveys, the discussions in the rec hall during the survey administration, and the feedback from the leaders while they reviewed the survey results were invaluable in developing a portrait of changes. This type of information helps to place static quantitative data into the context of ongoing organizational life. In essence, what I am talking about here is "ecological validity," which is to say, "the congruence between the environment as experienced by the [individual] and the properties of the environment the investigator assumes it has."[16] Particularly for understanding dynamic interpersonal issues, the results of a survey cannot be fully understood without getting out into the workplace to get an inside view of the daily rhythms of life.

ALLOWING FOR CHANGE IN THE MEANING OF MEASURES

Not only did the organization keep moving; the measures used to assess change also appeared to have a kind of motion of their own. More specifically, one impact of the Workplace Chemistry Initiative seemed to be changes in what some of the outcome measures *meant,* such that the very same questions were tapping a different set of issues at time 1 than at time 2. Since the changing organizational context was accompanied by changes in sensitivities, it was challenging to ascertain what a shift in ratings over time really signified. There is a odd irony here, as the intervention may have changed what the measures measured so that they no longer measured what they were designed to measure in order to measure any changes that resulted from the intervention . . . a wonderfully circular tongue twister.

There may be some positive "negative" results in the survey data. If we take the results for all the indicators of success at face value, some findings look quite distressing. The incidence of offensive behavior went up; sexual harassment seemed to increase. Yet from what we were told more informally, people were experiencing ChemPro as more informed and aware. Rich told us that the complaints of harassment that his office had fielded on a regular basis had virtually come to a halt. As discussed previously, the fact that whites and men reported observing a higher level of offensive behavior over time is noteworthy. It seems highly unlikely that there was an increase in offensive behavior only within earshot of white men, and more likely that the new ratings reflect changes in how these people evaluated the comments that had continuously surrounded them. The "negative" results may well be due to the elimination of previous blinders to the problems—and thus reflect a positive change in awareness and sensitivity.

There may also be some negative "positive" results. For example, some measures may have tapped into harsh, new understandings of what is really required in order to deal with an increasingly diverse set of coworkers. Thus, assessment results that look positive may not be good news. The finding that the predominantly white male departments considered themselves fairly accepting of diversity might, at first glance, seem positive, yet it could be a cause for serious concern. It is much easier to think that your unit is open to diversity when you have never had to face it. In Year 1, Processing rated itself more positively than other units in terms of receptivity to women—when just about everyone at ChemPro would have agreed that this was one of the least accepting corners of the plant. Not only were these self-assessments made in the absence of actual experience; these workers were perhaps confusing cohesion among current coworkers with openness to newcomers. Similarly, the camaraderie and low turnover in the male-dominated Maintenance Unit were, at one level, good news. However, the unit's lack of success in keeping its one woman worker was an *organizationally* significant concern. The findings for Processing and Maintenance raise questions about whether members of homogeneous groups are really equipped to rate themselves on issues of diversity. In both cases, workers' experiences of being "tight-knit" units may have clouded their awareness of how that cohesiveness shut others out. To be clear, I am not arguing that their ratings of openness were fabricated—rather that the operators and technicians had no benchmarks against which to understand their lack of receptivity to diversity.

At the same time that we suspected shifts in meanings, we needed to be careful about jumping too quickly from the original conceptualization of measures. While many people seemed to feel that the increased reporting of offensive behavior represented increased awareness, it still behooved us to be wary. The increases also might have reflected a backlash. It would not have been appropriate to explain away all negative feedback. It was also possible that the years of work on diversity issues had reduced the receptivity of some teams to workers from varied backgrounds and/or that the reporting of more negative results reflected a more realistic sense of the struggle involved in addressing daily challenges of working with a diverse team. The questions raised by the results cannot be answered glibly; they clearly need ongoing attention.

What I am suggesting here is that organizational change agents need to be mindful of how the changing context within and surrounding an organization affects *all* aspects of our work—including what our assessment tools might tap. The ambiguity about what findings might mean, however, should not immobilize us. In the case of ChemPro, no matter how the responses were interpreted, it was clear there were successes as well as important work still to be done to help workers deal effectively with diverse others. The main ecological lesson is that the context within which people respond to our questions shifts over time, and thus the meaning of what we ask can also shift. We need to consider our "conclusions" as hypotheses and proceed with a willingness to continually listen with openness and flexibility to feedback from varied sources.

ATTENDING TO SOCIAL LOCATIONS

The different patterns for different demographic groups and job categories at ChemPro underscore the importance of looking at how experience is shaped by one's social identity and social location—and the accompanying dynamics around access to power and resources. Assessments of change need to consider that workers' experiences are influenced by, among other things, their racial identity, their sex, the structure of their jobs, and their location within the hierarchy of the organization. At the same time, we need to be cognizant of the problems associated with assigning people to categories, as there is tremendous diversity among women and among people of different ethnic, cultural, and racial backgrounds.

In ChemPro's case, we did identify some differences between groups. Women started out feeling the most excluded and reported noteworthy improvements. There was increased sensitivity to racial and ethnic diversity, but people of color still felt intense scrutiny when in leadership roles. Many, of all races, felt that their own group was treated more unfairly than others. People at supervisory levels were the most positive about adapting to a changing work environment, while operators and techs reported more reluctance. People on the plant floor were less receptive to adapting to others. In sorting through implications of these findings, it is important to consider how the observed differences could be influenced by access to information and/or control over work. Although there were clearly improvements, groups lower in the social and organizational hierarchy faced more ongoing constraints.

It is also altogether possible that the ratings reflected different things in different departments. There were not enough women or people of color to do any statistical comparisons with white men on a department-by-department basis, but, from anecdotal responses, it was clear that life for women in Production was more stressful than for those in Administration; a person of color experienced a more welcoming work environment in Prepping than in Maintenance. To take into consideration the differences in lived experience for various groups (i.e., the phenomenology of work life) does not mean that we have to be able to dissect what elements are attributable, for example, to sex and which to position or which to race and which to social class. The confluence of race and/or sex with type of work, department, and job level replicates patterns of inequality in our society. It is not particularly useful to try to discern one-dimensional links—nor is it necessary to hone in on a single causal pathway. When varied markers of difference are interconnected, the impacts of various factors are impossible to fully disentangle.[17]

Our understanding of the experiences of marginalized groups is enhanced, however, when we recognize that race and ethnicity shape an *individual's* experiences and also define a *collective* social location that yields differential access to resources and opportunities. Too often differences that are influenced by a broad range of biased expectations, opportunity structures, and/or social constraints—and, in this case example, also segregated jobs—are reported as if they represent essential sex- or race-based differences.[18] Demographic differences on their own do not produce inequality. Rather, it is the differential treatment—and reactions of various demographic groups to that treatment—that shape many of the differences often attributed directly to membership in the group. Additionally, it is that shared *predicament* that typically contributes to social identification with the group. Further, when outlining ways to work with the *simultaneity* of various social identities in organizations, Holvino suggests that we need to pay attention to "the many ways in which difference and the social processes of race, gender, and class intertwine and 'move around,' as opposed to being localized in 'the oppressed' or 'the 'oppressor.'"[19] The complicated relationships among demographic group membership, social identity, formal job structure, and informal workplace dynamics are essential to consider when making sense of the impact of changes in team and organizational supports.

While ChemPro had benefited from the plantwide Workplace Chemistry Initiative and the HR attention to diversity concerns, the outcomes also reinforced the notion that ongoing work would be most beneficial if it included department-by-department approaches that attended to the unique culture of each unit and, while making room for tremendous variability within groups, that were sensitive to the ways that the lived experience of workers are affected by social identities such as gender, race, culture, ethnicity, sexual orientation, and disability status. In our final consultation with managers, the organizational leaders expressed their intention to adopt different approaches for the different areas within the plant and to proceed with sensitivity to how different people can experience the same environment quite differently from one another. These good intentions were hopeful, as were the initial plans to transform them into concrete action.

SYNTHESIS

The ecological lessons that emerge from looking at the organization as a whole revolve around seeing the change process as embedded in multiple contexts that are constantly changing—the context within which individuals sit, the context within which the organization sits, *and* the context within which any assessment is conducted. The ChemPro lessons also build on the principle of interdependence, which conceptualizes people and their relationships to their contexts as shifting with a perpetual motion that has a radiating impact—much as a mobile shifts in the wind. Organizational change agents need to work hard to get inside the texture and movement of daily work life within the organization. We may also need to settle for a close approximation, come to peace with the limitations of our measures, be flexible in how we understand "results," and accept the fact that there is no simple, single truth or source of change. While adopting this humble perspective, we can still use the insights gained from our efforts to understand the current state of the organization and to design plans for ongoing action.

equation for ongoing work

6

= connection + disruption

THE VISION SUPPORTED by the story of ChemPro is one of organizational transformation—not merely tinkering with isolated organizational practices but working to change the soul of the organization. It is not just about hiring a more diverse set of workers. It is not just about the adoption of new policies and procedures. It is not just a matter of treating everyone "the same." Unidimensional or static strategies simply cannot fully address dynamic problems. Returning to the imagery of chemistry, the work is about introducing elements that in interaction with one another have the potential to synthesize into something new—and about understanding that the process by which the elements are combined will determine whether they will produce an explosion or will work together to yield something more creative. The work with ChemPro illuminates the shift in paradigms from acontextual to systemic—and the shift in primary focus from content to process—that is required of researchers, consultants, and organization members interested in designing the inclusive workplace.[1]

It is useful to anchor this type of organizational change in a deep respect for human capacity and in empathy for divergent experiences of events, while also actively addressing the dynamics that create oppressive systems. Thus, our work has been grounded in a stance of *connected disruption,* which involves connecting to individuals while disrupting organizational and cultural arrangements, connecting to a shared humanity while challenging powerful blind spots supported by privilege. The multiyear effort at ChemPro holds many lessons for those committed to diversity work. In this final chapter, I will review the journey by returning to the vision for inclusive organizational settings that guided this work, summarizing the challenging dilemmas that emerged along the way, and discussing the countervailing forces working against

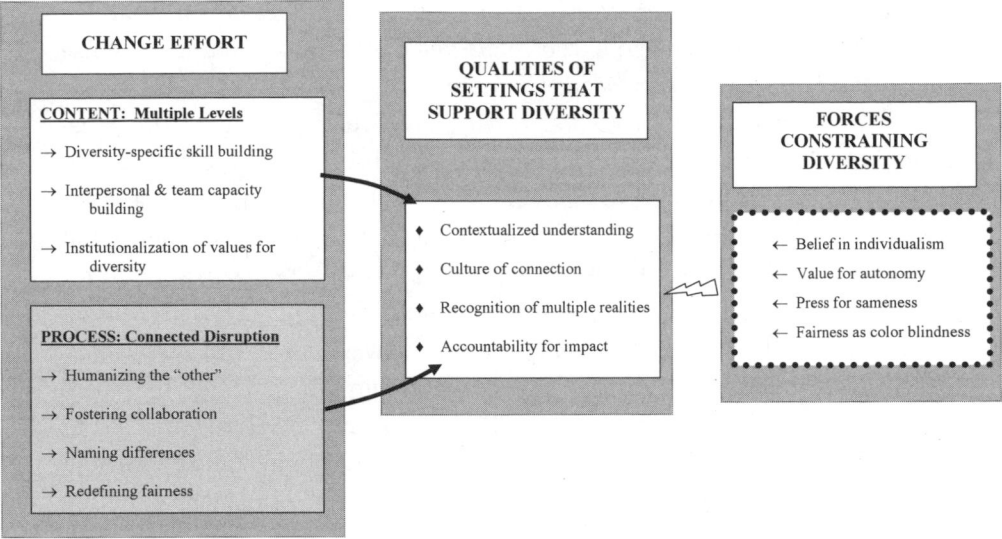

FIGURE 6.1   Connected Disruption and the Process of Change

change. Finally, I will return to the notion of *connected disruption* and expand on the process considerations that support such a stance (see figure 6.1).

qualities of diverse settings revisited

The vision that guided the Workplace Chemistry Initiative was to develop an organization that attended to contextual influences, embodied a culture of connection, recognized multiple realities, and held people accountable for their impact. One element of this vision involved fostering a *contextualized understanding* of organizational life. Becoming cognizant of context means recognizing how all workers fit into a maze of interpersonal and organizational influences.[2] As illustrated by this case study, teams that can work effectively across differences incorporate an understanding of how individual workers are affected by team dynamics, how team functioning is influenced by informal and formal organizational processes, and how work *within* the organization is facilitated or constrained by forces external to the organization—from family dynamics to workforce patterns to broader business pressures. Attending to context includes attention to informal norms, team relations, and formal institutional policies and procedures. It involves an expanded awareness of the historical and societal forces that have shaped current diversity dynamics.[3]

A *culture of connection* is the second setting characteristic and goes hand in hand with adopting a contextualized understanding of organizational life. A shift to an organizational *culture of connection* means incorporating the sense that what happens *between* people is as important as what happens *within* people. An organization that works toward effective diversity is an organization that cares about the spaces in between. Points of connection have qualities that transcend the particularities of the individual players involved and are enhanced by creating new settings where people can discover strengths and points of connection that they might not have previously realized. Support for connection can come in the form of more regular meetings, revised meeting structures, and regular training opportunities that enhance communication. A *culture of connection* is sustained by emphasizing the goals that members have in common and underscoring the fact that they need one another in order to reach those goals. In addition, such organizational cultures are supported by formal policies that institutionalize a value for community building.

The third important setting characteristic is the *recognition of multiple realities*. Rigid adherence to one way of operating has been found to characterize settings that are less supportive of diversity. For example, Cox suggests that cultures that have a narrow view of accepted behavior and that tend not just to describe broad goals but also to prescribe specific methodologies and tactical details (which he calls "high prescription" cultures) are not conducive to meaningful inclusion of a diverse membership.[4] He argues that low-prescription cultures, on the other hand, which set some core standards and superordinate goals but make room for varied ways of approaching the tasks at hand, are less judgmental and more inclusive. Within manufacturing, this is inherently tricky. At ChemPro, there is a specific pH at which a chemical mixture must be kept; there is a clearly defined temperature at which ingredients must be combined. Little or no variation can be tolerated, or the final product will be ruined. The Workplace Chemistry Initiative was not—in any way, shape, or form—about promoting sloppy operational standards. Rather, more phenomenologically, it was about validating varied subjective experiences of the work relationships and, where possible, varied approaches to workplace practices.

Organizations that support diversity provide settings where differences can be raised safely and where marginalized voices are heard. To do so, they are also settings that understand the accountability dynamics that can render some groups and perspectives less visible. The fourth core setting quality, *accountability for impact,* builds on the ecological notion that all members of an organization have an effect on others (as individuals and as a group), takes into account how power differences shape one's impact, and codifies responsibility for that impact. To accomplish this, it is critical to distinguish between *intentions* that drive individual and organizational behavior and the *impact* or effects of that behavior. The distinction between intent and impact is not new. Crosby and Cordova point out that businesses routinely assess whether their product improvements actually have the desired effect and that the legal community differentiates between "disparate treatment" and "disparate impact" in recognition that some policies that appear neutral can actually have different implications for people of different races or genders. They note that this distinction, however, can be more difficult to accept interpersonally because, at least in part, most people have learned that prejudice leads to discrimination, the extension of which is the belief that if we rid ourselves of biased attitudes, we will end discrimination.[5] However, discrimination *can* happen without prejudice, and negative impact *does* happen separately from mal-intent. Thus, we worked with ChemPro to use both formal and informal mechanisms to hold members accountable for their impact—with particular attention to the impact on previously invisible groups. Diversity efforts need to be backed up by institutional structures that support these alternative expectations. For example, organizations can incorporate accountability expectations into formal performance evaluations and reward structures, institute caucuses or affinity groups within organizations and give them a formal role in developing priorities, sponsor training, and/or organize settings for difficult dialogues.[6]

ecological reflections on emerging dilemmas

The Workplace Chemistry Initiative cultivated attention to context, connection, multiple realities, and impact throughout several threads of activities: a collaborative assessment process, plantwide training, team consultations, and attention to the institutionalization of organizational values in hiring and promotion practices, performance evaluations, and leadership development. As I traced the work with ChemPro in this book, I have noted dilemmas that emerged at each stage of the initiative (see figure 6.2). These ecologically grounded reflections combine to paint a dynamic picture of the challenges of organizational change.

Our initial task was to establish a shared understanding of the issues at ChemPro. Developing a nuanced sense of the organization required active recognition of the resources indigenous to the organization. Recognizing strengths was essential both for establishing a respectful relationship and for

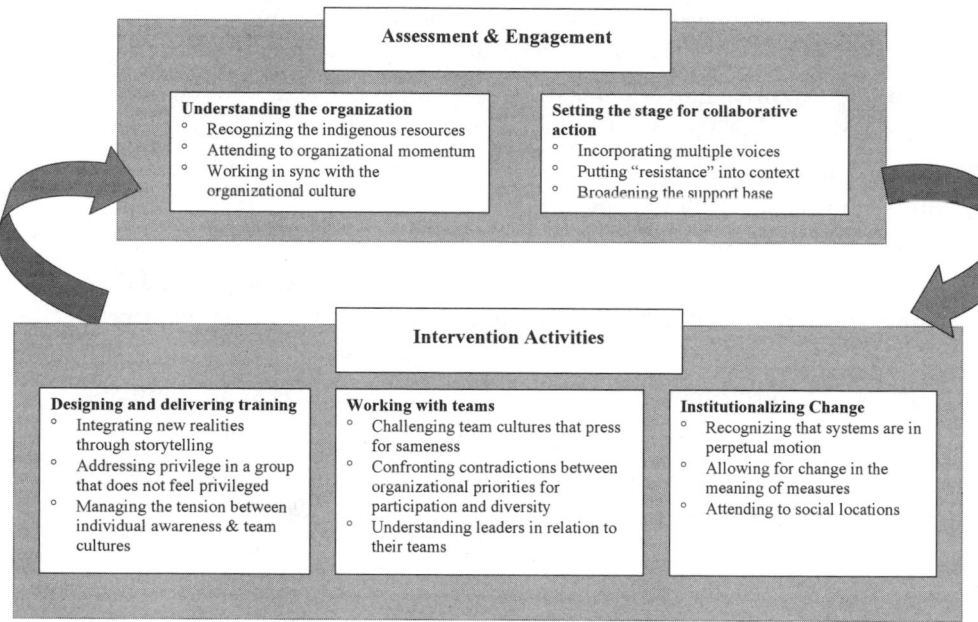

FIGURE 6.2 Ecological Reflections on Organizational Change

discovering the foundation on which to build. At the same time, it was critical to understand ChemPro as a system in motion, with a unique culture and
a momentum that predated that of any new initiative. As change agents, we
needed to understand the ongoing organizational journey—even while pre-
paring to intentionally nudge it off its current course.

The more active phase of setting the stage for change involved establishing partnerships in this disruptive effort. Building effective collaborations
meant reaching out to hear from people who had not been previously involved in determining the organizational narrative. Such a process can be
energizing as previously bit players begin to share more of the organizational
spotlight. Yet pulling in new "realities" also signals a change in business as
usual. The accompanying uncertainty about what the future holds can be
unsettling and have ripple effects that emanate out to all parts of an organization. Some pushback is natural. Understanding this phenomenon can help
to de-pathologize the reactance and put "resistance" into perspective. Being
empathetic about the experience of disruption while sustaining the commitment to bringing in new voices is part of the balancing act required when trying to build an ever-broadening support base for change.

As we began providing training to increase awareness of diversity issues and to build skills for working across differences, we encountered process dilemmas related to both how to reach individuals and how to create work contexts that would support change. An important goal of training was to shift the organizational conversation so that the processes that had previously silenced the nondominant voices could be challenged. It is no easy task, however, to discuss the dynamics of privilege in a group that does not in many senses feel privileged. Just because someone is white or male does not mean that s/he is immune to experiences of oppression—particularly if working in an hourly job on the floor of a manufacturing plant. Those who are challenging the dynamics that marginalize women and people of color can gain important partners if it can be done without invalidating the experiences of white men.

As we consulted with the teams themselves to support new ways of operating, different sorts of ecological lessons emerged. Each ChemPro team had adopted patterns, traditions, and unique ways of operating that needed to be navigated and respected in the process of change. On some units, it became apparent that team relationships were being shaped by organizational values for independence. Interestingly, some organizational "empowerment" initiatives that were geared toward increasing the involvement of workers, while well intended, actually worked against the broad inclusion of workers outside the dominant core group. We sought to make the contradictions apparent to managers. The leadership approaches required for redirecting team priorities changed with the specifics of each team and the demands on members of the group, both from within the team and from the broader organization.

Organizational change efforts are not complete unless they also attend to the institutionalization of new guiding values and ways of operating. As we traced organizational efforts toward recruitment, promotion, and retention, the dilemmas that became most apparent were related to the observation that systems are in perpetual motion. Nothing stands still—not even the meaning of our indicators of change. Organizations embody a swirl of activities, sensibilities, personalities, social identities, and priorities. Any change effort has to work in sync with that commotion and, at the same time, take into account that how individual workers respond will vary with their social location vis-à-vis such identities as race/ethnicity, sex, age, sexual orientation, and job position.

countervailing forces

Dynamics that cannot easily be seen, values that are not actively labeled, and assumptions that are not explicit enough to be questioned make change more difficult.[7] They are in a sense forces against change. Four such countervailing forces that ran through the process dilemmas at ChemPro included the belief in individualism, a value for autonomy, pressure for sameness, and the invoking of "color blindness" as a marker of fairness. Belief in the heroic power of individuals is an entirely acontextual perspective, and the person-centric prescriptions for change that emerge from beliefs in individualism are often barriers to organizational change.[8] Similarly, the go-it-alone nature of an emphasis on autonomy denies the interdependencies inherent in system dynamics. Inclusivity is further hampered within groups where there is pressure for sameness, since diversity is antithetical to the comfortable sense of order that comes with predictability and conformity. "Color blindness" implies that the emphasis on sameness is freeing; however, the disavowal of differences in power and of variation in experiences of the world is actually a stance that can preclude effective diversity.

These countervailing forces are rooted in the fundamental question of what constitutes "fairness." Is fairness about treating everyone the same way or about ensuring equal access to resources and opportunities? William Ryan, the writer who introduced the concept of "blaming the victim," contrasts a "fair play" with a "fair shares" perspective on fairness.[9] The fair play perspective stresses that individuals should have the freedom to pursue opportunities but assumes that there is no guarantee of success and that natural processes will determine who is most successful. From this perspective, inequality in the workplace is seen as not only tolerable but justified as long as all people have the opportunity to apply for the job. The fair shares conception of equality puts the emphasis on the resources necessary to succeed in the workplace. It is a commitment to the principle that all members of society "obtain a reasonable portion of the good the society produces."[10] This view is that inequality results from ignoring basic differences in power, opportunities, and access to resources; thus, to achieve equality, you must pay attention to both formal and informal workplace dynamics that might privilege one group over another. Along these lines, Rosenblum and Travis argue that "color blindness is not really a strategy of politeness; rather it is a strategy of power evasion. Since race clearly makes a difference in people's lives, pretending not to see it is a way to avoid noticing its effects."[11]

The conflict between these two perspectives is deep. In fact, from a fair play perspective, paying attention to different types of supports needed by different groups is seen as profoundly unfair, whereas, from a fair shares perspective, ignoring the different needs and barriers is seen as inherently unfair. Some of what gets coded as "resistance" is intertwined with these unspoken—and largely inaccessible—contrasting paradigms for thinking about equity. The fair play perspective is a worldview that embodies deep-seated values that can be forces against the type of change we were working on at ChemPro.[12] To rock a shared complacency with the individualistic values dominant in our society, organizational settings need to actively *counter* values that work against diversity, and they need to create a community of support for new ways of being.

connected disruption and the process of organizational change

The vision of enhanced chemistry through equity and inclusion is lofty, yet the actual process of fostering such organizational change is filled with subtle tensions that cannot be ignored. Addressing the emerging dilemmas and entrenched countervailing forces requires strong partnerships grounded in a stance that combines a sense of connection to members of all groups with a willingness to give voice to differences and hold people accountable in new ways (see table 6.1). In order to be transformative, a change effort needs to be humanizing and collaborative; yet nonetheless it needs to dispute assumptions, disrupt problematic patterns, and disturb complacency. Navigating system dynamics in a manner that is respectful yet bold enough to actually produce change entails a stance that combines *connection* with *disruption*.

CONNECTION
The connected side of this prescription involves humanizing the "other." This includes communicating empathy, respect, and appreciation, and attending to the ways that all workers are potential resources for the organization.[13] Extending this stance to diversity consultation entails bringing forth and appreciating the humanity of all organization members—both those who have been silenced and those who have enjoyed a more privileged hold on the organizational discourse. During the organizational change process, connection can be fostered through creating opportunities for sharing, promoting attention to the power of context, and adopting a nonjudgmental stance. It is also enacted through collaboration that recognizes organization members as partners in the process of change.

Members of groups with less power often suffer a combination of invisibility and gross stereotyping that denies their individuality. Their experiences

TABLE 6.1 · ELEMENTS OF CONNECTED DISRUPTION

CONNECTED DISRUPTION (FORCES FOR MEANINGFUL INCLUSION)		COUNTERVAILING FORCES (FORCES FOR EXCLUSION)	
Principles	*Practices*	*Values*	*Practices*
Humanizing the "other"	Appreciating the "other's" humanity Incorporating an understanding of context	Belief in individualism	Emphasis on individual change
Fostering collaboration	Focusing on shared aspirations and goals Honoring local knowledge and local contributions	Value for autonomy	Lack of accountability
Affirming differences	Creating opportunities for differences to surface Legitimizing multiple perspectives	Press for sameness	Rigid adherence to dominant norms
Redefining "fairness"	Acknowledging privilege Emphasizing accountability for impact	Fairness as color blindness	Blindness to differential privilege

are often unseen by majority group members, and it can feel risky to go public. When challenged to consider the marginalized experiences, dominant group members often fear they will be blamed and clumped together as "the oppressor." Getting beyond this potential standoff involves resisting the temptation to move further apart and, instead, moving close enough to see the humanity on the other side of the divide. For members of historically oppressed groups, entertaining the possibility of partnering with majority group members toward change requires a context that is truly validating and a connection at a human level that is not easy to achieve. For members of a dominant group, opening up to hear marginalized experiences involves something deeper than an intellectual appreciation for how minority experiences have been rooted in historical oppression and differential access to power.

Creating structures for safety and inclusion during an organizational change process are some of the scaffolding for finding common ground. In our assessment, we tried to develop an organizational portrait that was appreciative of the humanness of all workers involved. In the training and team consultations, we worked with participants to establish ground rules that would make the settings safer for sharing. We adopted a self-deprecating sense of humor about being "politically correct" to demonstrate a willingness to be self-critical and an intention to avoid self-righteousness. We worked with supervisors to get commitment to the initiative and assurances that there would be no backlash against those who participated. Warren, Keitha, and Rich stood behind these assurances.

I recently saw a bumper sticker that read, "The shortest distance between two people is a story." Organizations can help to shorten the distances between people by providing spaces for these stories. Many participants were more effectively introduced to new ways of viewing their coworkers through hearing about their lives than through didactic presentations about diversity. The personal stories grounded people's learning in connection and gave texture to the training. Not only did the formal aspects of the Workplace Chemistry Initiative provide such opportunities for storytelling, but the spaces around the edges (such as breaks, on-site assessment interviews, feedback sessions with individual units) were also transformed into opportunities for reaching across differences. For many women and participants of color, the workshops were the first time they had ever talked to white and/or male coworkers about their frustrations with biased treatment or their sense of aloneness in dealing with stereotypes about their group. The impact of hearing stories about the treatment of members of marginalized groups was sometimes transformative—and most powerful when the new insights were paired with more personal reactions to the injustice, whether that be outrage or just a sense of helplessness. It was at these moments that the marginalized perspectives were not only being heard by majority group members but were also being understood through connection. Empathy is not a distant fascination or depersonalized curiosity about the "other" but rather a sensibility with more heart. Additionally, a story that renders one particular coworker an "exception" while listeners hold onto preconceived judgments about race and/or gender in general is not going to move an organization forward. Connection to a shared humanity is a proactive process that comes from a position of humility and openness to questioning past assumptions.[14]

Connection is facilitated by embracing an ecological understanding of the multiple layers of influence on people and getting away from paradigms that focus exclusively on personality, individual capabilities, or even personal awareness. Understanding people in context opens up possibilities to connect to those you might initially be inclined to dismiss, avoid, and/or confront harshly. Contextual thinking helps to short-circuit temptations to pass judgment. If we had restricted our focus to personal skills, we would have missed team dynamics like those in Processing that could isolate members—particularly women—who made waves. If we had ignored outside forces, we would have missed the pressure on many white men from retired relatives who thought diversity meant that their old workplace was going downhill. We would have missed the worry in some black families that a promotion would mean becoming "one of them." If we had not looked at organizational arrangements, we would have missed the ways that decision-making strategies designed to empower workers actually conceded power to a dominant "in crowd."

While bringing *new* voices to the fore is a top priority in diversity work, I have been arguing throughout this book that connection to the experiences of majority group members is also important, as it helps enable them to move toward change without tripping over feelings of blame or shame. Some change agents operate as if power will concede nothing without a demand. There is certainly some history to support this belief, and adversarial action is sometimes the only effective method available. However, we worked from the belief that neither blame nor shame is a particularly effective motivator for *enduring* constructive action—particularly in an intact social system like an organization. In fact, they are probably more likely to produce anger and resentment than become the seeds for personal growth or openness to collaboration. What I am suggesting here is the usefulness of connecting to people's humanity and building on their good intentions rather than first pulling their mistakes or failings into the foreground. The connection can help provide a foundation for the challenges and confrontation that may follow. This is not just an idealistic stance; it is also a pragmatic one.

Connection is buoyed by collaboration and an honoring of local knowledge. To bring a wide range of people into the Workplace Chemistry process as partners, we shared our assessment observations with every unit in the plant—twice!—and worked to incorporate feedback before proposing an intervention plan. The initiative was vetted and sponsored by an existing cross-department team of workers. We had in-house partners as cotrainers who took the risk to model the unearthing of perspectives and experiences that had not been previously shared; their stories had a particularly profound impact. Organizational members were integrally involved in every aspect of intervention design and implementation.

Working from a position of connection means attending to all these interdependencies during the process of change, but it is also about integrating this sensibility into the daily functioning of teams and the organization as a whole. The connected part of the prescription for change is not just a stance for change agents. It is, perhaps even more importantly, an ongoing organizational shift from an individual lens to a community lens—that is, *collective attention to context* and the development of a *culture of connection*. This includes a sense of "being in it together" (in contrast to an "us vs. them" attitude), sharing goals, and valuing each team member's contributions to meeting those goals. It moves the organizational ethos from what's "unfair to me" to what's "good for the team." Not all types of connection are helpful, however. A focus on what brings people together should not be confused with minimizing differences. I am talking about connection that is empathic, reciprocal, and sustained over time but also attentive to the tangled web of organizational relationships and attuned to power dynamics—thus the pairing of connection with disruption.

DISRUPTION

There are a few lines in a poem by Pat Parker that have stuck with me over the years. While the poem is titled "For the White Person Who Wants to Know How to Be My Friend,"[15] it contains good advice that can generalize to many dimensions of difference. Parker counsels,

> The first thing you do is to forget that i'm Black.
> Second, you must never forget that i'm Black.

We can connect around what we have in common, but the connection is not complete unless we also accept that we are also profoundly different from one another. We are then challenged to hold onto both of these views at the same time. Basing connections only on similarities can deny critical differences tied to individuals' experiences and identities in the same way that "color blindness" ignores power differences.

Another way to think about this is to again invoke a narrative analogy.[16] Settings, in a sense, adopt a dominant story, and that story attaches meanings to behaviors. Unwelcoming settings are those where the prevailing story does not allow for variations based on experiences of members who bring different expectations, resources, or values and who thus might experience the world differently. Organizational change efforts that promote meaningful participation of diverse members uncover multiple stories or "realities" and thereby acknowledge variations on how a situation, an event, or an interaction can be experienced and how the variations are influenced by one's membership in various identity groups (e.g., based on gender, ethnicity, or race).[17] Accepting multiple "realities" can disrupt the power of a rigid dominant story and thereby create openings for other stories to be heard. Julian Rappaport describes this when he says, "the ability to tell one's story, and to have access to and influence over collective stories is a powerful resource."[18] Herein lies the critical and disruptive shift—from one story that defines normative expectations for everyone to multiple stories of shared legitimacy, from one dominant storyteller to multiple and equally valued weavers of tales.

As Reinharz notes, "When people do not name their own experience, others name it for them and obliterate it."[19] She goes on: "Diversity-related research that seeks to hear other people's voices requires understanding the relationship as one of speaking and listening and therefore requires us to understand who can speak to whom and be heard."[20] In order to hear voices that have been suppressed, we have to be able to create a context where the person can speak *and* where others can listen. This process may be facilitated by fostering connection. However, there is a disruptive side as well. More specifically, to make room for new "realities," change agents engage in disrupting patterns, relationships, and practices that define a single view as "natural" or more "real" (i.e., normative). This is a proactive process of making room for alternative views.

In our work, we emphasized the importance of collectively adopting a "both/and" perspective so that people could listen without feeling they had to relinquish their own views in order to hear those of others—even though revealing previously silent voices inevitably transforms the dominant organizational ethos. "Both/and" also allows for the honoring of alternative views without having to totally agree with or embrace them. The challenge is to allow seemingly contradictory perspectives to coexist. The spirit of this work is captured in a question posed by author Lillian Hellman: "Since when do we have to agree with people to defend them from injustice?"[21]

The importance of this multiplism is rooted in contextualist assumptions that challenge notions of uniformity across people, places, and times. It does not mean disavowal of white male experience but rather the *meaningful* inclusion of the experiences of women and people of color *and* the possibility for the alternative views to transform the majority view. The goal is not to flip the hierarchy of views. The shift toward "both/and" moves multiple perspectives side by side *and* into relationship with one another. This perspective stands in contrast to an "either/or" stance, where there is a press to determine which *one* of multiple experiences is the correct, legitimate, or *prevailing* one.

No matter how humanizing the process, revealing and elevating minority perspectives is inherently disruptive, as it puts previous "givens" into question. Making visible the perspectives and experiences of those who have been kept at the margins means reexamining values and assumptions at the core of how many in the majority have defined themselves and the world around them. It requires the majority group to tolerate an intense lack of certainty and what Sandra Bartkey has called "double ontological shock"—"first, the realization that what is really happening is quite different from what appears to be happening, and, second, the frequent inability to tell what is really happening at all."[22] This new questioning of previously taken-for-granted assumptions also challenges those who have carved out a relatively safe place at the margins to risk a new relationship to the setting. Dealing with this disruption may well require a particular type of tolerance for ambiguity and emotional intelligence, which have been suggested as characteristics of leaders and organizations that support diverse groups.[23]

I am also suggesting in this case study that while naming differences is important for creating workable settings where diverse groups can all contribute in meaningful ways, it is not sufficient. In fact, making differences more visible can sometimes result in highly charged, adversarial relations unless conditions are such that the forces that privilege one view over others are actively addressed. While discomfort with ambiguity and preferences for sameness may be the critical dynamics that push for a more uniform view, differential privilege is the central factor that determines which view or views predominate. The power structure of the organization, the distribution of power among participants, and the relative power within society can serve to privilege (or highlight) the positions and views held by one group over others even when the intentions are toward shared power.

A profound intervention in this direction is the shift to attending to impact. Focusing on *intent* tends to privilege the dominant group, as it allows the status quo to stay intact (i.e., people are not required to adjust to others as long as they mean well). Focusing on *impact* forces a setting to expand to really include the marginalized "realities" and thus confronts the very dynamics that have marginalized those experiences. Disruption is woven into the change in social order required when people are accountable in multiple directions for their impact on others. As Rob Hall describes, "Fundamental to the [accountability] process is the dominant group's acceptance that they cannot presume to know when their actions are being experienced as oppressive by the less dominant group but must seek information from, or be informed by, the less dominant group."[24] *Attention to impact* does not represent the standard hierarchical arrangement of organizational relationships, but rather a multidirectional accountability. Since the best (perhaps only) judges of impact on marginalized groups are those people or groups themselves, accountability changes the social arrangements.[25] Being accountable for your impact involves tremendous responsibility for your behavior beyond your own sense of what you meant to do.

The need for alternative procedures and supportive structures is intensified by the way the broader culture embraces values for independence that can work against accountability. Inherent in the shift to a focus on impact is a redefinition of "fairness" from the notion that everyone should be treated the same to the notion that everyone should have access to an environment that allows them to work to their full capacity. It is a shift from ensuring equal starting places to ensuring equal opportunities or "fair shares." It is a shift that emphasizes the power of context to shape those opportunities. It is also a shift from suggesting that people who are unhappy should speak up to, instead, expecting people to seek out and hear what others are saying.

CONNECTED DISRUPTION

Putting this all together yields *connected disruption*. To summarize: the stance of *connected disruption* involves humanizing the "other" (e.g., through storytelling, understanding the influence of context, and being nonjudgmental) and fostering collaboration (i.e., attending to shared goals, honoring local knowledge, and bringing organization members into the process as partners). Simultaneously, it involves developing settings that give voice to previously marginalized experiences (i.e., affirming differences, creating opportunities for talking *and* listening, and legitimizing "both/and") and shifting our definition of "fairness" (i.e., naming the privilege dynamics that have precluded attention to nondominant voices and shifting accountability). Confronting collective complacency with organizational arrangements that hinder meaningful involvement across differences involves a process of developing a disruptive edge yet doing so while staying in relationship with others. *Connected disruption* is about what change agents *do*—but, more importantly, it is also about what organization members *feel* or *experience* in the process of change. It is about the impact of the change process on those involved. It is about the relational field that surrounds the intervention.

The connection and the disruption are tightly interlinked. Attending to impact requires empathy—not sympathy, which embodies a hierarchy of caretaker and injured, but empathy, which incorporates a mutual respect and willingness to truly imagine how someone else's life might feel to that person. It is not easy to focus on how others experience or "construct" the meaning of your behavior, since you have much more control over your intent than your impact. It is disconcerting to learn that the effects of our actions ripple out in directions that we cannot control by simply being well-meaning. Some appreciation for good intentions may provide the connection needed for tolerating the disruption of being held accountable for impact. The accountability does not negate the empathy, nor does the appreciation negate the responsibility. Both empathy and attention to impact are consistent with the ecological requirement for understanding the legitimacy of participants' subjective *experiences* of events versus retaining a sole focus on external, measurable definitions.[26] Collaboration rooted in local knowledge is in sync with the requirement to name differences—both are built on an ecological appreciation for the power of context.[27]

To effectively open up organizational settings, there may, in fact, be a recursive relationship between the *connection* and the *disruption*. That is, some assurance of disruption may be necessary to allow marginalized groups to risk connection, while some assurance of connection may be necessary to allow majority groups to risk disruption. For example, early in our relationship with ChemPro, some workers of color were reluctant to "open Pandora's box"—clearly telling us that the known inequities were more tolerable than the risk of opening up to an uncertain outcome. Some evidence that there really would be a challenge to old patterns and support for new ones may have been a precondition for previously silent groups to risk sharing their alternative "realities."

Simultaneously, for the white men, connection may have been an important precondition for effectively shifting the focus to accountability and impact without triggering a destructive backlash. Agents working for change can support the participation of members of dominant groups through connection but be disruptive enough to challenge dominant *practices* that limit the participation of more marginalized members. Keitha reflected on differences between the Workplace Chemistry Initiative at ChemPro and some of the diversity work she witnessed at Corporate. Although Corporate had instituted a program that involved many more days of training than ours did, she said:

In a lot of ways I thought our program at ChemPro was more effective because we included the white males. [Corporate's] was definitely a blaming approach: "White males, you are the problem." I think that alienated people, made people think twice. To me, it was just not necessary . . . It was not pragmatic at all [because after the training] you had to go back and do damage control.

Connected disruption means understanding the dynamics that shape the behavior of dominant group members and that can blind them from recognizing privilege and the impact of their behavior. But it also means making room for people to make mistakes and to misunderstand—and joining with them to support their learning from these lapses versus dissolving into adversarial camps. It helps to assume that the intent of the dominant group member is not malicious, for then *connected disruption* can mean challenging people's behavior through a climate of learning and partnership. It is also very useful to separate blame from responsibility. Although an *individual* member of the majority group (i.e., white, male) is not necessarily to blame for inequalities, that person can still take responsibility for the power that privilege has given her/him to define whether or not others are treated as "outsiders." Change agents can simultaneously appreciate people's loyalty to team cultures and challenge them to open up to new possibilities. Through such approaches, we can combine disruption and connection by challenging culturally embedded practices while honoring individual humanity.

Sustained commitment to the change effort is critical both to the connected and disruptive elements of such a stance. This is not always easy, and there is an ongoing dynamic tension between the two sides of the *connected disruption*. When establishing connection, the pull is to collude and not be disruptive. When you are disruptive, you are a disquieting and uncomfortable influence. However, a truly empathic connection, where you work to understand how people can see and experience what they do without necessarily agreeing, can potentially create the leverage needed to effectively disrupt and work toward an effective alliance to deal with race and gender issues. There is an evolving process, an awkward process, of disconnecting from old norms like racial and sexual humor and then trying to find new, more inclusive and egalitarian ways to connect. It takes time.

We can carry a stance of *connected disruption* into the many aspects of the role of change agent. Through *connected disruption*, change agents can help people see the unseen and take the risk to address the unknown. Our work can be more consistently informed by the standpoint of marginalized groups. We can focus on labeling and challenging privilege at least as much as we have focused on describing the oppressed. We can wonder more actively about the perspectives of those who stand on the "fringe" and recognize "outliers" as important sources of information. In all the settings we work with (and in), we can strive to create cultures of connection and facilitate communities of support for alternative ways of approaching organizational work. Through active *connected disruption,* we can help to create exciting contexts for putting a value for diversity into action.

the consultant and connected disruption

Throughout this book, I have been reflecting on my experiences as a white, middle-aged, able-bodied, heterosexual female academic working with a predominantly white, male, blue-collar workforce. I have tried to distill lessons that can be useful for others working toward culture change in organizational systems. However, I would be remiss to ignore the ways that a consultant's ability to engage in *connected disruption* is profoundly affected by her/his own social identity and context.

For example, being white probably allowed me easier initial entry with management than might otherwise have been the case. My race may have given me permission to confront issues of racial and ethnic discrimination without being dismissed by whites as having a "personal agenda" or a "chip on my shoulder." However, my race also presented challenges in terms of earning the respect of people of color within the organization. Even if I earned some trust over time, I could never fully bridge the differences. Being a woman meant I needed to prove myself in ways that probably would not have been true for a male consultant. It might have been harder for the men at ChemPro to trust me. At the same time, my gender (and stereotypes about women) may have made it easier for people to reveal their vulnerabilities— allowing me to be confrontational and still stay in connection. Being heterosexual clearly made me a more comfortable presence for many people at ChemPro but did little for increasing the visibility of GLBT issues within the organization.

My work context also played a role. Being an academic initially fed some worries about being out of touch with the "real world," but it also provided me with considerable flexibility. As a full-time professor, I had the luxury of an income outside consultant fees, which meant my livelihood was not dependent on a certain pace of work. Additionally, while we hoped to reach some concrete benchmarks of success, we were not prisoners to a predetermined, unmoving finish line. I could approach the work as a learning experience for my students, for me, for my professional community, *and* for ChemPro. This gave us more freedom to revise and adapt our approach with the various punches that life was throwing ChemPro's way. This flexibility was only really possible because Warren, Keitha, and Rich valued the learning—but it was also enabled by my academic home.

My personal life was another relevant aspect of my context that brought with it advantages and barriers. I remember slipping out of early morning meetings at ChemPro to check on a child's fever, rushing home after an intense training workshop to make it to a parent-teacher conference, and operating on very few hours of sleep.[28] Even while the multiple demands were sometimes stressful, being married and having children put me on common ground with many at ChemPro and facilitated connection. My family also gave me significant supports that enabled me to do this work. I could not have made it out to the plant for a 7:00 a.m. shift change meeting and gotten two young children out the door if I was a single mother. I could not have done interviews on night shifts if my husband was not home to cook dinner and do bedtimes. Bill was not just a logistical helpmate on the home front; he was also a valuable resource for bouncing ideas back and forth and generating action plans. It is downright silly to think that any change agent acts alone; I would have had a lot less ability to either connect or disrupt if I did not have a community behind me.   .

The work of a consultant is not only influenced by who you are and the community that surrounds you; it is also affected by the story about you that is held within the organization. There are many at ChemPro who have told me they felt understood and respected, even though challenged, by me. For some, I was like a special aunt who could provide support during difficult times—in a way, I was both inside and outside the family and thus informed but relatively safe. For others, however, I was primarily a disruptive force—in part because of who I am but also in part because of the story that developed about me. One worker in Processing told me he was surprised at my relatively mild manner when he met me. He had imagined me a "monster" after hearing repeatedly, "If you don't work this out, we are going to bring Meg Bond in here." Some never saw me as anything but a bother, since no matter what stance I might adopt, I was still a signal of change.

As Shula Reinharz reminds researchers, "We must study who we are as well as who we are in relation to those whom we study." This clearly applies to change agents as well.

conclusion

ChemPro made a commitment to diversity among workers that lasted over time. I was fortunate to have been invited to come along on the journey. In the years working with ChemPro, I heard moving stories of transformation. Yet it was also quite clear that there were barriers to broader workplace change—some individually based, some systemic. The cutbacks and layoffs that plague all of manufacturing in the United States often left little energy for diversity. Organizational leaders made it clear that this work was essential for the survival of the organization, yet many—workers and managers—also believed a more active effort would be necessary to keep the commitment alive.

This was a real-world story—a messy story—not without bumps and bruises. I do not want to idealize the work described here. Rather I offer up this case example as a real-life effort to make a difference—one with many successes and creative approaches. I hope readers find lessons and insights they can use in their work. I hope this example makes clear the value of considering the interrelationships among personal identity, team dynamics, organizational procedures and culture, and the world outside the organization. I hope it drives home the importance of a long-term, multifaceted commitment to the process.

In spite of all its complexity, I truly believe that the Workplace Chemistry Initiative was worth all the time and energy. Keitha agreed:

> This initiative wasn't a luxury for us—to have you all come in—it was a necessity. That's the way I look at it. If you are not focused on the people side of business and you just focus on the product side, then you lose your ability to stay alive. If I was writing this book, I would make sure that you say that the Workplace Chemistry Project was critical for ChemPro. We needed to be very adaptive. We couldn't have done that without paying attention to the people part of the business—and diversity is a huge part of that. If we hadn't done this work, we weren't going to survive.

appendixes

appendix a: SURVEY OVERVIEW

goals

- To look at how employees of different races, ethnicities, genders, ages, and/or physical abilities experience life at ChemPro
- To gather information that will help guide future initiatives to improve the quality of work life

overview

The survey included measures of:

- Individual-level values that support diversity
- Team and organizational supports for diversity
- Quality of work life

individual values supportive of diversity

- *Conservatism about diversity* = the perspective that efforts to promote equity/diversity have gone too far and/or are unnecessary. These beliefs are often referred to as "backlash." A high score indicates strong endorsement of conservative beliefs.
- *Empathy* = the ability to put oneself in another's position and/or to listen and understand another person's perspective even when one disagrees. A very important perspective when dealing with people who come from different ethic, racial, or gender cultures. A high score indicates high empathy.
- *Concerns about adapting to differences* = attitudes about whether one should be asked to adapt to the needs of others (as opposed to feeling resentful if asked to change one self because of a coworker's preferences or needs). A high score indicates high resentment if asked to adapt to diverse needs of others.

team and organizational supports for diversity

DIVERSITY CLIMATE
(Items adapted from Riger et al. 1997 and Stokes et al. 1995; additional items designed specifically for ChemPro survey; subscales defined through factor analysis)

- *Good for diverse groups* = extent to which ChemPro is seen as a good place for various groups of people to work.
- *Commitment to equality* = perception regarding whether management is serious about treating people equally.
- *Support for diversity* = ratings of supervisors' value for and understanding of diverse workers.

RESPONSIVENESS TO CONCERNS
(Items adapted from Riger et al. 1997 remediation subscale; additional items designed specifically for ChemPro survey; subscales defined through factor analysis)

- *Reactions to harassment* = the likelihood that coworkers will challenge degrading comments and jokes.
- *Intolerance for sexual harassment* = the extent to which supervisors and coworkers communicate that sexual harassment will not be tolerated.
- *Inflexibility around work-life integration* = extent to which workers feel they can ask for flexibility to deal with issues outside work.

quality of work life

GENERAL
(Items adapted from the Hughes and Dodge 1997 and the Job Content Questionnaire designed by Karasek and colleagues 1985)

- *Satisfaction with current job*
- *Feeling respected*
- *Supervisor support*
- *Peer cohesion*

OBSERVATIONS OF TREATMENT OF OTHERS
(Items adapted from Riger et al. 1997, Stokes et al. 1995, and Donovan et al. 1998; additional items designed specifically for ChemPro survey; subscales defined through factor analysis)

- *Observations of harassment and discrimination* = ratings of extent the respondent has observed the harassment and/or discrimination of others based on their gender or race. A high score indicates greater observed harassment.

- *Observations of generally offensive behavior* = extent to which respondent has witnessed generally offensive, sexist, or racist jokes or comments. A high score indicates more frequent occurrence of offensive behavior.
- *Unfairness* = perceptions regarding whether some groups are treated more harshly than others.

OWN EXPERIENCES OF HARASSMENT AND DISCRIMINATION
(Items designed specifically for ChemPro survey)

- *Experiences of sexual harassment* = frequency of experiencing unwelcomed sexualized attention, touching, or pressure. A high score indicates greater frequency.
- *Experiences of gender harassment* = frequency of experiencing gender-based harassment or discrimination over the last year. A high score indicates greater frequency.
- *Experiences of racial harassment* = frequency of experiencing race-based harassment or discrimination over the last year. A high score indicates greater frequency.

TABLE B.1 · RATINGS OF TRAINING TOPICS AND ACTIVITIES

TRAINING TOPICS AND ACTIVITIES	N	RANGE	MEAN (S.D.)
Day #1–topics			
Various aspects of diversity among people	71	2–5	4.35 (.66)
Why organizational diversity is important for ChemPro	71	2–5	4.38 (.70)
The development of an inclusive and nonblaming definition of workplace diversity	70	2–5	4.24 (.71)
Day #1–activities			
Movie: *True Colors*	70	1–5	4.61 (.73)
BafáBafá simulation	68	1–5	3.72 (1.06)
Mobile making and discussion	69	1–5	3.57 (1.06)
Day #2–topics			
Your own values about gender	71	2–5	4.38 (.80)
Your own values about race	71	2–5	4.35 (.79)
How workers from different racial and ethnic backgrounds might experience ChemPro differently	71	3–5	4.42 (.65)
The unique concerns women face in the workplace	71	1–5	4.32 (.87)
What empathy is	71	3–5	4.21 (.72)
How multiple perspectives can coexist peacefully and productively (both/and perspective)	71	2–5	4.13 (.74)
Day #2–activities			
Cultural affirmations	70	1–5	4.30 (.86)
Circle of sharing	70	2–5	4.37 (.75)
Both/and activity	70	3–5	4.04 (.73)
Day #3–topics			
The impact that stereotyping has on everyday interactions at work in the real world	71	1–5	4.34 (.88)
How various forms of privilege affect work relations	71	2–5	4.15 (.84)
Recognition of your own sources of privilege	70	2–5	4.14 (.86)
The importance of focusing on impact (rather than intent)	70	2–5	4.31 (.71)

TABLE B.1 · *continued*

TRAINING TOPICS AND ACTIVITIES	N	RANGE	MEAN (S.D.)
Day #3—activities			
Stereotyping exercises	69	1–5	4.09 (.80)
Movie: *Color of Fear*	70	1–5	4.66 (.81)
The Race	70	1–5	4.09 (.96)
Day #4—topics			
The model of effective teams adopted by ChemPro	69	1–5	3.88 (.92)
Interpersonal patterns	70	1–5	3.96 (.84)
What it means to be accountable to teammates	69	1–5	4.14 (.93)
Skills of giving constructive feedback	69	2–5	4.03 (.79)
Day #4—activities			
Bridge it simulation	70	2–5	4.03 (.99)
Organizational culture/"cup" game	69	1–5	3.90 (1.06)
Sharing your heritage	70	1–5	4.66 (.81)

appendix b: TRAINING EVALUATION

Conservatism About Diversity

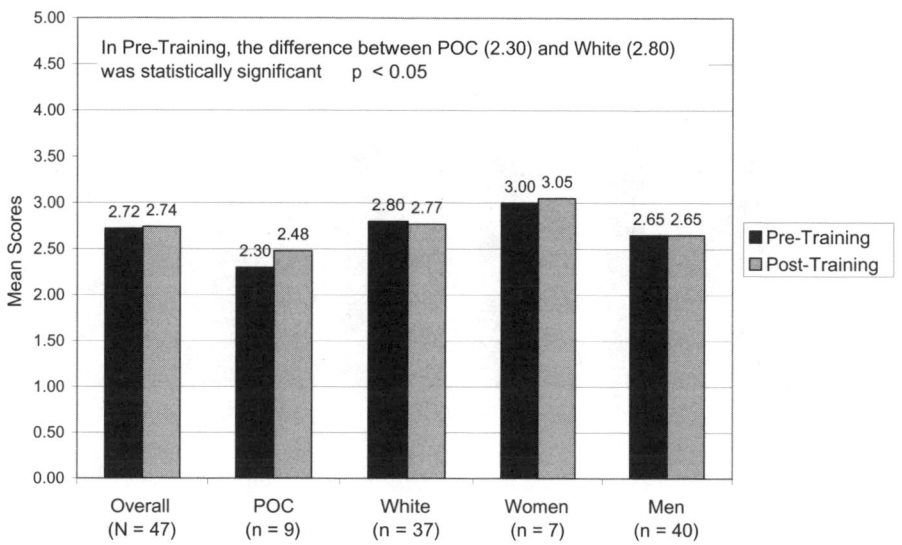

Conservatism About Diversity

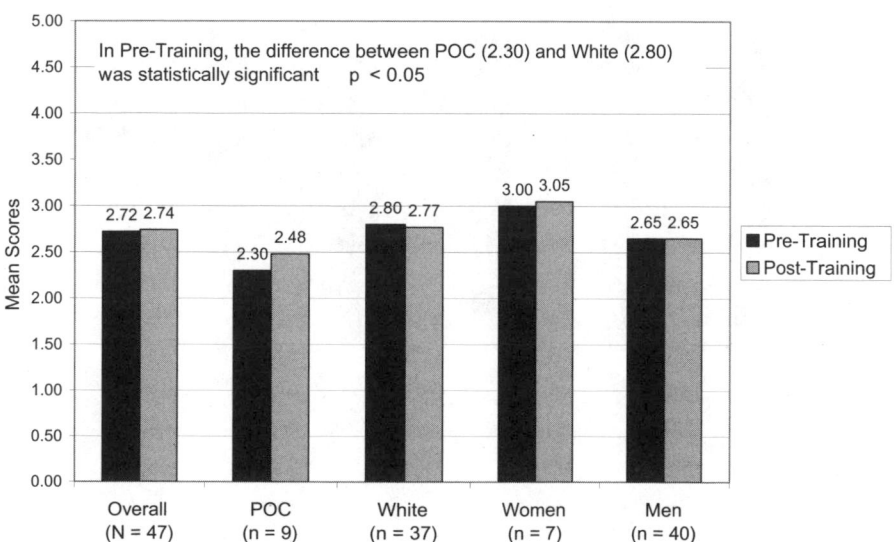

FIGURE B.1 Pre-post Means for the Overall Sample, as Well as by Race/Ethnicity and Gender

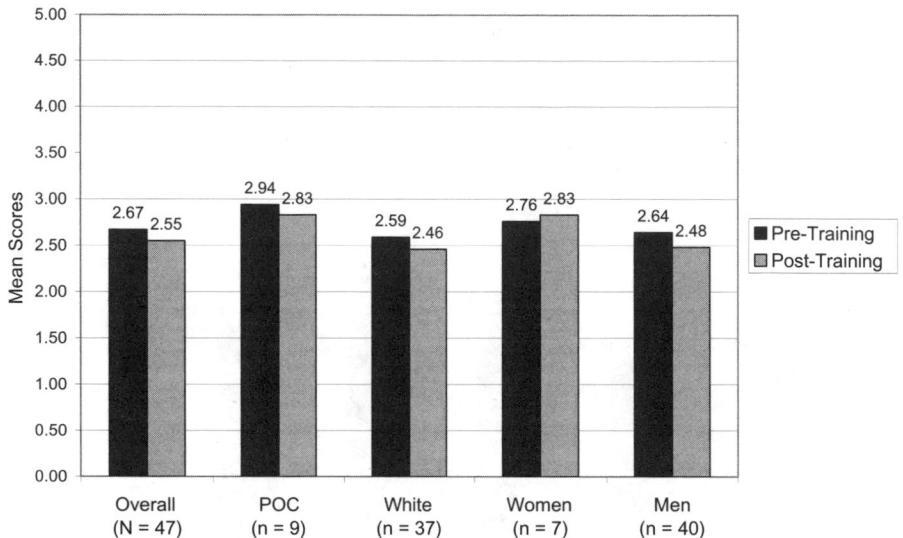

Concerns About Adapting to Differences

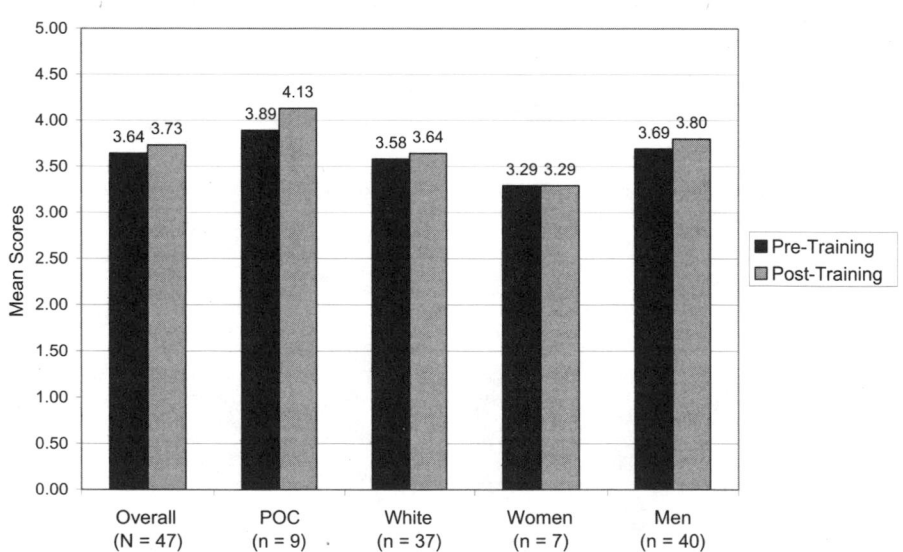

Satisfaction with Current Job

FIGURE B.1 *continued*

Feeling Respected

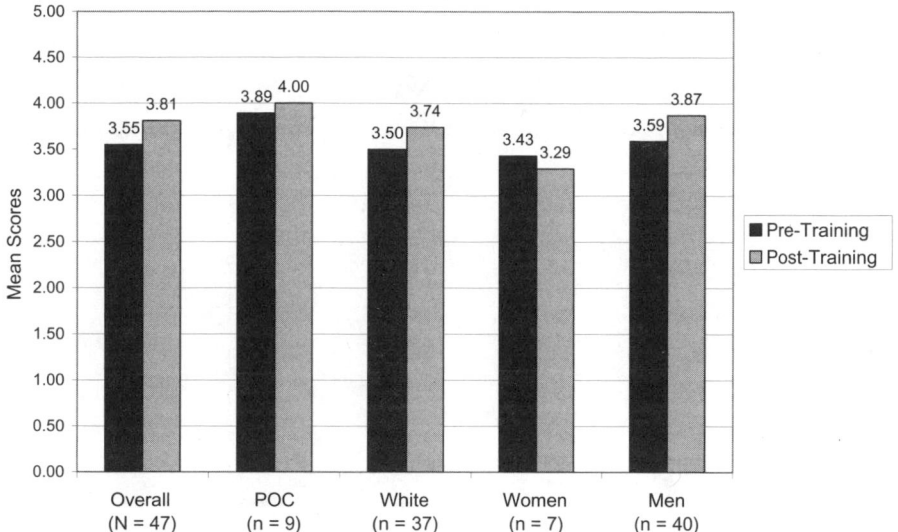

Peer Cohesion

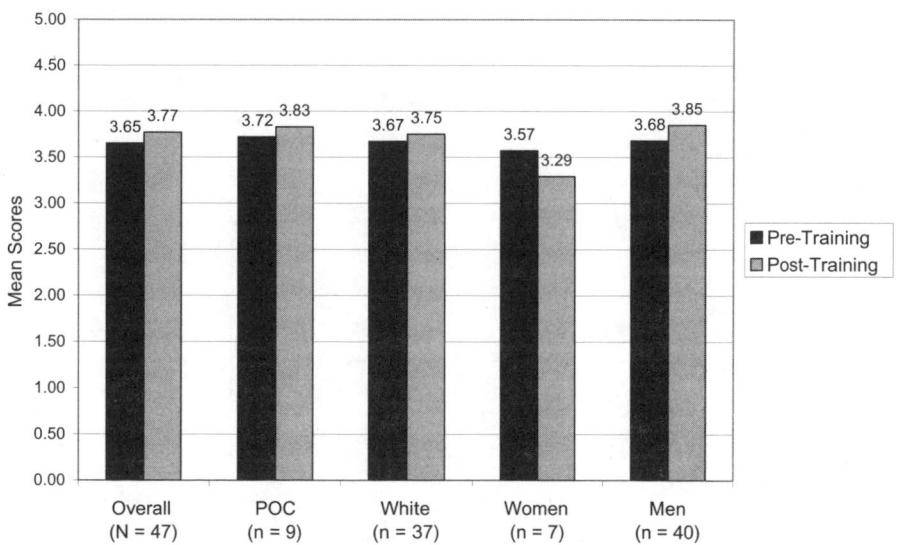

FIGURE B.1 *continued*

appendix c: SURVEY RESULTS FOR YEAR 1 AND YEAR 7

TABLE C.1 · COMPARISONS BY DEPARTMENT FOR YEAR 1

	MANUFACTURING 1	MANUFACTURING 2	FACILITIES	LABS	ADMIN	SIG
	$n = 26$	$n = 37$	$n = 20$	$n = 16$	$n = 16$	
Individual values						
Conservatism about diversity	2.93 (.76)	2.78 (.89)	2.85 (.72)	3.06 (.67)	2.37 (.82)	
Empathy	3.64 (.91)	4.31 (.76)	3.55 (.89)	3.94 (.93)	3.50 (.89)	.003
Concerns about adapting to differences	2.62 (.47)	2.44 (.62)	2.49 (.57)	2.43 (.46)	2.20 (.42)	
Team and organizational supports						
Good for diverse groups	3.60 (.64)	3.86 (.64)	4.00 (.62)	3.52 (.72)	3.39 (.65)	.026
Commitment to equality	4.10 (.69)	3.97 (.74)	4.08 (.89)	3.56 (1.08)	3.44 (.93)	.046
	3.72 (.80)	3.75 (.71)	3.63 (.74)	3.63 (.79)	3.83 (.65)	
Reactions to harassment	3.04 (.90)	3.09 (1.06)	3.20 (.98)	3.19 (1.03)	3.39 (1.16)	
Inflexibility around work-life integration	3.02 (1.13)	2.58 (1.00)	2.63 (1.15)	2.94 (.98)	2.43 (.97)	
Quality of work life						
Satisfaction with current job	3.88 (1.14)	3.89 (1.37)	3.39 (1.79)	2.94 (1.18)	2.94 (1.57)	.046
Feeling respected	3.60 (1.00)	3.91 (.95)	3.70 (1.17)	3.19 (1.05)	3.63 (.81)	
Supervisor support	3.96 (.73)	3.76 (.85)	3.66 (1.25)	3.45 (.87)	3.68 (.62)	
Peer cohesion	3.54 (.72)	3.66 (.78)	3.43 (1.10)	3.60 (.93)	3.53 (.56)	
Harassment and discrimination						
Observations of discrimination and harassment	2.14 (.96)	2.00 (.82)	1.98 (1.08)	2.27 (.81)	2.40 (.81)	
Observations of generally offensive behavior	1.36 (.68)	1.57 (.92)	1.72 (.22)	1.54 (.74)	1.92 (.98)	
Unfairness	2.25 (.78)	1.68 (.72)	1.83 (.78)	2.09 (.86)	2.46 (.84)	.007
Experiences of sexual harassment	1.03 (.08)	1.08 (.21)	1.15 (.29)	1.09 (.20)	1.36 (.66)	.017
Experiences of gender discrimination	1.25 (.68)	1.26 (.76)	1.05 (.22)	1.88 (1.03)	2.00 (1.37)	.002
Experiences of racial discrimination	1.92 (1.28)	1.37 (.71)	1.20 (.70)	1.38 (.81)	1.38 (.89)	.079

NOTE: Ns vary slightly from cell to cell.
NOTE: The table numbers are the mean rating of participants on scales that ranged from 1 to 5. The numbers in parentheses are the standard deviations.

TABLE C.2 · COMPARISONS BY DEPARTMENT FOR YEAR 7

	MANUFACTURING 1	MANUFACTURING 2	FACILITIES	LABS	ADMIN	SIG
	n = 38	*n* = 50	*n* = 18	*n* = 14	*n* = 26	
Individual values						
Conservatism about diversity	2.45 (1.04)	2.77 (.99)	2.69 (1.02)	2.52 (.84)	1.99 (.74)	.020
Empathy	3.63 (1.13)	3.88 (1.04)	3.89 (1.18)	3.71 (.99)	3.88 (1.21)	
Concerns about adapting to differences	2.54 (.83)	2.68 (.74)	2.38 (.66)	2.60 (.58)	2.09 (.61)	.018
Team and organizational supports						
Good for diverse groups	3.91 (.67)	3.48 (1.01)	3.94 (.87)	3.68 (.66)	4.20 (.57)	.005
Commitment to equality	3.67 (1.07)	3.15 (1.15)	3.47 (.95)	3.71 (.75)	4.37 (.82)	.000
Support for diversity	3.50 (.87)	3.13 (1.09)	3.86 (1.12)	3.71 (.96)	4.00 (.79)	.003
Reactions to harassment	3.18 (.94)	3.27 (1.29)	3.36 (.87)	3.46 (.82)	3.59 (.96)	
Inflexibility around work-life integration	3.05 (.98)	2.85 (.99)	2.55 (.89)	2.67 (.69)	2.19 (.83)	.006
Quality of work life						
Satisfaction with current job	3.89 (.86)	3.44 (1.09)	4.22 (1.00)	3.86 (.66)	4.07 (.79)	.011
Feeling respected	3.55 (1.00)	3.48 (.95)	3.72 (1.23)	3.64 (.93)	3.92 (.84)	
Supervisor support	3.68 (1.02)	3.34 (1.00)	4.23 (1.06)	4.02 (.76)	4.40 (.54)	.000
Peer cohesion	3.86 (.83)	3.55 (.93)	4.17 (.84)	3.79 (.87)	4.19 (.86)	.018
Harassment and discrimination						
Observations of harassment and discrimination	1.67 (.90)	1.82 (.99)	1.63 (.83)	2.01 (.77)	1.54 (.44)	
Observations of generally offensive behavior	1.91 (.81)	2.46 (1.20)	1.83 (.99)	1.79 (.78)	2.09 (.76)	.028
Unfairness	1.83 (.88)	1.91 (.81)	1.69 (.75)	1.86 (.89)	1.77 (.80)	
Experiences of sexual harassment	1.88 (.89)	1.92 (1.13)	1.50 (.92)	1.74 (.80)	1.60 (.65)	
Experiences of gender discrimination	1.24 (.47)	1.29 (.38)	1.11 (.36)	1.29 (.39)	1.15 (.26)	
Experiences of racial discrimination	1.13 (.47)	1.32 (.79)	1.22 (.55)	1.29 (.47)	1.27 (.60)	

NOTE: Ns vary slightly from cell to cell.

NOTE: The table numbers are the mean rating of participants on scales that ranged from 1 to 5. The numbers in parentheses are the standard deviations.

TABLE C.3 · HARASSMENT AND DISCRIMINATION: COMPARISONS BY RACE AND SEX

	OVERALL MEAN	POC	WHITE	SIG	WOMEN	MEN	SIG
Year 1	$n = 145$	$n = 21$	$n = 114$		$n = 26$	$n = 114$	
Year 7	$n = 165$	$n = 28$	$n = 122$		$n = 28$	$n = 131$	
Observations of harassment and discrimination							
Year 1	2.13 (.90)	2.20 (.86)	2.10 (.90)		2.73 (.78)	1.99 (.87)	< .001
Year 7	1.77** (.85)	1.68* (.74)	1.73** (.82)		1.77** (.83)	1.74* (.84)	
Observations of generally offensive behavior							
Year 1	1.60 (.87)	1.70 (1.03)	1.56 (.80)		1.81 (.74)	1.52 (.84)	
Year 7	2.10** (.98)	1.96 (.81)	2.13** (1.00)		1.96 (.84)	2.12** (1.01)	
Unfairness							
Year 1	2.00 (.80)	2.23 (.94)	1.94 (.77)		2.52 (.70)	1.88 (.78)	< .001
Year 7	1.89 (.84)	1.80 (.85)	1.87 (.82)		2.30 (.91)	1.78 (.79)	< .01
Experiences of sexual harassment							
Year 1	1.14 (.37)	1.10 (.15)	1.12 (.33)		1.21 (.34)	1.10 (.30)	
Year 7	1.25+ (.46)	1.29+ (.42)	1.21+ (.39)		1.24 (.35)	1.25** (.47)	
Experiences of gender discrimination							
Year 1	1.40 (.89)	1.30 (.66)	1.36 (.85)		2.38 (1.30)	1.15 (.51)	< .001
Year 7	1.26 (.67)	1.04* (.19)	1.28 (.63)	< .001	1.32** (.67)	1.25 (.68)	
Experiences of racial discrimination							
Year 1	1.45 (.92)	2.14 (1.06)	1.26 (.74)	< .001	1.62 (1.13)	1.39 (.83)	
Year 7	1.26* (.70)	1.39** (.88)	1.20 (.54)		1.18+ (.61)	1.28 (.73)	

+$p < .10$ for comparison of Year 1 vs. Year 7
*$p < .05$ for comparison of Year 1 vs. Year 7
**$p < .01$ for comparison of Year 1 vs. Year 7
NOTE: The table numbers are the mean rating of participants on scales that ranged from 1 to 5. The numbers in parentheses are the standard deviations.

TABLE C.4 · HARASSMENT AND DISCRIMINATION:
COMPARISONS BETWEEN MANAGERS AND HOURLY WORKERS

	MANAGERS	HOURLY WORKERS	SIG
Year 1	$n = 23$	$n = 110$	
Year 7	$n = 21$	$n = 110$	
Observations of harassment and discrimination			
Year 1	2.22 (1.05)	2.11 (.87)	
Year 7	1.67$^+$ (.67)	1.82* (.92)	
Observations of generally offensive behavior			
Year 1	1.83 (.76)	1.52 (.82)	
Year 7	2.11$^+$ (.64)	2.10** (1.10)	
Unfairness			
Year 1	1.71 (.72)	2.05 (.81)	
Year 7	1.43 (.55)	1.93 (.85)	< .05
Experiences of sexual harassment			
Year 1	1.10 (.26)	1.13 (.33)	
Year 7	1.19 (.32)	1.26** (.41)	
Experiences of gender discrimination			
Year 1	1.61 (1.03)	1.35 (.84)	
Year 7	1.19 (.51)	1.26 (.67)	
Experiences of racial discrimination			
Year 1	1.43 (.89)	1.43 (.88)	
Year 7	1.14 (.48)	1.27 (.70)	

$^+p < .10$ for comparison of Year 1 vs. Year 7
$*p < .05$ for comparison of Year 1 vs. Year 7
$**p < .01$ for comparison of Year 1 vs. Year 7
NOTE: The table numbers are the mean rating of participants on scales that ranged from 1 to 5. The numbers in parentheses are the standard deviations.

TABLE C.5 · RATINGS OF UNFAIR TREATMENT: ITEM BY ITEM ANALYSIS

ITEMS	POC	WHITE	SIG	WOMEN	MEN	SIG
Whites/Anglos seem to be penalized more for mistakes than nonwhite/non-Anglo employees in my department	1.64	2.38	**	2.36	2.29	
Women seem to be penalized more for mistakes than men in my department	1.50	1.80		2.32	1.65	***
In general, ChemPro is a good place for white men to work	4.29	3.87	*	4.00	3.93	
In general, ChemPro is a good place for nonwhite/people of color to work	3.37	4.07	***	3.96	3.94	

* $p < .05$; ** $p < .01$; *** $p < .001$

NOTE: The table numbers are the mean rating of participants on scales that ranged from 1 to 5. The numbers in parentheses are the standard deviations.

TABLE C.6 · SEXUAL HARASSMENT: ITEM BY ITEM ANALYSIS

EXPERIENCED ANY OF THE FOLLOWING AT CHEMPRO OVER THE LAST FIVE YEARS:	TOTAL N	FREQUENCY			% OF EACH POPULATION WHO HAVE EXPERIENCED THE PROBLEM			
		Never	1–2 times	Some to very frequently	% POC	% White	% Women	% Men
Year 1					n = 21	n = 112	n = 26	n = 112
Overall	139	108	19	12	33.3	18.8	38.5*	17.9*
Unwelcome suggestive looks or gestures	137	117	12	8	19.0	11.8	28.0*	1.8*
Unwelcome flirtation/sexual attention	139	130	6	3	0	6.3	23.1***	1.8***
Unwelcome pressure for dates	139	135	4	0	0	1.8	3.8	1.8
Uninvited and unwanted touching	139	126	9	4	14.3	8.0	19.2*	6.3*
Year 7					n = 28	n = 122	n = 28	n = 131
Overall	162	100	38	24	50.0	33.6	42.9	37.4
Unwelcome suggestive looks or gestures	161	110	32	19	46.4*	25.6*	28.6	32.3
Unwelcome flirtation/sexual attention	162	132	20	10	17.9	16.4	25.0	16.8
Unwelcome pressure for dates	162	154	2	6	3.6	4.9	.0	6.1
Uninvited and unwanted touching	162	143	12	7	14.3	9.8	21.4	9.2

*$p < .05$; **$p < .01$; ***$p < .001$.

notes

introduction (pages 1–25)

1. ChemPro is not the real name of the company, but rather one adopted for the purposes of this book. Essential information about the organization and the initiative are as reported here. However, some minor details have been altered to protect the confidentiality of the participants.

2. Lewin 1946.

3. United States Census Bureau 2004; United States Census Bureau n.d.; United States Census Bureau, Population Division 2001.

4. United States Department of Labor, Bureau of Statistics, Monthly Labor Review 2004.

5. Judy and D'Amico 1997.

6. United States Department of Labor, Bureau of Statistics, Monthly Labor Review 2005.

7. United States Department of Labor, Bureau of Statistics, Women's Bureau 2004.

8. Kuczynski 1999; McLeod et al. 1996; Watson et al. 1993.

9. Klonoff et al. 2000; Ensher et al. 2001.

10. Ng and Tung 1998.

11. Catalyst 2004; Hillman et al. 2002; Richard et al. 2002; Richard et al. 2003; Wright et al. 1995.

12. Bellinger and Hillman 2000.

13. Cox 1993; Jehn et al. 1999; Kochan et al. 2003; Riordan 2000.

14. Jehn 1995; Lau and Murnighan 1998.

15. Tsui et al. 1992.

16. http://www.eeoc.gov/.

17. Chubb 2004.

18. Bond and Keys 1993; Foster-Fishman and Keys 1997.

19. Bond 1995;1999; Bond and Keys 2000; Cox 1993; Kelly et al. 1994.

20. Kochan et al. 2003.

21. Kochan et al. 2003, p. 17.

22. Thomas and Ely 1996, 2001.

23. Harrison et al. 1998.

24. See, for example, Jackson and Associates 1992.

25. Gottfredson 1992; Bond and Pyle 1998a.

26. See Litvin 2006 for an in-depth and critical discussion of the business case for diversity.

27. See the work of Claude Steele and colleagues on "stereotype threat," Steele et al. 2002.

28. See Bell and Nkomo 2003; Chrobot-Mason and Ruderman 2004; Cokley et al. 2004.

29. Miller 1976.

30. Bond and Punnett 2006; Clark et al. 1999; Krieger 2003.

31. Rayman 2001.

32. Kelly 1968, 1979; Kelly et al. 1994; Trickett 1986.

33. C.f. Cox 1993; Stockdale and Crosby 2004.

34. For example, Gridley and Turner 2005; Nelson and Prilleltensky 2005; Trickett 1994.

35. Trickett 1996.

36. Bronfenbrenner 1979; Kelly 1966; Kelly et al. 2000.

37. Levine and Perkins 1997, p. 144.

38. Holahan and Spearly 1980; Kelly 1968; Trickett et al. 1972.

39. Holahan and Spearly 1980; Kelly 1968; Kingry-Westergaard and Kelly 1990.

40. Hartstock 1998.

41. Wright, adapted from Allmond et al. 1979.

42. Bond 1999.

43. C.f. Katz and Kahn 1978; Pyle and Bond 1997.

44. Bond 1999; Bond and Keys 1993.

45. E.g., Sherif et al. 1961.

46. Watts, Trickett, and Birman 1994, p. 464.

47. C.f. Rosabeth Moss Kanter's classic 1977 book, *Men and Women of the Corporation.*

48. Bond 1999.

49. In fact, some of the material in chapter 2 draws heavily on a coauthored paper: Bond and Pyle 1998b. Permission was obtained from coauthor and publisher.

50. I owe many thanks to the following students and collaborators: Beth Adler, Dianne Cazeca, Jennifer Gooch, Raji Kanniyapan, Yael Keren, Steven Lockney, Erin Lynch, William Madsen, Eileen Maloney, Gabriela Pashturro, Manjula Sastry, Robin Toof, Ana Valdez, Melissa Wall, and Jamie Weller.

51. Bond and Pyle 1998b; Pyle and Bond 1997.

52. See, for example, Roosevelt Thomas's classic 1991 book, *Beyond Race and Gender.*

53. For example, Hayles and Russell 1997.

54. See, for example, Linnehan and Konrad 1999.

55. Bond and Pyle 1998a; Pyle and Bond 1997.

56. Oxtoby et al. 2002, p. 2.

chapter 1: chempro (pages 26–49)

1. Census information is available at http://www.census.gov.

2. Bond and Pyle 1998b.

3. Senge 1990, pp. 56–57.

4. For example, Jackson and Associates 1992; Families and Work Institute 1993.

5. Trickett 1986, p. 190.

6. Lewin 1946 as reprinted in 1997, p. 42.

chapter 2: catalysts for change (pages 50–81)

1. Bartunek et al. 1994; Bartunek and Louis 1996; Rappaport 1994; Reinharz 1992.

2. Cox 2001; Chrobot-Mason and Ruderman 2004; Thomas and Ely 1996.

3. It was approved by the university's Institutional Review Board (IRB), which reviews all university-sponsored research proposals for the purpose of protecting the rights of individuals who are subjects of any research conducted by faculty, staff, students, or others.

4. Eisenhardt 1989; Lincoln and Guba 1985.

5. See, for example, Elvira and Graham 2002.

6. Bartunek et al. 1994; Bond and Keys 1993; Fine et al. 1990; Kossek and Zonia 1993.

7. Ogbu 1993.

8. For example, Fuehrer and Schilling 1988; Gilligan 1982; Tannen 1990, 1994.

9. Clayton and Crosby 1992.

10. Fine 1995.

11. Blau et al. 2002; Pyle and Bond 2002.

12. Greenwood and Levin 1998.

13. See, for example, the classic book Toward a New Psychology of Women by Jean Baker Miller (1976).

14. Fiske 1993, 2000.

15. Eberhardt and Fiske 1994, p. 204; see also Fiske 1993.

16. Kelly 1986; Vincent and Trickett 1983.

17. Reinharz 1994, p. 194.

18. Reinharz 1994.

19. Trickett et al. 1994b, p. 23.

20. C.f. Bartunek 2003; Bartunek and Louis 1996; Walsh 1987.

21. Bond and Pyle 1998b; Katz and Kahn 1978; Vincent and Trickett 1983.

22. Prilleltensky and Nelson 2002, p. 27.

chapter 3: formulas for action (pages 82–120)

1. See appendix A for an outline of the survey.

2. See chapter 5 and appendix C with the Year 1 survey results.

3. This group included Raji Kanniyapan, Yael Keren, Manjula Sastry, Steven Lockney, and Erin Lynch.

4. See Bond 1999.

5. BafáBafá is copyrighted by Simulation Training Systems (www.simulation trainingsystems.com).

6. Akutawaga 1952.

7. *The Color of Fear* is available from StirFry Seminars and Consulting (www.stir fryseminars.com). Our use of the film at ChemPro was in accordance with their use agreement, which specifies that the corporate purchaser is "limited to viewing The Films for use within the institution on the following conditions: (1) The Films were purchased by the institution; (2) no admission is charged, and (3) the showing is limited to a presentation for staff members and/or students within the institution, and is used to discuss the issue of improving race relations."

8. Vasquez 2006.

9. This exercise has been adopted by many others, sometimes also called the "privilege line."

10. The interviewers for this assessment were Gabriella Pashturro and William C. Madsen.

11. A table with mean ratings of all topics and training activities can be found in appendix B.

12. Francescato 2006.

13. See appendix B for pre and post-training comparisons by race and gender.

14. Reinharz 1994; Bond 1997; Bond, Belenkyi and Weinstock 2000.

15. Essed 1991; Tatum 1999.

16. Brewer and Miller 1984; Brewer 2000.

17. Rappaport 1995.

18. For example, Fiske 1993; Miller 1976; Mulvey et al. 2000.

19. Adapted from Merriam-Webster: http://www.m-w.com/dictionary/privilege.

20. Fine 1997, p. 57.

21. There is wonderful work on developing critical consciousness for the oppressed, including the groundbreaking work by Freire (1972) and more recent work by Watts, Griffith, and Abdul-Adil (1999). What I am suggesting here is that perhaps we can also teach a form of social critique to the majority group to help break down forms of oppression.

chapter 4: out of the laboratory (pages 121–167)

1. Berg 1994; de Shazer 1985.

2. For example, Bryson 1995.

3. Kellogg 2004.

4. Lewin 1943, as republished in 1997, pp. 42–43.

5. The work of the Public Conversations Project is a useful model here. Information can be found at: www.publicconversations.org.

6. This exercise drew on an imaging exercise designed by Blake, Mouton, and Sloma (1965) to address intergroup conflicts.

7. MacKinnon 1979, p. 27.

8. Eisenberg 1998.

9. See official EEOC definition at http://www.eeoc.gov/types/sexual_harassment .html.

10. Families and Work Institute 1993; Katz and Kahn 1978; Tsui et al. 1992.

11. Scott 1994.

12. See Bond and Pyle 1998a.

13. The sameness perspective is akin (although not identical) to William Ryan's (1981, 1994) "fair play" perspective. Difference paradigms are akin to Ryan's "fair shares" perspective, where the primary concern is with the distribution of resources and "the assurance is that everyone has enough" (1994, p. 28). See also Lykes et al. 1996.

14. Scott 1994, p. 362.

15. Jackson and Ruderman 1995.

16. C.f. Kelly et al. 1994; Schneider 1987.

17. E.g., Bond and Keys 1993; Cornell Empowerment Group 1989; Swift and Levin 1987; Rappaport 1990; Serrano-Garcia 1984.

18. E.g., Chrobot-Mason and Ruderman 2004; Cox 2001; Loden and Rosener 1991.

19. Eisenberg 1998.

20. Phillip Mann, e-mail communication, April 22, 1998.

chapter 5: synthesis (pages 168–207)

1. Holvino et al. 2004.

2. For testing the significance of changes in plant demographics over time, a series of z-tests were conducted comparing the proportions for the three measurement points for each demographic group. None of the changes were statistically significant using a $p < .05$ criterion.

3. Again, we requested and received approval from the Institutional Review Board at UMass Lowell for the survey work.

4. See appendix A for an outline of the survey and information about the sources for the various scales utilized.

5. For the statistical comparisons of mean ratings of diversity values, team and organizational supports, general quality of working life, and discrimination/harassment, analysis of variance (ANOVA) tests were conducted between specific groups (i.e., whites vs. POC; men vs. women; managers vs. workers) and between times (i.e., Year 1 and Year 7).

6. See appendix C for comparisons by departments.

7. It is worth noting that the scales for inflexibility around work-life integration used in Year 1 and Year 7 were not identical.

8. See appendix C for comparisons by departments.

9. This should, however, be interpreted with caution, since the supervisor scales used in Year 1 and Year 7 were slightly different.

10. See appendix C for comparisons by departments.

11. See appendix C for an item-by-item analysis for unfair treatment.

12. See appendix C for an item-by-item analysis for sexual harassment.

13. See appendix C for more details.

14. Holvino et al. 2004, p. 250.

15. Banyard and Miller (1998) argue this is particularly true for understanding issues of diversity.

16. Bernal et al. (1995) summarize the definition proposed by Bronfenbrenner (1979). See also Reppucci 1990.

17. For example, Bond and Keys 1993.

18. See Barnett and Rivers 2005.

19. Holvino 2001, p. 26.

chapter 6: equation for ongoing work = connection + disruption (pages 208–227)

1. Pyle and Bond 1997; Harrell and Bond 2006; Rappaport 1990.

2. Bond and Keys 1993; Harrell and Bond 2006; Kelly et al. 1994; Riger 1993.

3. Harrell and Bond 2006.

4. Cox 1993, p. 169.

5. Crosby and Cordova 1996.

6. C.f. Bond 1997.

7. Rao et al. 1999; Fletcher 1999.

8. Rao et al. 1999.

9. Ryan 1981, 1994.

10. Ryan 1981, p. 9.

11. Rosenblum and Travis 2006, p. 189.

12. See Bailyn 1993.

13. Connection is emphasized in many feminist writings as critical to nurturing the empowerment of women (e.g., the work of the Wellesley Stone Center; see Jordan et al. 1991) and in work on women's ways of knowing (Belenky et al. 1986; Belenky et al. 1997).

14. Harrell and Bond 2006.

15. Parker 1999.

16. Reinharz 1992; Rappaport 1995; Thomas and Rappaport 1996; White and Epston 1990.

17. See, for example, Harrell and Bond 2006; Mulvey et al. 2000.

18. Rappaport 1995, p. 802.

19. Reinharz 1994, p. 182.

20. Reinharz 1994, p. 195.

21. Hellman 1976, p. 85.

22. Bartkey 1990, p. 18.

23. Cox 1993; Cherniss 2002; Cherniss and Goldman 2001.

24. Hall 1996, p. 213.

25. Tamasese and Waldegrave 1993.

26. Bond and Pyle 1998b; Holahan and Spearly 1980; Kelly 1968.

27. Harding 2004; Kingry-Westergaard and Kelly 1990; Russo and Dabul 1994.

28. Perhaps a testimony to the fact that such early mornings are not in my normal repertoire is the fact that I locked my key in my car more often during the period of these consultations than I ever have either before or since. This was both a source of some embarrassment and an opportunity to bond with the Security staff, who helped me out repeatedly.

references

Akutawaga, R. 1952. *Rashomon and seventeen other stories.* New York: Liveright Publishing Co.

Allmond, B., W. Buckman, and H. Gofman. 1979. *The family is the patient: An approach to behavioral pediatrics for the clinician.* St. Louis: The C. V. Mosby Company.

Bailyn, L. 1993. *Breaking the mold: Women, men and time in the new corporate world.* New York: Free Press.

Banyard, V., and K. Miller. 1998. The powerful potential of qualitative research for community psychology. *American Journal of Community Psychology* 26 (4), 485–505.

Barnett, R. C., and C. Rivers. 2005. *Same difference: How gender myths are hurting our relationships, our children, and our jobs.* New York: Basic Books.

Bartkey, S. L. 1990. *Femininity and domination: Studies in the phenomenology of domination.* New York: Routledge.

Bartunek, J. 2003. *Organizational and educational change: The life and role of a change agent group.* Mahwah, N.J.: Lawrence Erlbaum Associates.

Bartunek, J., P. Foster-Fishman, and C. Keys. 1994. Using collaborative advocacy to foster intergroup cooperation: A joint insider-outsider investigation. *Human Relations* 4, 701–732.

Bartunek, J., and M. Louis. 1996. *Insider-outsider team research.* Thousand Oaks, Calif.: Sage Publications.

Belenky, M., L. Bond, and J. Weinstock. 1997. *A tradition that has no name: Nurturing the development of people, families, and communities.* New York: Basic Books.

Belenky, M. F., B. M. Clinchy, N. R. Goldberger, and J. M. Tarule. 1986. *Women's ways of knowing.* New York: Basic Books.

Bell, E. L., and S. M. Nkomo. 2003. Our separate ways: Barriers to advancement. In R. Ely, E. Foldy, and M. Scully (eds.), *Reader in gender, work and organization* (pp. 343–361). Malden, Mass.: Blackwell Publishing.

Bellinger, L., and A. J. Hillman. 2000. Does tolerance lead to better partnering? The relationship between diversity management and merger and acquisition success. *Business and Society* 39, 323–337.

Berg, I. K. 1994. *Family based services: A solution-focused approach.* New York: W. W. Norton.

Bernal, G., J. Bonilla, and C. Bellido. 1995. Ecological validity and cultural sensitivity for outcome research: Issues for the cultural adaptation and development of psychosocial treatments with Hispanics. *Journal of Abnormal Child Psychology* 23, 67–83.

Blake, R., J. Mouton, and R. Sloma. 1965. The union-management intergroup laboratory: Strategy for resolving intergroup conflict. *Journal of Applied Behavior Science* 1, 25–57.

Blau, F. D., M. Ferber, and A. Winkler. 2002. *The economics of women, men, and work.* 4th ed. Upper Saddle River, N.J.: Prentice-Hall.

Bond, L. A., M. F. Belenky, J. S. Weinstock. (2000). The listening partners program: An initiative toward feminist community psychology in action. *American Journal of Community Psychology* 28 (5), 697–730.

Bond, M. A. 1995. Prevention and the ecology of sexual harassment: Creating empowering climates. *Prevention in Human Services* 12 (2), 147–173.

Bond, M. A. 1997. Race, gender, and community: Creating contexts for diversity within community psychology. Presidential column in *The Community Psychologist* 30 (4), 3–7.

Bond, M. A. 1999. Gender, race, and class in organizational settings. *American Journal of Community Psychology* 27 (3), 327–355.

Bond, M. A., and C. Keys. 1993. Empowerment, diversity and collaboration: Promoting synergy on community boards. *American Journal of Community Psychology* 21 (1), 37–58.

Bond, M. A., and C. Keys. 2000. Strengthening parent-community member relations on agency boards: A comparative case study. *Mental Retardation* 38 (5), 422–435.

Bond, M. A., and L. Punnett. 2006. Expanding our understanding of the psychosocial work environment. In Bond et al., *Compendium of diversity-related measures for research in occupational health.* Cincinnati, Ohio: National Institute for Occupational Safety and Health (NIOSH.).

Bond, M. A., and J. L. Pyle. 1998a. Diversity dilemmas at work. *Journal of Management Inquiry* 7 (3), 252–269.

Bond, M. A., & J. L. Pyle. 1998b. The ecology of diversity in organizational settings: Lessons from a case study. *Human Relations,* 51 (5), 589–623.

Brewer, M. 2000. Reducing prejudice through cross-categorization: Effects of multiple social identities. In S. Oskamp (ed.), *Reducing Prejudice and Discrimination* (pp. 165–184). Mahwah, N.J.: Lawrence Erlbaum Associates.

Brewer, M., and N. Miller. 1984. Beyond the contact hypothesis: Theoretical perspectives on desegregation. In M. Brewer and M. Brewer (eds.), *Groups in contact: The psychology of desegregation* (pp. 281–302). San Diego: Academic Press.

Bronfenbrenner, U. 1979. *The ecology of human development: Experiments by nature and design.* Cambridge, Mass.: Harvard University Press.

Bryson, J. 1995. *Strategic planning for public and nonprofit organizations: A guide to strengthening and sustaining organizational achievement.* San Francisco: Jossey-Bass.

Catalyst. 2004. *The bottom line: Connecting corporate performance and gender diversity.* Available at catalystwomen.org.

Cherniss, C. 2002. Emotional intelligence and the good community. *American Journal of Community Psychology* 30 (1), 1–11.

Cherniss, C., and D. Goldman (eds.). 2001. *The emotionally intelligent workplace: How to select for, measure, and improve emotional intelligence in individuals, groups, and organizations.* San Francisco: Jossey-Bass.

Chrobot-Mason, D., and M. Ruderman, 2004. Leadership in a diverse workplace. In M. Stockdale and F. Crosby (eds.), *The psychology and management of workplace diversity* (pp. 100–121). Malden, Mass.: Blackwell Publishing.

Chubb Group of Insurance Companies. 2004. *Employment practices: Liability survey findings.* Warren, N.J. http://csi.chubb.com.

Clark, R., N.B. Anderson, V. Clark, and D. R. Williams, 1999. Racism as a stressor for African Americans. *American Psychologist* 54 (10), 805–816.

Clayton, S., and F. Crosby. 1992. *Justice, gender and a*ᵃ*rmative action.* Ann Arbor: University of Michigan Press.

Cokley, K., G. Dreher, and M. Stockdale. 2004. Toward the inclusiveness and career success of African Americans in the workplace. In M. Stockdale and F. Crosby (eds.), *The psychology and management of workplace diversity* (pp. 168–190). Malden, Mass: Blackwell Publishing.

Cornell University Empowerment Group. 1989. *Networking bulletin: Empowerment and family support* (Vol. 1, No. 1). Ithaca, N.Y.: Author.

Cox, T. 1993. *Cultural diversity in organizations: Theory, research and practice.* San Francisco: Berret-Koehler Publishers.

Cox, T. H. 2001. *Creating the multicultural organization: A strategy for capturing the power of diversity.* San Francisco: Jossey-Bass.

Crosby, F., and D. J. Cordova. 1996. Words worth of wisdom: Toward an understanding of affirmative action. *Journal of Social Issues* 52 (4), 33–49.

de Shazer, S. 1985. *Keys to Solution in Brief Therapy.* New York: W. W. Norton.

Donovan, M. A., F. Drasgow, and L. J. Munson. 1998. The perceptions of fair treatment scale: Development and validation of a measure of interpersonal treatment in the workplace. *Journal of Applied Psychology* 83 (5), 683–692.

Eberhardt, J., and S. Fiske. 1994. Affirmative action in theory and practice: Issues of power, ambiguity, and gender versus race. *Basic and Applied Social Psychology* 15 (1 & 2), 201–220.

Eisenberg, S. 1998. *We'll call you if we need you: Experiences of women working construction.* Ithaca, N.Y.: ILR/Cornell University Press.

Eisenhardt, K. 1989. Building theories from case study research. *Academy of Management Review* 14 (4), 532–550.

Elvira, M., and M. Graham. 2002. Not just a formality: Pay system formalization and sex-related earnings. *Organization Science* 13 (6), 601–618.

Ensher, E., E. Grant-Vallone, and S. Donaldson. 2001. Effects of perceived discrimination on job satisfaction, organizational commitment, organizational citizenship behavior and grievances. *Human Resources Development Quarterly* 12 (1), 53–72.

Essed, P. 1991. *Understanding everyday racism: An interdisciplinary theory.* Newbury Park, Calif.: Sage Publications.

Families and Work Institute. 1993. *The national study of the changing workforce.* New York: Families and Work Institute.

Fine, M. 1995. *Individual and social resilience in the face of discrimination.* Presentation at the American Psychological Association National Convention, New York, N.Y.

Fine, M. 1997. Witnessing whiteness. In M. Fine, L. Weiss, L. Powell, and L. M. Wong (eds.), *Off white* (pp. 57–65). New York: Routledge.

Fine, M. G., F. L. Johnson, and M. S. Ryan. 1990. Cultural diversity in the workplace. *Public Personnel Management* 19 (3), 305–319.

Fiske, S. 1993. Controlling other people: The impact of power on stereotyping. *American Psychologist* 48, 621–628.

Fiske, S. 2000. Interdependence and the reduction of prejudice. In S. Oskamp (ed.), *Reducing prejudice and discrimination* (pp. 115–136). Mahwah, N.J.: Lawrence Erlbaum Associates.

Fiske, S., and S. Neuberg. 1990. A continuum of impression formation, from category-based to individuating processes: Influences of information and motivation on attention and interpretation. In M. Zanna (ed.), *Advances in experimental social psychology* (pp. 1–74). San Diego: Academic Press.

Fletcher, J. 1999. *Disappearing acts: Gender, power, and relational practices at work.* Cambridge, Mass.: MIT Press.

Foster-Fishman, P., and C. Keys. 1997. The person/environment dynamics of employee empowerment: An organizational culture analysis. *American Journal of Community Psychology* 25, 345–370.

Francescato, D. 2006. Salient characteristics of European community psychology: Past achievements, future challenges. Keynote address at the International Conference on Community Psychology, San Juan, Puerto Rico, June.

Freire, P. 1972. *Pedagogy of the oppressed.* Harmondsworth: Penguin.

Fuehrer, A., and K. Schilling. 1988. Sexual harassment of graduate students: The impact of institutional factors. *The Community Psychologist* 21 (2), 12–13.

Gilligan, C. 1982. *In a different voice: Psychological theory and women's moral development.* Cambridge, Mass.: Harvard University Press.

Gottfredson, L. S. 1992. Dilemmas in developing diversity programs. In S. E. Jackson and Associates (eds.), *Diversity in the workplace: Human resources initiatives* (pp. 279–305). New York: Guilford Press.

Greenwood, D., and M. Levin. 1998. *Introduction to action research: Social research for social change.* Thousand Oaks, Calif.: Sage Publications.

Gridley, H., and C. Turner. 2005. Gender, power, and community psychology. In G. Nelson and I. Prilleltensky (eds.), *Community psychology: In pursuit of liberation and well being* (pp. 364–381). London: McMillan.

Hall, R. 1996. Partnership accountability. In C. McLean, M. Carey, and C. White (eds.), *Men's ways of being* (pp. 211–238). Boulder, Colo.: Westview Press.

Harding, S. 1987. *Feminism and methodology.* Bloomington: Indiana University Press.

Harding, S. 2004. Rethinking standpoint epistemology: What is "strong objectivity"? In S. Hesse-Biber and M. Yaiser (eds.), *Feminist perspectives on social research* (pp. 39–64). New York: Oxford University Press.

Harrell, S., and M. A. Bond. 2006. Listening to diversity stories: Principles for practice in community research and action. *American Journal of Community Psychology* 36 (3/4).

Harrison, D. A., K. H. Price, and M. P. Bell. 1998. Beyond relational demography: Time and the effects of surface- and deep-level diversity on work group cohesiveness. *Academy of Management Journal* 41 (1), 96–107.

Hartstock, M. 1998. *The feminist standpoint revisited*. Boulder, Colo: Westview Press.

Hayles, V. R., and A. M. Russell. 1997. *The diversity directive: Why some initiatives fail and what to do about it*. Chicago: Irwin/ASTD.

Heller, K. 1989. The return to community. *American Journal of Community Psychology* 17, 1–16.

Hellman, L. 1976. *Scoundrel time*. New York: Bantam Books.

Hillman, A. J., A. A. Cannella, and I. C. Harris. 2002. Women and racial minorities in the boardroom: How do directors differ? *Journal of Management* 28 (6), 747–763.

Holahan, C. J., and J. L. Spearly. 1980. Coping and ecology: An integrative model for community psychology. *American Journal of Community Psychology* 8, 671–685.

Holland, J. L. 1985. *Making vocational choices*. 2nd ed. Englewood Cliffs, N.J.: Prentice-Hall.

Holvino, E. 2001. Complicating gender: The simultaneity of race, gender, and class in organization change(ing). Simmons Graduate School of Management, Center for Gender in Organizations, working paper #14.

Holvino, E., B. Ferdman, and D. Merrill-Sands. 2004. Creating and sustaining diversity and inclusion in organizations: Strategies and approaches. In F. Stockdale and F. Crosby eds., *The psychology and management of workplace diversity* (pp. 245–276). Oxford: Blackwell Publishing.

Hughes, D., and M. A. Dodge. 1997. African American women in the workplace: relationships between job conditions, racial bias, and perceived job quality. *American Journal of Community Psychology* 25 (5), 581–599.

Jackson, S. E. 1991. Team composition in organizational settings: Issues in managing an increasingly diverse workforce. In S. Worchel, W. Wood, and J. Simpson (eds.), *Group Process and Productivity.* (pp. 138–173). Beverly Hills, Calif.: Sage Publications.

Jackson, S. E., and Associates (eds.) 1992. *Diversity in the workplace: Human resources initiatives*. New York: Guilford Press.

Jackson, S. E., and M. N. Ruderman (eds.). 1995. *Diversity in work teams: Research paradigms for a changing workplace*. Washington, D.C.: American Psychological Association.

Jehn, K. A. 1995. A multi-method examination of the benefits and determinants of intragroup conflict. *Administrative Science Quarterly* 40, 256–282.

Jehn, K. A., G. B. Northcraft, and M. A. Neale. 1999. Why differences make a difference: A field study of diversity, conflict, and performance in work groups. *Administrative Science Quarterly* 44, 741–763.

Jordan, J., A. Kaplan, J. B. Miller, I. Stiver, and J. Surrey. 1991. *Women's growth in connection: Writings from the Stone Center.* New York: Guilford Press.

Judy, R., and C. D'Amico. 1997. *Workforce 2020: Work and workers in the 21st century.* Washington, D.C.: Hudson Institute.

Kanter, R. M. 1977. *Men and women of the corporation.* New York: Basic Books.

Karasek, R. A. 1985. *Job content instrument: Questionnaire and user's guide.* Los Angeles: Department of Industrial and Systems Engineering.

Katz, D., and R. L. Kahn. 1978. *The social psychology of organizations.* New York: Wiley.

Kellogg Foundation. 2004. *Logic model development guide.* www.wkkf.org/Pubs/Tools/Evaluation/Pub3669.pdf.

Kelly, J. G. 1966. Ecological constraints on mental health services. *American Psychologist* 21, 535–539.

Kelly, J. G. 1968. Toward an ecological conception of preventive interventions. In J. Carter (ed.), *Research contributions from psychology to community mental health* (pp. 75–99). New York: Behavioral Publications.

Kelly, J. G. 1979. Taint what you do, it's the way that you do it. *American Journal of Community Psychology* 7, 244–258.

Kelly, J. G. 1986. Content and Process: An ecological view of the interdependence of practice and research. *American Journal of Community Psychology* 14, 581–605.

Kelly, J. G., S. Azelton, R. Burzette, and L. Mock. 1994. Creating social settings for diversity: An ecological thesis. In T. Trickett, D. Birman, and R. Watts (eds.), *Human diversity: Perspectives on people in context* (pp. 424–451). San Francisco: Jossey-Bass.

Kelly, J. G., A. M. Ryan, B. E. Altman, and S. Stelzner. 2000. Understanding and changing social systems: An ecological view. In J. Rappaport and E. Seidman (eds.), *The handbook of community psychology.* (pp. 133–159). New York: Plenum.

Khatiwada, I., S. Palma, S. Sum, and M. Trubbsky. 2001. *Foreign immigration and its contributions to population and labor force growth in Massachusetts and the U.S.: A recent assessment of 2000 census and CPS survey findings.* Publication of the Center for Labor Market Studies, Northeastern University.

Kingry-Westergaard, C., and J. G. Kelly. 1990. A contextualist epistemology for ecological research. In P. H. Tolan, C. Keys, F. Chertok, and L. Jason (eds.), *Researching community psychology: The integration of theories and methods* (pp. 23–31). Washington D. C.: American Psychological Association.

Klonoff, L., and H. Landrine. 1995. The schedule of sexist events: A measure of lifetime and recent sexist discrimination in women's lives. *Psychology of Women Quarterly* 19 (4), 473–492.

Klonoff, E. A., H. Landrine, and R. Campbell. 2000. Sexist discrimination may account for the well known gender differences in psychiatric symptoms. *Psychology of Women Quarterly* 24, 93–99.

Kochan, T., K. Bezrukove, R. Ely, S. Jackson, A. Joshi, K. Jehn, J. Leonard, D. Levin, and D. Thomas. 2003. The effects of diversity on business performance: Report of the diversity research network. *Human Resource Management* 42 (1), 3–21.

Kossek, E., and S. Zonia. 1993. Assessing diversity climate: A field study of reactions to employer efforts to promote diversity. *Journal of Organizational Behavior* 14, 61–81.

Krieger, N. 2003. Does racism harm health? Did child abuse exist before 1962? On explicit questions, critical science and current controversies: An ecosocial perspective. *American Journal of Public Health* 93 (2), 194–199.

Kuczynski, S. 1999. If diversity, then higher profits? *HR Magazine* 44 (13), 66–74.

Lau, D. C., and J. K. Murnighan. 1998. Demographic diversity and faultiness: The compositional dynamics of organizational groups. *Academy of Management Review* 23, 325–340.

Levine, M., and D. V. Perkins. 1997. *Principles of community psychology: Perspectives and applications.* 2nd ed. New York: Oxford University Press.

Lewin, K. 1946. Action research and minority problems. *Journal of Social Issues* 2, 34–46.

Lewin, K. 1997. Behavior and development as a function of the total situation. Reprinted from a 1943 essay in K. Lewin, *Resolving social conflicts and field theory in social science.* Washington, D.C.: American Psychological Association.

Lincoln, Y. S., and E. Guba. 1985. *Naturalistic inquiry.* Beverly Hills, Calif.: Sage Publications.

Linnehan, F., and A. M. Konrad. 1999. Diluting diversity. Implications for intergroup inequality in organizations. *Journal of Management Inquiry* 8 (4), 339–414.

Litvin, D. 2006. Diversity: Making space for a better case. In P. Prasad, J. Pringle, and A. Konrad (eds.), *Handbook of workplace diversity.* London: Sage Publications.

Loden, M., and J. B. Rosener. 1991. *Workforce America! Managing employee diversity as a vital resource.* Burr Ridge, Ill.: Irwin.

Lykes, B., A. Banuazizi, R. Liem, and M. Morris. 1996. *Myths about the powerless: Contesting social inequalities.* Philadelphia: Temple University Press.

MacKinnon, C. 1979. *The sexual harassment of working women.* New Haven, Conn.: Yale University Press.

McLeod, P. L., S. A. Lobel, and T. Cox, Jr. 1996. Ethnic diversity and creativity in small groups. *Small Group Research* 27, 248–264.

Miller, J. B. 1976. *Toward a new psychology of women.* Boston: Beacon Press.

Mulvey, A., M. Terenzio, J. Hill, M. Bond, I. Huygens, H. Hamerton, and S. Cahill. 2000. Stories of relative privilege: Power and social change in feminist community psychology. *American Journal of Community Psychology* 28 (6), 883–911.

Nelson, G., and I. Prilleltensky (eds.) 2005. *Community psychology: In pursuit of liberation and well being.* London: McMillan.

Neville, H. A., L. L. Roderick, G. Duran, R. M. Lee, and L. Browne. 2000. Construction and initial validation of the Color-Blind Racial Attitudes Scale (CoBRAS). *Journal of Counseling Psychology* 47, 59–70.

Ng, E. S., and R. L. Tung. 1998. Ethno-cultural diversity and organizational effectiveness: A field study. *International Journal of Human Resource Management* 9, 980–995.

Ogbu, J. U. 1993. Difference in cultural frame of reference. *International Journal of Behavior Development* 16 (3), 483–506.

Oxtoby, D. W., W. A. Freeman, and T. F. Block. 2002. *Chemistry: Science of Change.* 4th ed. Pacific Grove, Calif.: Brooks/Cole.

Parker, P. 1999. *Movement in Black.* Ithaca, N. Y.: Firebrand Books.

Prilleltenski, I., and G. Nelson. 2002. *Doing psychology critically: Making a difference in diverse settings.* New York: Palgrave Macmillan Publishers.

Pyle, J. L., and M. A. Bond. 1997. Workforce diversity: Emerging interdisciplinary challenges. *New Solutions* 7 (2), 41–57.

Pyle, J. L., and M. A. Bond. 2002. Gender and ethnic divisions in the U.S. labour force. In William Lazonick (ed.), *The international encyclopedia of business and management: Handbook of economics.* London: International Thompson Publishing Company.

Rao, A., R. Stuart, and D. Kelleher. 1999. *Gender at work: Organizational change for equality.* West Hartford, Conn.: Kumarian Press.

Rappaport, J. 1990. Research methods and the empowerment social agenda. In P. Tolan, C. Keys, F. Chertok, and L. Jason (eds.), *Researching community psychology: Issues of theory and methods.* Washington, D.C.: American Psychological Association.

Rappaport, J. 1994. Empowerment as a guide to doing research: Diversity as a positive value. In E. Trickett, R. Watts, and D. Birman (eds.), *Human diversity: Perspectives on people in context* (pp. 359–382). San Francisco: Jossey-Bass.

Rappaport, J. 1995. Empowerment meets narrative: Listening to stories and creating settings. *American Journal of Community Psychology* 23, 795–807.

Rayman, P. 2001. *Beyond the bottom line: The search for dignity at work.* New York: Palgrave.

Reinharz, S. 1992. *Feminist methods in social research.* New York: Oxford University Press.

Reinharz, S. 1994. Toward an ethnography of "voice" and "silence." In E. Trickett, R. Watts, and D. Birman (eds.), *Human diversity: Perspectives on people in context* (pp. 178–200). San Francisco: Jossey-Bass.

Reppucci, N. D. 1990. Ecological validity and the deritualization of process. In P. Tolan, C. Keys, F. Chertok, and L. Jason (eds.), *Researching community psychology: Issues of theory and methods* (pp. 160–163). Washington, D.C.: American Psychological Association.

Richard, O. C., T. A. Kochan, and A. McMillan-Capehart. 2002. The impact of visible diversity on organizational effectiveness: Disclosing the contents in Pandora's black box. *Journal of Business and Management* 8, 1–26.

Richard, O., A. McMillan, K. Chadwick, and S. Dwyer. 2003. Employing an innovative strategy in racially diverse workforces: Effects on firm performance. *Group and Organization Management* 28 (1), 107–126.

Riger, S. 1993. What's wrong with empowerment. *American Journal of Community Psychology*, 21 (3), 279–292.

Riger, S., J. Stokes, S. Raja, and M. Sullivan. 1997. Measuring perceptions of the work environment for female faculty. *The Review of Higher Education* 21 (1), 63–78.

Riordan, C. 2000. Relational demography within groups: Past developments, contradictions, and new directions. In G. R. Ferris (ed.), *Research in personnel and human resource management* 19 (pp. 137–73). New York: Elsevier Science Publishing.

Rosenblum, K. E., and T. C. Travis. 2006. *The meaning of difference: American constructions of race, sex and gender, social class and sexual orientation*. New York: McGraw Hill.

Russo, N. F., and A. J. Dabul. 1994. Feminism and psychology: A dynamic interaction. In E. Trickett, R. Watts, and D. Birman (eds.), *Human diversity: Perspectives on people in context* (pp. 81–100). San Francisco: Jossey-Bass.

Ryan, W. 1981. *Equality*. New York: Pantheon.

Ryan, W. 1994. Many cooks, brave men, apples, and oranges: How people think about equality. *American Journal of Community Psychology* 22 (1), 25–36.

Schneider, B. 1987. The people make the place. *Personnel Psychology* 40, 437–453.

Scott, J. 1994. Deconstructing equality-versus-difference; or, The uses of poststructuralist theory for feminism. In A. C. Herman and A. J. Stewart (eds.), *Theorizing feminism: Parallel trends in the humanities and social sciences*. Boulder, Colo.: Westview Press.

Senge, P. 1990. *The fifth discipline: The art and practice of the learning organization*. New York: Bantam, Doubleday, Dell Publishing Group.

Serrano-Garcia, I. 1984. The illusion of empowerment: Community development within a colonial context. *Prevention in Human Services* 3 (2/3), 173–200.

Sherif, M., O. J. Harvey, B. J. White, W. Hood, and C. Sherif. 1961. *Intergroup conflict and cooperation: The robbers cave experiment*. Norman: University of Oklahoma Institute of Intergroup Relations.

Steele, C., S. Spencer, and J. Aronson. 2002. Contending with group image: The psychology of stereotype and social identity threat. *Advances in Experimental Social Psychology* 34, 379–440.

Stockdale, M., and F. Crosby. (eds.) 2004. *The psychology of workplace diversity*. Malden, Mass.: Blackwell Publishing.

Stokes, J., S. Riger, and M. Sullivan. 1995. Measuring perceptions of the working environment for women in corporate settings. *Psychology of Women Quarterly* 19, 533–549.

Swift, C., and G. Levin. 1987. Empowerment: An emerging mental health technology. *Journal of Primary Prevention* 8, 71–94.

Tamasese, K., and C. Waldegrave. 1993. Cultural and gender accountability in the "Just Therapy" approach. *Journal of Feminist Family Therapy* 5 (2), 29–45.

Tannen, D. 1990. *You just don't understand: Women and men in conversation*. New York: Ballantine Books.

Tannen, D. 1994. *Talking from 9 to 5*. New York: William Morrow Press.

Tatum, B. 1999. *Why are all the black kids sitting together in the cafeteria?* New York: Basic Books.

Thomas, D. A., and R. Ely. 1996. Making differences matter: A new paradigm for managing diversity. *Harvard Business Review* 74 (5), 79–90.

Thomas, D., and R. Ely. 2001. Cultural diversity at work: The effects of diversity perspectives on work group processes and outcomes. *Administrative Science Quarterly* 46 (12), 229–73.

Thomas, E., and J. Rappaport. 1996. Art as community narrative: A resource for social change. In B. Lykes, A. Banuazizi, R. Liem, and M. Morris (eds.), *Myths about the powerless: Contesting social inequalities* (pp. 317–336). Philadelphia: Temple University Press.

Thomas, R. 1991. *Beyond race and gender: Unleashing the power of your total workforce by managing diversity*. New York: AMACOM.

Thomas, R. 1992. Managing diversity: A conceptual framework. In S. E. Jackson and Associates (eds.), *Diversity in the workplace: Human resources initiative* (pp. 13–35). New York: Guilford Press.

Trickett, E. 1986. Consultation as a preventative intervention: Comments on ecologically based case studies. *Prevention in Human Services* 4 (3/4), 187–204.

Trickett, E. 1994. Human diversity and community psychology: Where ecology and empowerment meet. *American Journal of Community Psychology* 22 (4), 583–592.

Trickett, E. 1996. A future for community psychology: The contexts of diversity and the diversity of contexts. *American Journal of Community Psychology* 24 (2), 209–234.

Trickett, E., J. G. Kelly, and D. Todd. 1972. The social environment of the high school: Guidelines for organizational change and organizational development. In S. G. Golan and Eisdorfer (eds.), *Handbook of community mental health* (pp. 331–406). New York: Appleton-Century-Crofts.

Trickett, E., J. G. Kelly, and T. Vincent. 1985. The spirit of ecological inquiry in community research. In D. Klein and E. Susskind (eds.), *Community research: Methods, paradigms, and applications* (pp. 5–38). New York: Praeger.

Trickett. E., R. Watts, and D. Birman. 1994a. *Human diversity: Perspectives on people in context*. San Francisco: Jossey-Bass.

Trickett, E., R. Watts, and D. Birman. 1994b. Toward an overarching framework for diversity. In E. Trickett, R. Watts, and D. Birman. (eds.), *Human diversity: Perspectives on people in context* (pp. 7–26). San Francisco: Jossey-Bass.

Tsui, A. S., T. D. Egan, and C. A. O'Reilly III. 1992. Being different: Relational demography and organizational attachment. *Administrative Science Quarterly* 37, 549–579.

Unger, R. 1992. Will the real sex differences please stand up? *Feminism and Psychology* 2, 231–238.

United States Census Bureau. 2004. *Annual estimates of the population by race alone and Hispanic or Latino origin for the United States and states: July 1, 2004.* Retrieved December 3, 2005, from http://www.census.gov./popest/states/asrh/SC-EST2004-04.html.

United States Census Bureau. 2004. *U.S. Interim projections by age, sex, race, and Hispanic origin.* Retrieved December 2005 from http://www.census.gov/ipc/www/usinterimproj/.

United States Census Bureau, Population Division. 2001. *Rankings and comparisons population and housing tables (PHC-T series).* Retrieved December 12, 2005, from http://www.census.gov/population/www/cen2000/tablist.html.

United States Department of Labor, Bureau of Labor Statistics, Monthly Labor Review. 2004. *Labor force characteristics of foreign-born workers in 2004.* Retrieved December 2005 from http://www.bls.gov/cps/.

United States Department of Labor, Bureau of Labor Statistics, Monthly Labor Review. 2005. *The employment situation: October 2005.* Retrieved December 2005 from http://www.bls.gov/ces/691-5902.

United States Department of Labor, Bureau of Labor Statistics, Women's Bureau. 2004. *Quick facts on women in the labor force in 2004.* Retrieved December 3, 2005, from http://www.dol.gov/wb/factshets/Qf-laborforce-04.html.

Vasquez, H. 2006. Facing resistance in waking up to privilege. *American Journal of Community Psychology* 35 (3–4).

Vincent, T., and E. Trickett. 1983. Preventive interventions and the human context: Ecological approaches to environmental assessment and change. In R. D. Felner, L. A. Jason, J. Moritsugu, and S. Farber (eds.), *Preventive psychology: Theory, research and practice* (pp. 67–86). New York: Pergamon Press.

Walsh, R. T. 1987. The evolution of the research relationship in community psychology. *American Journal of Community Psychology* 15, 773–88.

Watson, W. E., K. Kumar, and L. K. Michaelsen. 1993. Cultural diversity's impact on interaction process and performance: Comparing homogeneous and diverse task groups. *Academy of Management Journal* 36, 590–602.

Watts, R. 1994. Paradigms of diversity. In E. Trickett, R. Watts, and D. Birman (eds.), *Human diversity: Perspectives on people in context* (pp. 49–80). San Francisco: Jossey-Bass.

Watts, R., E. Trickett, and D. Birman. 1994. Conclusion: Convergence and divergence in human diversity. In E. Trickett, R. Watts, and D. Birman (eds.), *Human diversity: Perspectives on people in context* (pp. 452–464). San Francisco: Jossey-Bass.

Watts, R., D. Griffith, and J. Abdul-Adil. 1999. Sociopolitical development as an antidote for oppression: Theory and action. *American Journal of Community Psychology* 27 (2), 255–271.

White, M., and D. Epston. 1990. *Narrative means to therapeutic ends.* New York: W. W. Norton.

Wright, L., and M. Leahey. 2005. *Nurses and families: A guide to family assessment and intervention.* Philadelphia: F. A. Davis Company.

Wright, P., S. P. Ferris, J. S. Hiller, and M. Kroll. 1995. Competitiveness through management of diversity: Effects on stock price valuation. *Academy of Management Journal* 38, 272–09.

index

workplace chemistry

Joan —
All the best
in your work.